Ski Touring Guide
To New England
Fourth Edition
1979

edited by
Katey Ziegler

 published by
Eastern Mountain Sports, Inc.
Peterborough, New Hampshire

designed and produced by
MITCHELL & WEBB, INC.
Boston, Massachusetts

Copyright © 1979 by Eastern Mountain Sports, Inc.
First edition copyright © 1972
Second edition copyright © 1973
Third edition copyright © 1976
All rights reserved
Printed in the United States of America
ISBN 0-910146-23-3

front cover photo: **Fletcher Manley**
back cover photo: **Ozzie Sweet**

*This book is dedicated
to Rye Ellen and Aran.*

Foreword

As the popularity of cross-country skiing in New England continues to grow, so does the need for comprehensive, up-to-date information on places to ski. Eastern Mountain Sports published the First Edition of the *Ski Touring Guide to New England* in 1972 to fill that need with the help of employees and the suggestions and recommendations of our customers. This Fourth Edition provides fully updated information on previously listed trails, and many new touring areas as well as completely new sections on Cape Cod and Rhode Island.

EMS thanks all employees, customers, and others who have given time and information toward the preparation of this *Guide*. We hope it helps New England ski tourers find trails to their liking.

Credit for the publication of this guide goes to Alan McDonough and Roger Furst, President and Vice President of EMS, who through the years have continued to give their support to the project.

EMS extends special thanks to Katey Ziegler, our editor, who has done an excellent job of collecting, checking, organizing, writing, and revising descriptions of hundreds of touring areas. Her diligence has greatly improved this edition over previous ones.

Margaret Murphy
EMS Publications Manager

Acknowledgments

Special thanks are extended to the many people who submitted information. Their contributions were essential to the writing of this book.

I greatly appreciate the work of Margaret Murphy, who coordinated publication at Eastern Mountain Sports; Meg Schwarz of the Appalachian Mountain Club, for editing and proofreading; and Bob Webb, Gretchen Gearhart, and others at Mitchell & Webb, Inc., for their work on design and production. The section on Abandoned Railroad Grades was written by John Reading of Railroad Enthusiasts, Inc. His help with this and previous editions has been invaluable.

I am indebted to Medora Bass, Jean Turnbull, and Ethel MacAdam, who wrote and edited the first two editions of this **Guide**.

Lastly, this edition could not have been written without the help of my husband, Don, who endured months of inconvenience and remained supportive, and my parents, who provided shelter when we traveled, and helped with the children.

Katey Ziegler
September, 1979

Table of Contents

Introduction 1

Chapter 1 Maine 11
    Maine State Map **15**
    Maine Trails **16**

Chapter 2 New Hampshire 31
    Northern New Hampshire Regional Map **37**
    Northern New Hampshire Trails **38**
    Southern New Hampshire Regional Map **67**
    Southern New Hampshire Trails **68**

Chapter 3 Vermont 95
    Northern Vermont Regional Map **99**
    Northern Vermont Trails **100**
    Central Vermont Regional Map **111**
    Central Vermont Trails **112**
    Southern Vermont Regional Map **129**
    Southern Vermont Trails **130**

Chapter 4 Massachusetts 145
    Northeastern Massachusetts Regional Map **149**
    Northeastern Massachusetts Trails **150**
    Southeastern Massachusetts and
        Rhode Island Regional Map **169**
    Southeastern Massachusetts and
        Rhode Island Trails **170**
    Western Massachusetts Regional Map **187**
    Western Massachusetts Trails **188**

Chapter 5 Connecticut 215
    Connecticut State Map **219**
    Connecticut Trails **220**

Ski Touring Abandoned Railroad Grades 240

Contributing to Future Editions 251

Bibliography 253

Index to Trails 257

List of Maps

Maine 15
University Forest **25**
Holbrook Island Sanctuary **29**

Northern New Hampshire 37
Pemi Trail **47**
Mount Moosilauke **59**

Southern New Hampshire 67
Mount Pawtuckaway Area **79**
Hyland Hill **81**
Skatutakee and Thumb Mountains **83**
Winn and Rose Mountains **85**
Purgatory Falls **89**

Northern Vermont 99

Central Vermont 111

Southern Vermont 129
Broad Brook Trail **139**

Northeastern Massachusetts 149
Oak Hill **153**
Manning State Forest **155**
Lowell-Dracut State Forest **157**
Boxford State Forest and Boxford Wildlife Sanctuary **161**
Crane Pond Wildlife Management Area **164-165**

Southeastern Massachusetts and Rhode Island 169

Western Massachusetts 187
R.R.R. Brooks Trail **189**
Notch Road, Bellows Pipe Trail, and Hopper Trail **192-193**
D.A.R. State Forest **198-199**
Conway State Forest **201**
Stratton Mountain Tour **207**
Mount Orient and Poverty Mountain **211**

Connecticut 219
Seth Low Pierrepont State Park **229**
Collis P. Huntington State Park **231**
Osbornedale State Park **233**
Wadsworth Falls State Park **235**
Mansfield Hollow State Park **237**

Abandoned Railroad Grades 241

Ski Touring Guide
To New England
INTRODUCTION

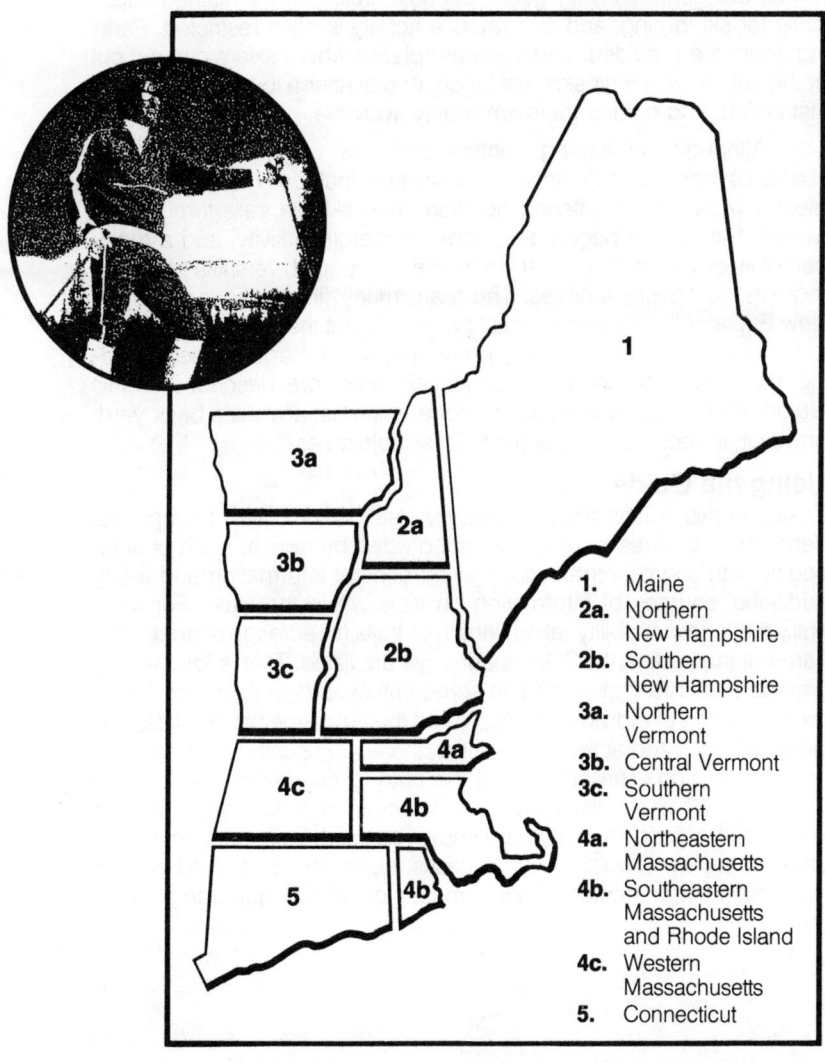

1. Maine
2a. Northern New Hampshire
2b. Southern New Hampshire
3a. Northern Vermont
3b. Central Vermont
3c. Southern Vermont
4a. Northeastern Massachusetts
4b. Southeastern Massachusetts and Rhode Island
4c. Western Massachusetts
5. Connecticut

The first edition of the *Ski Touring Guide to New England* was compiled and printed in 1972 to meet a growing need for information on where to ski. At that time, the number of skiers in New England was still comparatively small, though growing rapidly, and there were very few touring centers or organized programs. The first edition was primarily a listing of skiable public lands, wildlife sanctuaries, and wilderness trails.

Subsequent editions have documented the growth of the sport with increased listings of all types of trails and touring areas. The greatest growth, however, has been in the number of ski touring centers with systems of maintained trails, special activities, and facilities for skiers. There are several advantages to skiing at touring centers. Snow conditions are generally very good, because trails are maintained especially for ski touring, and snowmobile activity is often restricted. Parking areas are provided, and there are places where skiers can get out of the cold to wax their skis, eat lunch, or rest after a long tour. Rentals, instruction, and guided tours are widely available.

Although ski touring centers comprise a greater number of entries as their numbers grow, this *Guide* still includes many non-commercial areas, some offering no more than skiable trails through the woods. Ski touring began as a non-commercial activity, and a major part of its growth in this country has been as a quiet, versatile sport that requires no special facilities. There are many fine areas for skiing in New England that have no formal programs, but these are often harder to find because they are rarely promoted. A number of these, including mountain trips for the experienced skier, are described in this *Guide*. As long as skiing can be done in almost anyone's back yard, however, a book can only begin to list skiable areas.

Using the Guide

Entries in this edition are arranged by state. In turn, New Hampshire, Vermont, and Massachusetts are subdivided by region. Each chapter begins with a state introduction, giving general information and listing additional sources of information on trails within the state. For each entry the location, ability rating, length of trails (or acreage of area), and name of the pertinent USGS quadrangle are listed. This is followed by general area information and, in some entries, a description of the ski route or listing of individual trails. Where there are special facilities, services, or organized activities for skiers, these are usually listed in a separate paragraph. The last part of the entry gives driving and parking directions. When necessary, a map has been included. Trails that are known to be good for skiing are shown as solid lines; parking is indicated by the symbol ⓟ . In most cases, the reader is referred to other sources (touring centers, hiking maps, or USGS quadrangles) for maps.

Trail ability ratings are approximate, especially since snow conditions can drastically alter the level of difficulty of a trail. A trail suited to novices in powder snow can be very difficult to negotiate when covered by ice or crust. Generally, trails recommended to novices are suited to those who have skied a couple of times and have mastered the snowplow on gentle slopes. Intermediates have greater control over their skis on most types of terrain. Advanced skiers can handle steep, rugged terrain and are experienced in a variety of snow conditions.

Trail mileages refer to the length of a trail, one way, unless specifically stated as a round-trip distance. An increasing number of ski touring centers are using kilometers (abbreviated km) to measure their trails. When distances are given in kilometers here, they are followed by approximate mileages in parentheses.

Each entry lists the U.S. Geological Survey topographic maps covering that area. USGS maps are helpful in finding a route or estimating the difficulty of a trail. They have contour lines showing steepness and are usually colored to indicate woods and fields. They also show many old roads and trails. Maps may be obtained from the U.S. Geological Survey, 1200 South Eads Street, Arlington, Virginia 22202. Write for an index and order form.

Because it has great impact on the trails and land, snowmobile use is discussed in almost every entry. Snowmobiles tend to compact the snow, making hard, narrow tracks, These tracks can be useful in deep powder snow, where breaking trail can be very tiring, but they can be annoying, or even dangerous, in icy or crusty conditions. Sharing a trail with snowmobiles can also be unpleasant due to noise and exhaust. Because snowmobile use is heaviest in most areas on weekends, these places are best avoided at such times. In many public lands, however, there are now separate trails or sections for snowmobiling and skiing.

Many variables, beyond the scope of this book, affect trail use. A guide cannot rate an individual's skiing ability. A guide cannot predict snow conditions (for example: trails with stream crossings or trails over old railroad grades that still have ties are particularly affected by inadequate snow cover). Factors such as these should be taken into account in deciding whether or not to ski a particular trail at a given time.

Though every effort has been made to insure the accuracy of information in this edition, many things are subject to change, and it is impossible to guarantee that they will be exactly as they are described here. Trails may be rerouted. Programs or facilities at ski touring centers may change. Trail fees may vary. Occasionally, a touring center will go out of business or a public area will be closed to skiing. It is helpful to call an area before skiing to confirm the information given.

Other Places to Ski

There are many ways of finding good trails and areas for ski touring beyond those listed in this book. Chapter introductions suggest sources of trail information in each state. In addition, there are other valuable guides to ski trails. The *Ski Touring Guide,* published annually by the Ski Touring Council, has descriptions of trails and touring centers throughout the United States and Canada. Most entries are from the northeast, and there is an especially good section on New York state. *Ski Touring in New England and New York,* by Lance Tapley, is an introductory book on ski touring, written for skiers in the northeast. There are chapters on places to ski in each state. The *25 Ski Tours* series from New Hampshire Publishing includes maps, driving directions, and detailed trail information for selected tours in a particular state or region. The *Guide to Cross-Country Skiing,* published each year by *SKI* Magazine, includes feature articles, plus sections on places to ski in the United States and Canada. The National Ski Touring Operators Association (NSTOA) prints a map of ski touring locations in the northeast, and the Eastern Ski Map, primarily a listing of alpine ski areas, also shows some touring centers. A number of regional guides and maps include listings of ski touring areas. Magazines and newspapers often have articles and where-to-ski sections. *Nordic Skiing* has a "Tracks to Try" section each season, and *Country Journal* and other regional magazines frequently have special articles and listings.

A brief search will usually turn up several possibilities for ski touring in any neighborhood, even in populated areas. Most cities and towns have some parks and forest land set aside for general recreation, and many of these have trails and open areas suitable for ski touring. Check with town recreation departments or conservation commissions. State and federal lands are usually open to ski touring, and most states issue brochures describing their parks, forests, and recreation facilities. Private reservations and wildlife sanctuaries frequently have good ski touring, but some restrict public access; get permission from landowners before skiing in these areas.

Golf courses are ideal for ski touring, especially for beginners, since the slopes are usually gentle and there are large open areas. They are frequently located near urban areas and may be among the largest tracts of open land in these areas. Be sure to stay off the greens; the vegetation there is unusually sensitive and may be damaged if the snow is compacted. For this reason, some golf courses are not open for ski touring. Check with the management before skiing.

In northern New England, ponds and lakes are often used for ski touring. Since they are flat and open, they provide good skiing for beginners, and the scenery can be lovely. Skiing on ice can be risky, though. Do not go out early in the season, and avoid places where there is moving water or changing water levels (as in reservoirs). Ski during cold weather, and look for ice fishing shacks or fresh snowmobile tracks as signs that the ice is thick enough. When in doubt, don't go.

Along the coast, beaches provide excellent skiing, but good snow conditions are rare. Head out immediately after a storm, before the snow is melted or blown away, and get permission before skiing on private land.

Bicycle paths and bridle trails are often excellent for ski touring because they tend to be wide and well graded.

Though it is often assumed that hiking trails are good for skiing, this is frequently not true, especially in mountainous areas. Hiking trails are often narrow and twisting and may be too rocky or steep for ski touring. Even a short stretch over rough terrain, or one difficult stream crossing, may make it impossible to ski further on a trail. Some hiking trails are good for ski touring, however, and these usually have one advantage over other ski trails: they are described in one of the several dozen hiking guides that cover various parts of New England. These guides can be very helpful to skiers planning their own routes, especially to those who have some familiarity with the area described. Most hiking guides are listed in the state introductions. Two books that cover all of New England are *Hiking Trails in the Northeast,* by Thomas A. Henley and Neesa Sweet, and *Eastern Trips and Trails,* by Bill Thomas. The New England Trail Conference publishes an annual report, "New England Trails," that lists current conditions of major trails and other sources of trail information. They also issue a map, "Hiking Trails of New England," showing general routes of major trails (it does not show enough detail to be used without other guides or maps) and highway access. It includes a list of trail maintaining organizations and a bibliography. The trail report is $1.00; the map $.50. Write to the Secretary, New England Trail Conference, Box 8001, Cranston, Rhode Island 02920.

USGS topographic maps are excellent for finding skiable trails. These maps show roads and trails, buildings, streams and ponds; and most are colored to indicate woods and fields. Almost every New England quadrangle shows some old roads or trails, or potentially good open areas. By interpreting a map's contour intervals, it is possible to estimate the steepness of a trail and to get an idea of its terrain. Keep in mind that some of these maps are fairly old and do not show developments such as new interstate highways, reservoirs, or houses. The old 15' series of maps is being replaced by 7½' maps that show smaller areas in greater detail.

The U.S. Army Corps of Engineers permits ski touring around their 31 reservoirs in Vermont, New Hampshire, Massachusetts, and Connecticut. Maps are available for areas where there are designated snowmobile trails. There are marked ski trails at Surry Mountain Lake in Keene, New Hampshire; Hodges Village Dam in Oxford, Massachusetts; Knightville Dam in Huntington, Massachusetts; and Birch Hill Dam in Royalston, Massachusetts; however, there are no maps of the designated trails. Most of the other reservoirs have old roads and trails that are also suitable for ski touring. Write to the Corps for their pamphlet, "Lakeside Recreation in New England," or for off-road vehicle trail guides for specific areas, at 424 Trapelo Road, Waltham, Massachusetts 02154.

Environmental Impact

Though ski touring is generally a sport with minimal environmental impact, the large number of skiers using some trails has created problems of overuse. Snow compaction can damage vegetation, particularly in sensitive areas such as golf greens, beaches, and alpine areas. There are a number of places, primarily in populated areas, that are not listed in this *Guide* due to the landowner's or managing agency's concern about this problem.

Dogs can also damage woods and wildlife, and in areas where more than one party are skiing, they can ruin the track and annoy other skiers. In general, ski touring centers and wildlife sanctuaries do not allow dogs on the trails; they are prohibited in some other areas as well.

Litter can be a serious problem, in part because it is not especially visible in winter. Trash that is buried in the snow goes unnoticed by skiers but is found in the spring, lying on the ground or caught in bushes. Bring all trash back from the trail, and dispose of it properly. Fires, excessive noise, and damage to areas near the trails are also potential problems. When skiing, please have respect for the environment, and leave the woods intact.

Safety

New England winters can be harsh, and weather can change rapidly. Though light clothing is usually all that is necessary while in motion, stopping promotes rapid cooling. Bring extra clothing to wear while not actively skiing, or in case of a change in weather. Do not ski alone outside well-traveled areas. When skiing with a large group or on an extended tour, bring basic emergency equipment. An emergency ski kit should generally include an emergency ski tip, a flashlight, a first aid kit, a repair kit (including extra binding parts), extra food, matches, and a map and compass. When skiing in areas that have a sign-in procedure, be sure to register and to sign out after returning. Remember that it gets dark early in winter, and plan trips to end well before sunset. Check equipment before skiing, so problems can be discovered before they cause trouble on the trail. The Nordic Ski Patrol sends patrollers on Ski Touring Council and AMC trips and is willing to cooperate with other organized groups.

Two excellent books on winter mountaineering and another on alpine ski touring have information pertinent to safety and wilderness touring: *Winter Hiking and Camping,* published by the Adirondack

Mountain Club; *Mountaineering: The Freedom of the Hills,* edited by Peggy Ferber, and *Wilderness Skiing,* by Lito Tejada-Flores and Allen Steck.

Courtesy

Most rules of courtesy are designed to promote safety and protect the environment; a side benefit is usually greater enjoyment for everyone concerned. Most ski touring centers, and other areas where there are large numbers of skiers, have specific regulations, but all skiers should be aware of general recommendations.

Damage to groomed ski tracks can be annoying or dangerous; do not walk on tracks or allow dogs on them, and fill in holes made by a fall. On hills, give the right-of-way to skiers going downhill. If passing skiers call "track," step to the right to let them by. Ski in control at all times, even if its means sidestepping or removing skis to get by a difficult section of trail.

In places that have a sign-in system, be sure to sign out after finishing a tour so patrollers will not be concerned that people are still out on the trail. When skiing on private property, respect landowners' rights and stay on marked trails.

Basic Information

There are many excellent sources of information on ski touring equipment, techniques, and waxing. Among the best books are *Cross-Country Skiing Today,* by John Caldwell; *Complete Cross Country Skiing and Ski Touring,* by William J. Lederer and Joe Pete Wilson; *Steve Reischl's Ski-Touring for the Fun of It,* by Cortlandt Freeman; and *Ski Touring in New England and New York,* by Lance Tapley. A good introductory pamphlet, "Touring on Cross-Country Skis," is available free from Sun Life of Canada, U.S. Headquarters, One Sun Life Executive Park, Wellesley Hills, Massachusetts 02181.

Instruction is offered by most ski touring centers, and many of the organizations that sponsor trips also have workshops covering basic technique.

Racing, Ski Orienteering, and Organized Trips

Cross-country ski racing has rapidly expanded in popularity during the past few years. There are now many races held annually in New England, from family-oriented fun races to highly competitive events. Many ski touring centers sponsor races; check individual entries and contact the centers for more specific information.

The best source of information on racing is the United States Ski Association (USSA), Box 777, Brattleboro, Vermont 05301. They administer major Nordic events throughout the country, which presently include the Bill Koch Youth Ski League, the Travelers PEP Ski Touring Series, the Great American Ski Chase, the "Dannon Series," and the National Cross-Country Championships. The Bill Koch Ski League is for children through 13 years of age; it involves instruction and club activities as well as races. There are presently four Travelers events: the Travelers Derby, Salisbury, Connecticut; the Cummington Farm Bread Race, Cummington, Massachusetts; the Paul Revere Cup, Fort Devens, Massachusetts; and the Washington's Birthday Race, Brattleboro, Vermont. Great American Ski Chase races in the east are the Hennessy Cognac American Ski Marathon, South Lincoln to Brandon, Vermont; and the Fleischmann's Margarine Ski Marathon, Waterville Valley, New Hampshire. The USSA also issues an organizer's manual on Cross-Country Citizen Racing.

Ski orienteering is becoming a popular activity in some areas. As a competitive sport, it combines route finding with a map and compass and ski touring. Participants ski to a number of controls (checkpoints), choosing routes and locating the controls with the aid of a map and compass. A skier's time is adjusted according to mistakes made in finding or recording the controls. A few touring centers in New England offer ski orienteering activities. A good booklet is "Ski Orienteering," by Bjorn Kjellstrom, which costs $.50 from Silva, Inc., Highway 39 North, La Porte, Indiana 46350; or from the American Orienteering Service, 308 West Fillmore, Colorado Springs, Colorado 80907.

Many ski clubs and other trail organizations sponsor ski trips, most of which are open to non-members. These are a good way to learn about new trails, get skiing experience with a group, and meet other skiers. Among the organizations sponsoring trips are the Appalachian Mountain Club (5 Joy Street, Boston, Massachusetts 02108; or Pinkham Notch Camp, Gorham, New Hampshire 03581); the Ski Touring Council; and American Youth Hostels.

The Ski Touring Council publishes an annual schedule of ski touring events including trips, workshops, races, and ski orienteering events. It also has information on organizations with ski touring programs, Nordic Ski Patrol schedules, and Eastern Professional Ski Touring Instructors (EPSTI) schedules.

Ski Touring Organizations

Several organizations have been formed to promote ski touring or to provide a particular service to the skiing community.

The Ski Touring Council is a non-commercial, non-profit organization founded in 1962 to reintroduce ski touring as a recreational sport. It sponsors workshops and trips and cooperates with many other outdoor groups. The Council has two publications: the *Ski Touring Guide,* which gives basic ski touring information and describes places to ski, and a schedule of ski touring trips and other activities. Both are issued annually. The Council also offers advice to individuals or organizations who wish to start ski touring programs. For further information, contact the Ski Touring Council, c/o Rudolf Mattesich, West Hill Road, Troy, Vermont 05868.

The National Ski Touring Operators Association (NSTOA) is a professional organization of ski touring operators formed to promote the sport of ski touring. They have set standards for trail markings currently used by a number of ski touring centers. A 4" by 4" blue diamond is used to indicate a ski touring trail. Standard alpine trail difficulty markers have been adopted to show difficulty ratings on touring trails. NSTOA issues a map, the "Ski Touring Guide and Directory," each year. Write to NSTOA, Bretton Woods, New Hampshire 03575. There is a $.25 postage charge.

The Eastern Ski Association (ESA), a division of the United States Ski Association, is a non-profit organization that promotes Alpine and Nordic skiing through competitive and recreational programs. ESA is an especially good source of information on citizens' races and racing programs. It issues and distributes many booklets, pamphlets, and brochures on technique, etiquette, safety, equipment, trail maintenance and layout, where to ski, schedules of racing events, and ESA's involvement in public land use planning. These are available on request. For information, contact the Eastern Office, Eastern Ski Association, 22 High Street, Brattleboro, Vermont 05301.

Eastern Professional Ski Touring Instructors, Inc. (EPSTI) was founded in 1973 to teach and certify ski touring instructors. Candidates must participate in a pre-examination course and pass a two-day comprehensive examination (skiing and teaching ability, plus written examination). Many touring centers are now offering EPSTI certified instruction. Skiers looking for certified instruction may refer to entries in this *Guide,* or inquire at individual touring centers. Experienced skiers interested in becoming certified instructors may contact EPSTI, P.O. Box 97, Londonderry, Vermont 05148. The teaching manual costs $8.50, and may be ordered from the same address.

The National Ski Patrol System's Nordic Ski Patrols presently include over 300 patrollers in 23 patrols throughout New England. Patrollers are trained in advanced and backwoods first aid and rescue. They tour at ski touring centers, accompany groups on outings, and patrol citizens' races and ski jump contests. Anyone interested in joining a patrol should contact Dave Shaeffer, Eastern Division Nordic Advisor, 57-14th Street, Wheeling, West Virginia 26003, to be put in contact with a local patrol.

American Youth Hostels (AYH) operates a network of hostels across the United States where members using non-motorized forms of transportation may stay overnight. A number of New England hostels are open in winter and offer ski touring on nearby trails. These include the Bantam Lake Youth Hostel, Lakeside, Connecticut; Mitchell College Youth Hostel, New London, Connecticut; Camp Karu, Washington, Massachusetts (see entry for Bucksteep Manor); Friendly

Crossways Youth Hostel, Littleton, Massachusetts; Train Hostel, East Bridgewater, Massachusetts; Hy Land Youth Hostel, Hyannis, Massachusetts; University of Rhode Island Youth Hostel, Kingston, Rhode Island; Ammonoosuc Campground Youth Hostel, Twin Mountain, New Hampshire; Waterville Valley Bunkhouse, Waterville Valley, New Hampshire; Gray Ledges, Grantham, New Hampshire (see individual entry); Ragged Edge Youth Hostel, Danbury, New Hampshire; Mrs. Farrell's Youth Hostel, Winooski, Vermont; Ski Hostel Lodge, Waterbury Center, Vermont (see individual entry); Old Homestead Youth Hostel, Warren, Vermont; Schoolhouse Youth Hostel, Rochester, Vermont; Ludlow Youth Hostel, Ludlow, Vermont; and home hostels in Bolton, Connecticut and Dudley, Massachusetts. Overnight fees are somewhat higher in winter due to heating costs; most are between $3 and $5. For an information package on hostels in New England (or anywhere else in the world), send a stamped, self-addressed envelope to the AYH at 251 Harvard Street, Brookline, Massachusetts 02146, or P.O. Box 10392, Elmwood, Connecticut 06110.

New Information

Help keep the *Ski Touring Guide to New England* up to date by sending in comments, suggestions, and additional information. New entries are welcome, and feedback on present information is equally important. Even suggesting minor changes in a ski route or stating that a particular description is still accurate is very helpful. See the section on "Contributing to Future Editions" at the back of the book.

Ski Touring Maine

CHAPTER 1

Maine

Maine has few developed ski touring trails — possibly because the vast wilderness boasts plenty of natural skiing opportunities. Ski touring is permitted in state parks, but snowmobile use is heavy here. The White Mountain National Forest in Maine has a number of skiable trails, although many are also open to snowmobiles. The Forest Service issues a map showing designated snowmobile trails and is developing a winter recreation map that will include a large number of ski trails. For copies of either map, write to the U.S. Forest Service, P.O. Box 638, Laconia, New Hampshire 03246.

The following guides to hiking trails in Maine may be useful to the ski tourer. All have detailed trail descriptions and maps, though none evaluates the trails specifically for ski touring. It is best to consult topographic maps or to have summer experience on a trail before attempting it on skis. Keep in mind that, although negotiating stream crossings and finding parking areas may not pose a problem for summer hikers, they can be very difficult in winter.

The AMC *Maine Mountain Guide* describes trails in mountain areas throughout the state. It includes several excellent maps (Carter-Mahoosuc, Katahdin, Mount Desert Island, Weld, and Rangeley-Stratton), which may be purchased separately. The introductory section entitled "Maine's Mountains in Winter" is particularly helpful.

The *Guide to the Appalachian Trail in Maine* covers all of the Appalachian Trail in Maine and a few side trails from the New Hampshire border to Katahdin. Though the Appalachian Trail generally traverses mountain areas, some parts are gentle enough to ski. Good possibilities for skiing are Sections 2 (Abol Bridge to Nahmakanta Lake), 3 (Nahmakanta Lake to Kokadjo-B Pond Road), 4 (Kokadjo-B Pond Road to West Branch Ponds Road), 7 (Bodfish Farm to Monson), 8 (Monson to Blanchard), 11 (Kennebec River at Caratunk to Long Falls Dam Road), 14 (Maine Highway 4 to Maine Highway 17), and 16 (Andover-B Hill Road to Maine Highway 5). Refer to the guidebook for trail descriptions and maps before skiing.

Fifty Hikes in Maine, by John Gibson, describes day hikes and a few backpacking trips in the Maine mountains. Though most are too steep for skiing, some of the beginner trips merit investigation.

Short Walks Along the Maine Coast, by Ruth and Paul Sadlier, and *Walking the Maine Coast,* by John Gibson, include many trips that would be good on skis or snowshoes.

The *Guide to Baxter State Park and Katahdin,* by Stephen Clark, contains excellent general information as well as trail descriptions. Most trails are too steep to ski.

Maine Ski Touring Areas

1. Baxter State Park, Millinocket 16
2. Little Lyford Pond Camps, Brownville 16
3. The Birches Ski Touring Center, Rockwood 17
4. Squaw Mountain Ski Area, Greenville 17
5. Saddleback Mountain Ski Area, Rangeley 18
6. Carrabassett Valley Touring Center, Carrabassett 18
   Narrow Gauge Cross-Country Trail, Bigelow 19
7. Deer Farm Ski Touring Center, Kingfield 19
8. Mount Blue State Park, Weld 20
9. Pineland Ski Club/Akers Ski, Andover 20
10. Sunday River Ski Touring Center, Bethel 21
11. Evergreen Valley Ski Touring Center, East Stoneham 21
12. Mount Abram Ski Slopes, Locke Mills 22
13. Teddybear Touring Trails, North Turner 22
14. Auburn Ski Touring Center, Auburn 23
15. Sebago Lake State Park, Naples 23
16. Bradbury Mountain State Park, Pownal 23
17. Hermon Meadow Ski Center, Bangor 24
18. University Forest, Stillwater 24
19. Camden Hills State Park, Lincolnville 26
    Camden Snow Bowl, Camden 26
20. Holbrook Island Sanctuary, Brooksville 28
21. Acadia National Park, Bar Harbor 27
22. Moosehorn National Wildlife Refuge, Calais and Dennysville 28

Maine

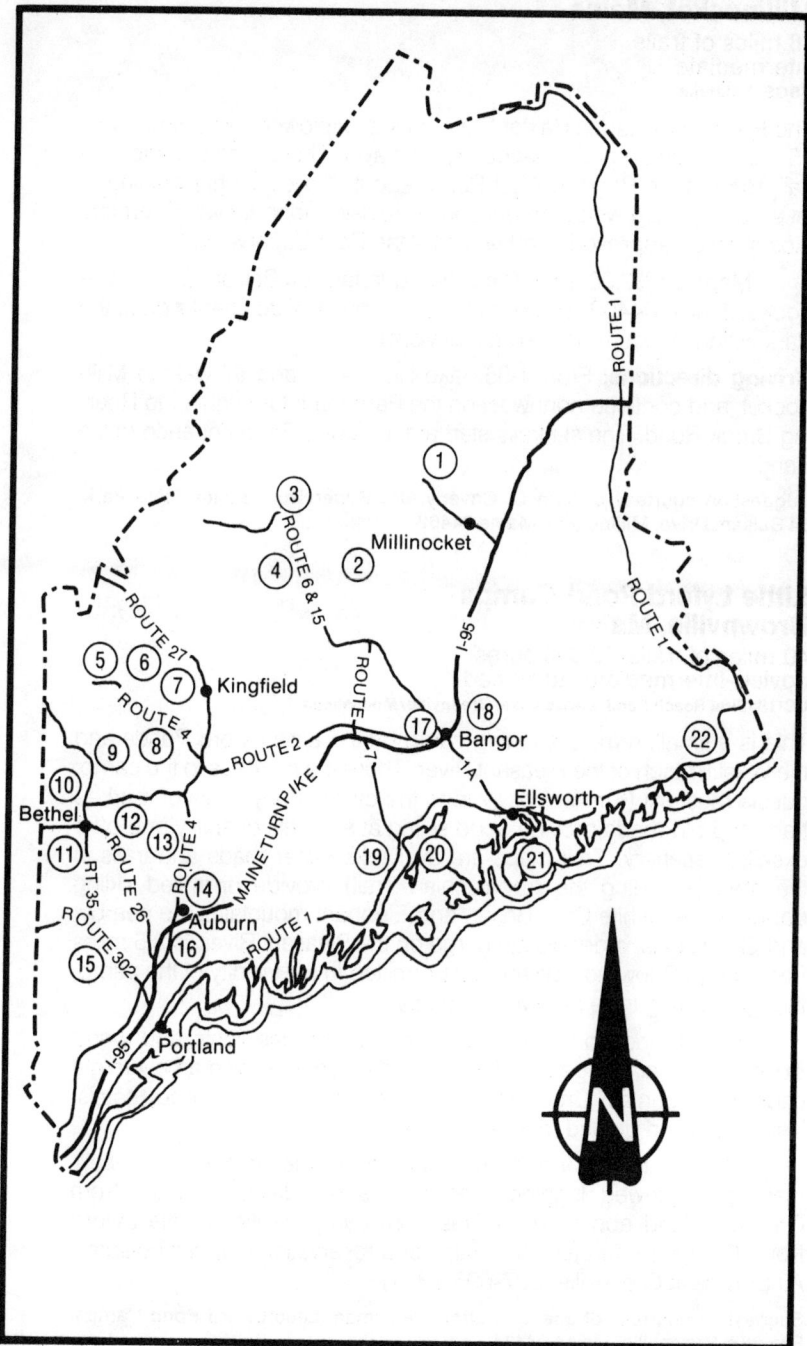

Baxter State Park
Millinocket, Maine
48 miles of trails
intermediate
USGS: Katahdin

The Perimeter Road in Baxter State Park is unplowed, providing about 45 miles of excellent cross-country ski travel. There is also a short ski trail from Togue Pond to Abol Pond, about 3 miles. Skiers wishing to take day trips are welcome but should register upon arrival. Overnight trips must be approved in advance by the Park Supervisor.

Maps are $2.00 at the Park Headquarters, 64 Balsam Drive, Millinocket, Maine 04462. There is also a 12 minute slide orientation to the Park which is recommended for all visitors.

Driving directions: From I-95, take Routes 11 and 57 west to Millinocket, and continue northwest on the Park road; turn right onto Roaring Brook Road. The ski trails start at the Togue Pond entrance to the Park.

Suggestion courtesy of Irvin C. Caverly, Jr., Supervisor, Baxter State Park, 64 Balsam Drive, Millinocket, Maine 04462.

Little Lyford Pond Camps
Brownville, Maine
40 miles of trails/30,000 acres
novice-intermediate-advanced
USGS: First Roach Pond/Sebec Lake/Greenville/Moosehead

This is a small, remote sporting camp by the Little Lyford Ponds and the West Branch of the Pleasant River. There are no roads to the camp; guests must ski (6 miles) or fly in to the camp. Forty miles of marked trails and old roads provide good skiing at all levels of ability and offer excellent scenery. Trail maps are available. Other roads and trails in the area (including the Appalachian Trail) provide unlimited skiing opportunities. White Cap, Baker, and Elephant mountains are nearby; and Gulf Hagas, a deep slate gorge on the Pleasant River, is 2.5 miles from camp. Snowmobiles are not permitted in the vicinity of the camp, though outlying trails receive some use.

Accommodations are in log cabins with gas lights and wood stoves. The main lodge has dining facilities. There is also an overnight cabin on Mountain Brook Pond. Limited ski and snowshoe rentals, instruction, and guided tours are offered.

The 6-mile ski trip in from the Brownville area is on a well-marked, unplowed logging road and is not difficult. Planes from Greenville land about 10 minutes from camp. Write to Little Lyford Pond Camps for further information and reservations, or call Folsom's Air Service in Greenville (207-695-2821).

Suggestion courtesy of Joel and Lucy Frantzman, Little Lyford Pond Camps, Box 688, Brownville, Maine 04414.

The Birches Ski Touring Center
Rockwood, Maine
10+ miles of trails
novice-intermediate-advanced
USGS: Rockwood

Situated on the shore of Moosehead Lake, The Birches offers ski touring on 10 miles of groomed trails and several miles of maintained wilderness trails. These connect with an extensive system of old logging roads and a 200-mile network of groomed snowmobile trails that extends into Quebec.

The Touring Center is operated by North Country Outfitters, and offers rentals and instruction. Guided tours include day trips and six-day tours in the Moosehead-Allagash region. The Birches has heated housekeeping cabins that sleep from two to eight people.

Driving directions: From I-95, take the Moosehead Lake Region exit at Newport. Follow Routes 7 and 11 north to Route 23. Continue to Guilford, then take Routes 6 and 15 through Greenville to Rockwood. Cross the Moose River bridge and continue for 2 miles on a dirt road to The Birches.

Suggestion courtesy of John Willard, Jr., The Birches Ski Touring Center, Rockwood, Maine 04478 (207-534-7305).

Squaw Mountain Ski Area
Greenville, Maine
45 miles of trails
novice-intermediate-advanced
USGS: Greenville/Moosehead Lake

This alpine area is owned and managed by the state of Maine. Fifteen miles of trails are marked and maintained; others are unmarked. There are also numerous open areas for skiing. Trails go along the west ridge of Squaw Mountain, commanding views of Moosehead Lake, Katahdin, and the Mount Kineo region. Terrain varies from mountainous topography to flat farmland. Snowmobile use is moderate.

Ski tourers may use the facilities of the base lodge, where rentals and instruction are available. Squaw Mountain Lodge offers meals and lodging.

Driving directions: From I-95, exit at Newport and take Route 7 north to Dover-Foxcroft. Then take Routes 6 and 15 northwest through Greenville. The Squaw Mountain access road is 6 miles north of Greenville.

Suggestion courtesy of Squaw Mountain Ski Area, P.O. Box 503, Greenville, Maine 04441 (207-695-2272).

Saddleback Mountain Ski Area
Rangeley, Maine
25 miles of trails
novice–intermediate
USGS: Rangeley

Saddleback Mountain has a number of marked trails that wind through primarily wooded areas and have commanding views of the Rangeley Lakes. Skiers may use the facilities of the base lodge. Accommodations are available nearby.

Driving directions: From Exit 12 on the Maine Turnpike, near Auburn, go north on Route 4. The Saddleback access road branches right about 1 mile south of Rangeley.

Carrabassett Valley Touring Center
Carrabassett, Maine
80 km (50 miles) of trails
novice–intermediate–advanced
USGS: Stratton

The Carrabassett Valley Touring Center is located 1 mile south of Sugarloaf Mountain on part of Maine's Public Reserved Land. The varied trail network encompasses 80 km of trails on all types of terrain. For novices there are wide, graded trails along the old Narrow Gauge Railroad Bed (see separate entry) or winding cedar bog trails. There are jeep trails and steep vertical ascents for more advanced skiers. Most trails are groomed, although some, including a section of the Appalachian Trail, are left for wilderness skiing. All are well marked, and maps are sold at the Touring Center.

The new ski touring lodge uses wood and passive solar heating and includes a warming room and a cafeteria with homemade food. The ski shop offers retail sales, rentals, instruction, and repairs. Special activities include moonlight tours, races, and waxing clinics. There is a fee for trail use.

Driving directions: From Kingfield, take Routes 16 and 27 north about 15 miles and turn left at the ski touring sign, 1 mile before Sugarloaf Ski Area. The lodge is ½ mile from the main road.

Suggestion courtesy of Muffy Patten, Carrabassett Valley Touring Center, Carrabassett, Maine 04947 (207-237-2205).

Narrow Gauge Cross-Country Trail
Bigelow, Maine
6½ miles, one way
novice-intermediate
USGS: Stratton

The Narrow Gauge Trail runs along the Carrabassett River, across gentle terrain. It follows an old narrow gauge railroad bed. During winters with heavy snowfall, numerous deer yarding areas may be seen, and moose are often spotted. Small animal tracks abound. Snowmobiles are rarely used on the trail. Trail maps are available at the Carrabassett Valley Touring Center.

Driving directions: From Kingfield, take Routes 16 and 27 north. Go past the entrance to Sugarloaf Mountain Ski Area and about 300 yards beyond the Carrabasset River. To the right, there is an old railroad bed and several cabins grouped around the abandoned Bigelow Station. Park as far off the road as possible. If skiing the route one way, leave a car at the Red Stallion Hotel in the Valley Crossing Shopping Center, south of Sugarloaf Ski Area on Routes 16 and 27.

Suggestion courtesy of Brud and Scotty Folger, University of Maine, Orono, Maine.

Deer Farm Ski Touring Center
Kingfield, Maine
30 miles of trails
novice-intermediate-advanced
USGS: Kingfield/Little Bigelow Mtn.

Deer Farm trails run over logging roads and hiking trails, through the foothills of the Longfellow Mountains. Trails skirt mountain lakes and ponds and command scenic views of the Carrabassett Valley and surrounding 4000-foot mountains. The trail network covers several thousand acres, and many trails loop back to the Touring Center. The system is bisected by the 45th parallel, giving skiers an opportunity to stand halfway between the equator and the north pole. Trails are well marked and labeled according to degree of difficulty. They are groomed, and tracks are set on the main-line trails. Maps may be purchased for $.45. Snowmobiles are prohibited. In order to ensure a wilderness experience, daily registrations are limited to five skiers per square mile. The Deer Farm system connects to Carrabassett Valley Touring Center (see separate entry).

Facilities include a heated ski shop and waxing room. Rentals, instruction, guided tours, moonlight tours, and luncheon tours are offered. There is a trail fee of $1.50. Accommodations at Deer Farm Camps include individual heated log cabins with running water, and a dining room.

Driving directions: From Kingfield, take Route 27 north 1 mile. Turn left at the Deer Farm sign and continue 2½ miles to the Touring Center, at the end of the road.

Suggestion courtesy of Larry Minnehan, Deer Farm Ski Touring Center, P.O. Box 78, Kingfield, Maine 04947 (207-265-2241).

Mount Blue State Park
Weld, Maine
15 miles of trails
intermediate-advanced
USGS: Mount Blue

Mount Blue State Park has long trails through wooded, mountainous areas and shorter, gentler trails in the Lake Webb vicinity. The hilltops offer excellent views. Snowmobile use is quite heavy in this area, especially on weekends. Trail maps are available at Park headquarters, or may be obtained by writing to the Bureau of Parks and Recreation, Department of Conservation, State House, Augusta, Maine 04333.

Driving directions: From I-95, take Exit 12 near Auburn to Route 4. Take Route 4 north to Wilton, then Route 156 northwest to Weld. Follow the signs for Mount Blue State Park. Park in the plowed area near the headquarters.

Suggestion courtesy of Tom Cieslinski, Maine Department of Conservation, Augusta, Maine.

Pineland Ski Club/Akers Ski
Andover, Maine
130 acres
novice-intermediate-advanced
USGS: Old Speck

The Andover area offers well-maintained novice and racing loops. Trails are marked and traverse hard- and softwood forest. There are good views of Andover Valley, the village, and an earth satellite station. Snowmobiles are prohibited on ski trails, except for maintenance. Trail maps are available at Akers Ski.

Akers Ski shop has a waxing room and a warming room, and offers rentals. Instruction may be arranged. There is a $2.00 trail fee.

Driving directions: From Route 2 between Bethel and Rumford, follow Route 5 north to Andover. In Andover, follow signs to Akers Ski shop, where trails begin. Park alongside Pine Street, in the center of town, or in the school lot if classes are not in session.

Suggestion courtesy of Leon Akers, Akers Ski, Andover, Maine 04216.

Sunday River Ski Touring Center
Bethel, Maine
40 km (25 miles) of trails
novice-intermediate-advanced
USGS: Bethel

Sunday River trails start at the Sunday River Inn and go through primarily wooded areas with scattered overlooks of the surrounding mountains and valleys. One trail ends at a covered bridge over the Sunday River; another winds 5 miles into the mountains to a high camp lunch shelter. Trails are groomed and identified by standard NSTOA markings. A trail map is available at the ski shop. Guided tours may be arranged to the upper end of the valley along routes used by the Hurricane Island Outward Bound School.

The Sunday River Inn has overnight accommodations in dorms and private rooms. Facilities include a complete ski shop, a waxing room, and a snack bar. Rentals, EPSTI affiliated instruction, and guided tours are available at the shop. There is night skiing by kerosene lamps and a bonfire every Friday. Nordic NASTAR races are held every weekend, USSA sanctioned races throughout the season, and an annual citizens' race in March. There is a daily area use fee with family and season memberships available.

Driving directions: From the Maine Turnpike (I-95), take Exit 11 for Gray and follow Route 26 north for about 45 miles to Bethel. From Bethel, take Routes 2, 5, and 26 toward Rumford; after about 3 miles, turn left to the Sunday River Ski Area. Follow this road for 2½ miles to the touring center at the Inn.

Suggestion courtesy of Sunday River Ski Touring Center, Sunday River Inn, RFD 2, Box 141, Bethel, Maine 04217 (207-824-2410).

Evergreen Valley Ski Touring Center
East Stoneham, Maine
25 miles of trails
novice-intermediate-advanced
USGS: Center Lovell/Speckled Mountain

Evergreen Valley maintains a large network of trails that connect with many others in the White Mountain National Forest. The trails are well marked and groomed, and maps are available. The new Adams Mountain Trail (6 miles) goes along a ridge from the summit of Adams Mountain, commanding excellent views of the White Mountains. To reach the summit, cross-country lift tickets may be purchased at the alpine ski area. Snowmobiles are not permitted on ski trails.

The Ski Touring Center has a waxing room and sells hot beverages and cross-country equipment and accessories. Rentals and instruction are offered. Special activities include guided tours, moonlight tours, citizens' races, and a Washington's Birthday race. There is a $2.00 trail fee.

Driving directions: From Route 5 in Stoneham, follow signs to Evergreen Valley.

Suggestion courtesy of Evergreen Valley Ski Touring Center, East Stoneham, Maine 04231 (207-928-3300).

Mount Abram Ski Slopes
Locke Mills, Maine
2-mile trail
novice-intermediate
USGS: Bryant Pond/Greenwood

Mount Abram maintains one trail for ski touring, which goes from the base lodge through stands of hardwoods and firs. It is marked with signs, and snowmobiles are prohibited. There are also logging roads in the area.

Ski tourers may use the facilities of the alpine ski area. The ski shop has sales and rentals of ski touring equipment. There is no trail fee.

Driving directions: From the Maine Turnpike (I-95), take Exit 11 at Gray and drive north on Route 26 to Locke Mills.

Suggestion courtesy of Jean Anton, Mount Abram Ski Slopes, Locke Mills, Maine 04255 (207-875-2601).

Teddybear Touring Trails
North Turner, Maine
10 miles of trails
novice-intermediate-advanced
USGS: Buckfield

Located at Bear Pond Park, Teddybear offers a variety of trails over hilly, mostly wooded terrain, with some fields and a frozen lake. Trails are groomed and marked according to difficulty, and maps are available. There are additional unmarked trails in the area which offer further skiing possibilities. Snowmobiles are not permitted on Teddybear trails.

Beverages and snacks are served at the Bear's Den, and rentals and instruction are available. The trail fee is $2.00. Teddybear is open on weekends and holidays and during school vacation weeks.

Driving directions: From the Maine Turnpike (I-95), take Exit 12 at Auburn. Go north on Route 4 to North Turner and turn left (west) onto Route 219. Continue for 1 mile to the Park.

Suggestion courtesy of Cecil and Ellie Wheeler, Auburn, Maine (207-783-1037). (Teddybear, 224-8275.)

Auburn Ski Touring Center
Auburn, Maine
10–15 miles of trails
novice–intermediate–advanced
USGS: Lewiston

Trails from Auburn Ski Touring Center wind through woods and fields over varied terrain. One trail follows the Androscoggin River, affording views of Gulf Island Dam. Trails are marked according to degree of difficulty and are shown on a trail map. Snowmobiles are not allowed on the trails.

Facilities include a snack bar and a waxing hut. Ski accessories, rentals, and instruction are available. There is a $2.00 trail fee.

Driving directions: From Route 4 in Auburn, turn onto North River Road at Wendy's Hamburger. Continue for 3 miles to the Touring Center.

Suggestion courtesy of Auburn Ski Touring Center, North River Road, Auburn, Maine 04210 (207-782-1360).

Sebago Lake State Park
Naples, Maine
3 miles, round trip
novice
USGS: Sebago Lake

The Sebago Lake ski touring trail goes from the parking area through mature mixed hardwood and evergreen forests to a beach in the day-use area of the Park. It is marked with signs, and a trail map is available. There is some snowmobile use from neighboring properties.

Driving directions: Sebago Lake State Park is off Route 35 between Raymond and Naples.

Suggestion courtesy of Thomas Cieslinski, Maine Department of Conservation, Augusta, Maine.

Bradbury Mountain State Park
Pownal, Maine
2 miles, round trip
novice–intermediate
USGS: Freeport

The Bradbury Mountain Trail has been designated specifically for ski touring. The first half mile is fairly gentle and easy; the second half is a steep climb to the summit of a 460-foot mountain. Return via the same route. The trail is marked with signs, but there is no map available. Snowmobiles have separate trails in other sections of the Park, and are not permitted on the ski trail.

Driving directions: Bradbury Mountain State Park is located on Route 9 in Pownal. Parking is limited.

Suggestion courtesy of Thomas Cieslinski, Maine Department of Conservation, Augusta, Maine.

Hermon Meadow Ski Center
Bangor, Maine
10 miles of trails/300 acres
novice–intermediate
USGS: Bangor

The Hermon Meadow Golf Club becomes a ski touring center in the winter, with trails over the rolling terrain of the golf course and surrounding wooded areas. Trails are marked and shown on a map. Snowmobiles are not permitted in the area, except to set tracks.

The Ski Center has a snack bar, waxing rooms, and rest rooms. Rentals and instruction are offered, and there is a $.75 trail fee.

Driving directions: From I-95 heading north, take the Hermon exit and go north on Coldbrook Road to Hermon Corner. From I-95 heading south, take the Union Street exit and follow Route 222 to the Pleasant Mill Dairy. Turn left onto Billings Road and continue to Hermon Corner.

Suggestion courtesy of Winthrop S. Pike, Hermon Meadow Ski Center, RFD #2, Bangor, Maine 04401 (207-848-3741).

University Forest
Stillwater, Maine
3½ miles
novice–intermediate
USGS: Orono

This is the primary training course for the University of Maine and is almost always in excellent condition. The trail traverses gently rolling terrain through forests and over meadows. The land is a game preserve. Occasional snowmobiles may be encountered.

Driving directions: North of Bangor, take the Stillwater Avenue exit from I-95. Turn right and drive 1 mile. Turn right again into the University Forest.

Suggestion courtesy of Brud and Scotty Folger, University of Maine, Orono, Maine.

University Forest

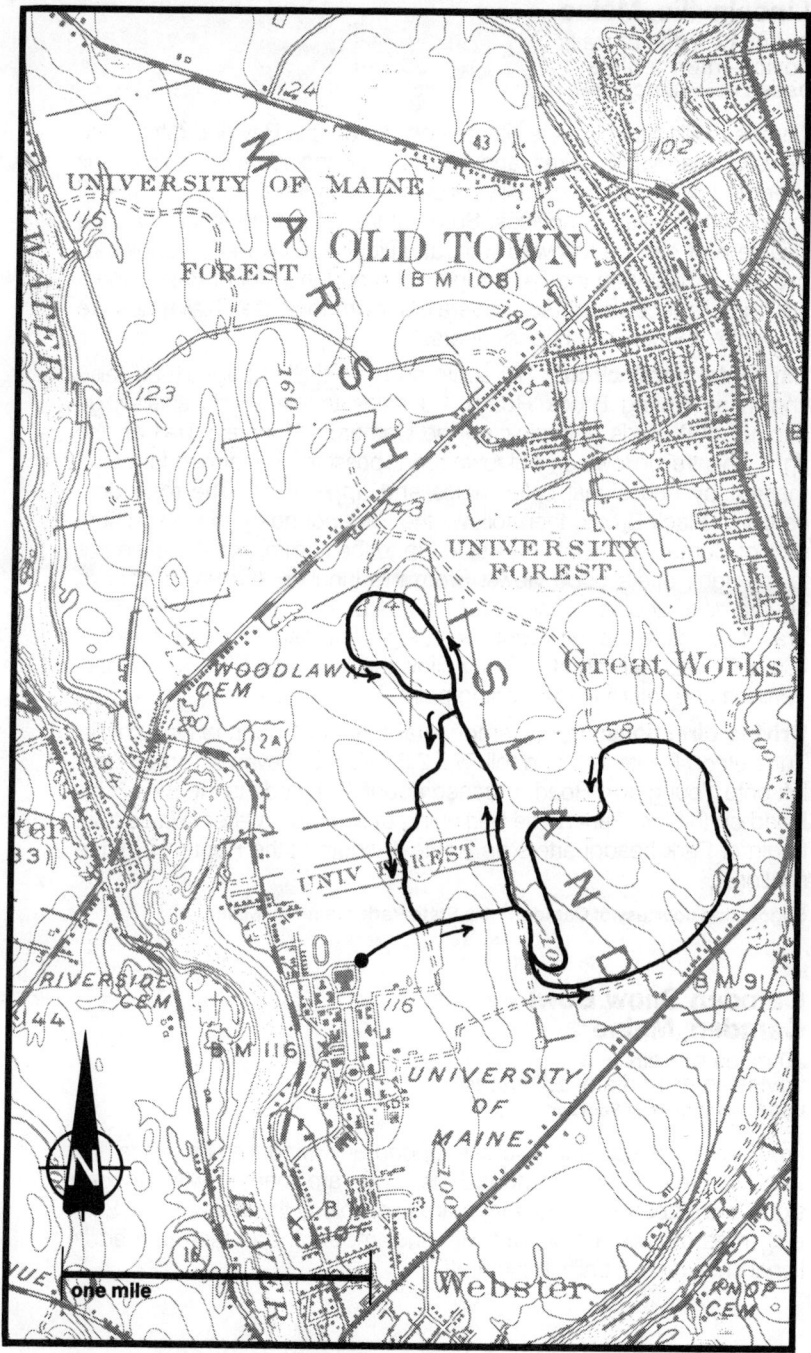

25   Maine

Camden Hills State Park
Lincolnville, Maine
about 12 miles of trails
novice–intermediate
USGS: Lincolnville/Camden

Camden Hills State Park is situated on Penobscot Bay and offers nice views of nearby hills, lakes, and ocean. Trails include a 6½-mile circuit over old town roads and easily-followed hiking trails. All but ½ mile of this circuit is suited to novices. Some of the other trails in the Park are skiable and can be followed without difficulty in the winter. Snowmobile use is heavy on the Ski Lodge Road and the Mount Battie Road. Hiking trails receive light to moderate snowmobile use. Trail maps are available at State Park headquarters.

Ski route, north circuit: Ski south on the old Ski Lodge Road (also known as Spring Brook Road) 1.3 miles to the picnic shelter; go another 100 yards and pick up the Cameron Mountain Trail on the right. This trail follows an old town road, passing abandoned farmland marked by occasional cellar holes and apple trees. The road descends to Black Brook, then follows the Park boundary to the southern side of Cameron Mountain. A side trip to the summit, off the main trail to the right, offers good views. From this junction, the trail descends 300 yards to another junction; turn left here. After ½ mile, the Sky Blue Trail diverges to the left. Continue straight another ¼ mile to the junction of Zeke's Trail, and turn left. Follow this trail to the Ski Lodge Road. Turn left and return to the starting point.

Driving directions: From Camden, take Route 1 north to Lincolnville. Turn left on Route 173 and follow it 2.3 miles to Steven's Corner. Bear left onto Youngtown Road; proceed about 100 yards to the Ski Lodge Road on the left. Park at the beginning of this road. Other skiable trails begin at Park headquarters on Route 1, south of the Route 173 intersection.

Suggestion courtesy of Camden Hills State Park, Camden, Maine.

Camden Snow Bowl
Camden, Maine
20 miles of trails
novice–intermediate–advanced
USGS: Camden/West Rockport

From the base lodge, trails cross a pond and wind through fields and wooded areas in the Camden Hills. They are marked with wooden signs and ribboned posts; maps are available at the Snow Bowl. Several miles of trails are shared with snowmobiles, and there are additional snowmobile trails in the area.

Ski tourers may use the facilities of the Camden Snow Bowl, which include a lodge with a fireplace and a cafeteria. Rentals and instruction are offered. Special activities include full moon tours and the annual Goose River Cross-Country Meet in February.

Driving directions: From Route 1 in Camden, take Hosmer Pond Road for 3 miles to the Snow Bowl.

Suggestion courtesy of Wendy Frutchy, Camden Snow Bowl, P.O. Box 456, Camden, Maine 04843 (207-236-4418).

Acadia National Park
Bar Harbor, Maine
36 miles of trails
novice-intermediate
USGS: Mt. Desert

Mount Desert Island has a large network of carriage roads that are designated for separate use by skiers and snowmobilers. The carriage roads are wide and not too steep and marked with rustic wooden signs. Thirty miles of carriage roads in the area of Sargent and Penobscot mountains, west of Eagle Lake and Jordan Pond, are set aside for ski touring and snowshoeing. Snowmobiles are prohibited in this area, which is bounded by Route 198 on the west, Route 233 on the north, and Route 3 on the south.

Another area that is set aside for ski touring includes 6 miles of carriage roads around Witch Hole Pond near the Hulls Cove Visitor Center. It is bounded by Route 3 to the north, the Park Loop Road to the east, and Route 233 to the south.

Most of the hiking trails on Mount Desert Island are too steep and narrow for ski touring, although some of the gentler trails are worth exploring. One possibility is the trail from the Asticou Inn (Northeast Harbor) to Jordan Pond, about 4 miles, round trip. This is a gentle trail through the woods and should be easy to follow as the snow is not exceptionally deep.

The best trail maps of the island are the AMC Mount Desert Island map and the USGS Mt. Desert quadrangle. The trails are described in the AMC *Maine Mountain Guide* and the AMC *Trail Guide to Mount Desert Island and Acadia National Park*. Other trail maps, some showing the designated ski and snowmobile routes, are available locally.

Snow conditions are unpredictable: check current conditions before setting out.

Driving directions: From I-95, take Route 1A southeast to Ellsworth. From Ellsworth, take Route 3 to Mount Desert Island. See a map for directions from here.

Suggestion courtesy of Acadia National Park, RFD #1, Box 1, Bar Harbor, Maine 04609 (207-288-3338).

Holbrook Island Sanctuary
Brooksville, Maine
1230 acres
novice
USGS: Cape Rosier

This is an area of wooded, rocky shoreline along Penobscot Bay. There are gentle trails and abandoned roads winding across hilly terrain. Snowmobiling is prohibited.

Driving directions: Follow Route 1 north to Orland, then take Route 175 south to North Brooksville. Follow signs to Cape Rosier. Park alongside the road.

Suggestion courtesy of Tom Cieslinski, Maine Department of Conservation, Augusta, Maine.

Moosehorn National Wildlife Refuge
Calais and Dennysville, Maine
40 miles of trails
novice-intermediate
USGS: Calais/Devils Head/Red Beach (Baring)
Pembroke/Whiting/Gardner Lake (Edmunds)

Moosehorn National Wildlife Refuge is divided into two separate areas totalling over 22,000 acres. The Baring Division is larger, and has headquarters and a visitor center in Calais; the Edmunds Division is in Dennysville and Edmunds, about 25 miles south, and includes a state-managed camping and recreation area along Whiting Bay. Both areas are on low, gently rolling coastal terrain. Panoramic views are limited, since the higher elevations are only 100-200 feet above sea level. There are some good views of Whiting Bay, however. Trails in both divisions are gravel roads, well marked, wide, and easy to follow. They wind through dense forest, primarily coniferous, with some areas of mixed hardwood and relatively open country. Trail maps of both areas are available at no cost. Snowmobiles are permitted on designated routes, but are not allowed in the wilderness areas (which are open to ski touring). There is occasional conflict of use on weekends and evenings; skiers may check at the Refuge headquarters for current information.

Driving directions: From Calais, travel north on Route 1, then turn left onto Charlotte Road for a total of 6 miles. Refuge signs (Baring Division) are posted from here. Parking is permitted at Refuge headquarters, or at any of the gates along Charlotte Road or Route 191 if they are sufficiently plowed. The Edmunds Division is about 3 miles south of Dennysville on Route 1.

Suggestion courtesy of Douglas M. Mullen, Refuge Manager, Moosehorn National Wildlife Refuge, Calais, Maine 04619.

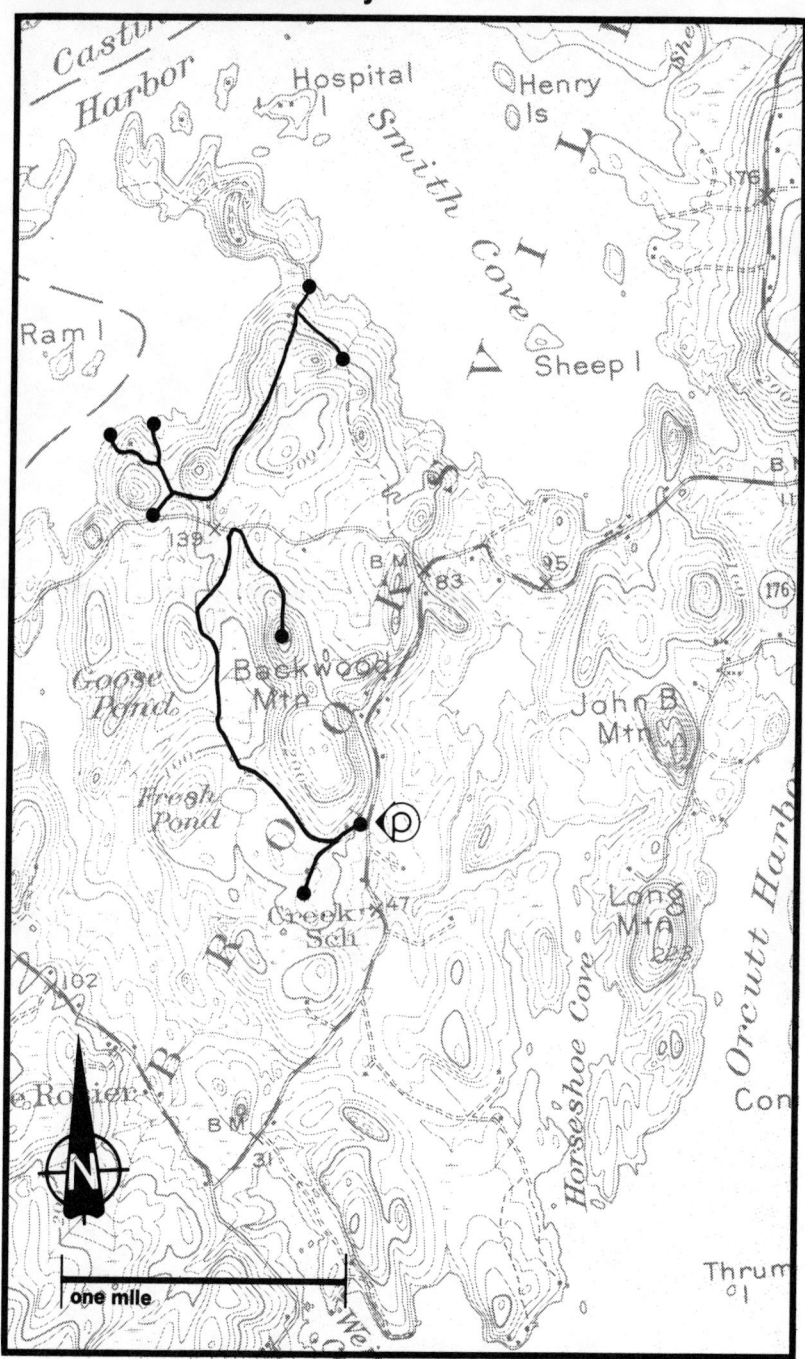

Holbrook Island Sanctuary

Ski Touring New Hampshire
CHAPTER 2

New Hampshire

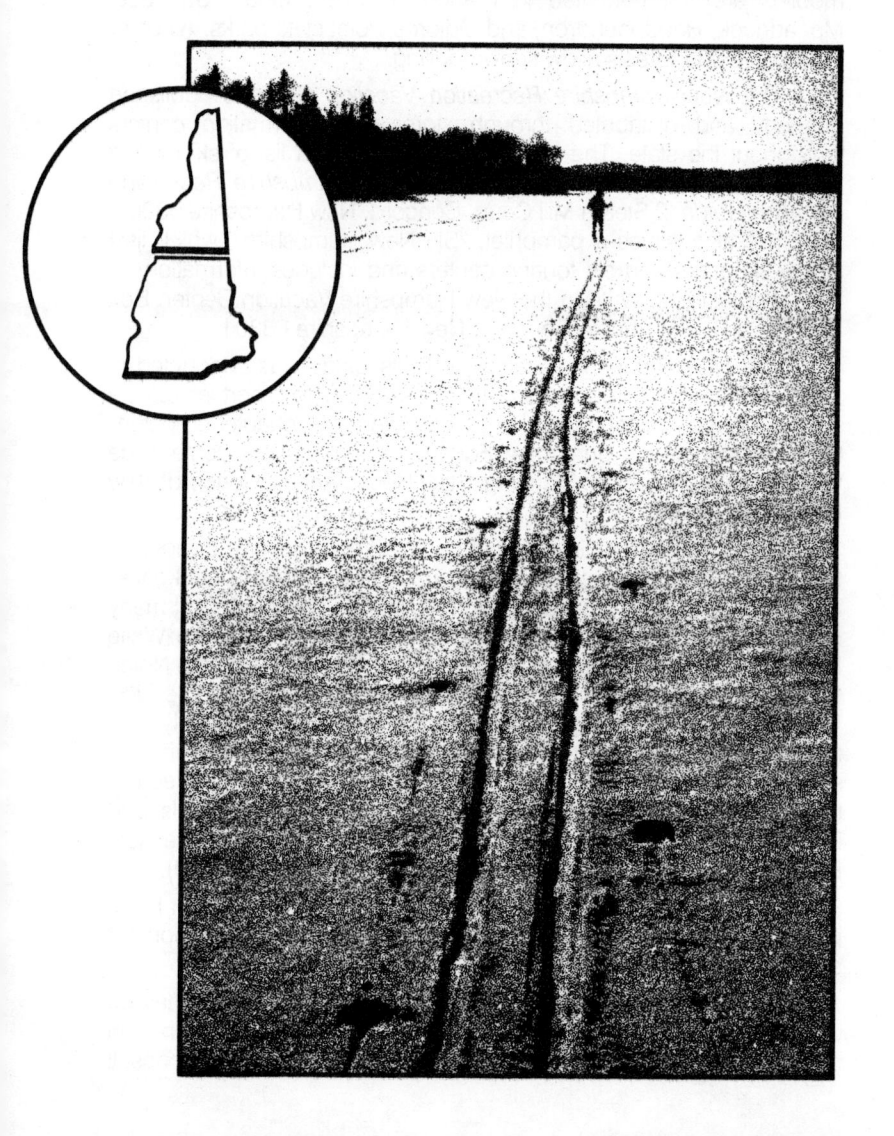

Ski touring is permitted in all New Hampshire state parks and forests, and four have developed ski touring trails: Mount Sunapee, Franconia Notch, Monadnock, and Bear Brook state parks (see individual entries). The state of New Hampshire prints maps of these parks and issues a pamphlet, *The Clean Getaway,* which describes each state park. Write to the Department of Resources and Economic Development, Division of Parks, State House Annex, Concord, New Hampshire 03301, for trail maps, or to the Department of Resources and Economic Development, Division of Economic Development, P.O. Box 856, Concord, New Hampshire 03301, for the pamphlet. Snowmobiles are not permitted in Franconia Notch, Mount Sunapee, Monadnock, Rhododendron, and Odiorne Point state parks. All other state parks and forests allow snowmobiling.

The *New Hampshire Recreation Vacation Guide* is published quarterly and distributed through stores and information centers throughout the state. The winter edition includes a list of ski touring areas in New Hampshire. Write to the *New Hampshire Recreation Vacation Guide,* 2 Steam Mill Court, Concord, New Hampshire 03301. The state also issues a pamphlet, "Ski New Hampshire," which lists alpine ski areas and ski touring centers and includes information on trails and facilities. Write to the New Hampshire Vacation Center, Box 856, State House Annex, Concord, New Hampshire 03301.

The New Hampshire Statewide Trails Study was conducted in 1973, and a lengthy report was issued in 1974. This report includes a short section on ski touring trails, plus an interesting chapter on potential trails for various purposes. For further information, contact the Office of Comprehensive Planning, State House Annex, Concord, New Hampshire 03301.

The White Mountain National Forest offers extensive opportunities for experienced skiers, including possibilities for long backpacking trips. Some good tours are described in the following pages; many others are possible. An excellent source of information in the White Mountains is the Appalachian Mountain Club (AMC) at Pinkham Notch Camp, Gorham, New Hampshire 03581 (603-466-2721). The U.S. Forest Service is also a good source of information, particularly pertaining to snowmobile use in the White Mountains (they are permitted in some areas, not in others). The Forest Service issues a winter recreation map that shows many ski touring trails and snowmobile trails, and includes other relevant information. Contact the U.S. Forest Service, P.O. Box 638, Laconia, New Hampshire 03246 (603-524-6450).

25 Ski Tours in the White Mountains, by Sally and Daniel Ford, includes maps, driving directions, and detailed trail information for selected tours in New Hampshire.

The following guides to hiking trails in New Hampshire may be useful to the ski tourer. All include trail descriptions and maps, though none evaluates trails specifically for ski touring. It is best to consult topographic maps or to have summer experience on a trail before attempting it on skis. Keep in mind that although negotiating stream crossings and finding parking areas may not pose problems for summer hikers, they can be very difficult in winter.

The AMC *White Mountain Guide* is the most comprehensive book on New Hampshire trails. In addition to trails in the White Mountains, it covers trails in mountain regions (such as Monadnock and Sunapee) further south. An excellent series of maps (Grand Monadnock, Mount Cardigan, Chocorua-Waterville, Franconia Region, Mount Washington Range, Carter-Mahoosuc, and Pilot) comes with the book; these also may be purchased separately. There is a short section entitled "White Mountains in Winter" at the end of the book.

The *Guide to the Appalachian Trail in New Hampshire and Vermont* covers the Appalachian Trail through the White Mountains. This is an especially rugged section of trail, and very little is skiable. A couple of sections south of Mount Moosilauke may be suitable.

Fifty Hikes: Walks, Day Hikes and Backpacking Trips in New Hampshire's White Mountains, by Daniel Doan, describes many possible hiking trips in the White Mountains area. Though most of the terrain is too steep, several areas are skiable in whole or in part. The Wildcat River–Bog Brook Loop is fine for skiing, though longer than the route described in the book, since the access road is not plowed all the way. The Old Mast Road is skiable; there is parking on the road north of Wonalancet near the trail sign. The Kelly Trail follows a brook and is therefore rough for skiing unless there is good snow cover. Black Pond, via the Wilderness Trail, is excellent for skiing. The Three Ponds Trail and the East Pond Trail are both good possibilities, though the latter has one steep section that may be difficult to descend. Other trails to investigate are Sabbaday Falls (the Sabbaday Brook Trail), the Rail n' River Forest Trail, the Crew-Cut Trail from Pinkham Notch, the Carrigain Notch Trail to Desolation Shelter (see entry in this Guide for Wilderness Trail–Carrigain Notch–Sawyer River Road), and the lower trail on Mount Pequawket (Kearsarge North). Refer to *Fifty Hikes* for trail descriptions, maps, and driving directions.

Fifty More Hikes in New Hampshire, by Daniel Doan, *25 Walks in the Dartmouth–Lake Sunapee Region,* by Mary L. Kibling, and *25 Walks in the Lakes Region,* by Paul H. Blaisdell, include a number of trips with ski touring potential.

Off the Beaten Path: Short Hikes in the White Mountains, by John Henderson, describes 26 hikes under 5 miles in length. Many of these are rated easy to moderate in difficulty and are potentially good for ski touring.

The SLA *Trails Guide,* published by the Squam Lakes Association, describes trails in the lakes area and in the Ossipee Mountains. It comes with a map that may be purchased separately.

Franconia Notch: An In-Depth Guide, edited by Diane M. Kostecke, includes a map of the Franconia Notch area and some trail descriptions. The *Monadnock Guide,* edited by Henry I. Baldwin, gives a history and natural history of Mount Monadnock, as well as trail descriptions. The AMC Grand Monadnock map is included with the book. The *Monadnock Guide* and *Franconia Notch* are both published by the Society for the Protection of New Hampshire Forests. For a brochure describing their publications, write to them at 5 South State Street, Concord, New Hampshire 03301.

The *Guide to the Metacomet—Monadnock Trail in Massachusetts and New Hampshire* covers about 16 miles of trail in southern New Hampshire. See entry under Western Massachusetts.

The Randolph Mountain Club publishes a waterproof map, "Randolph Valley and the Northern Peaks," that shows the northern Presidentials in greater detail than the AMC Mount Washington map.

Northern New Hampshire Ski Touring Areas

1. Wilderness Ski Area, Dixville Notch   *38*
2. York Pond Trail, Lancaster/Berlin   *38*
   Kilkenny Area, Kilkenny/Berlin/Randolph   *39*
3. Nansen Ski Club Touring Trails, Berlin   *40*
4. Pine Mountain, Martin's Location   *41*
5. Nineteen-Mile Brook Trail to Carter Notch,
   Pinkham Notch   *41*
6. Pinkham Notch Area, Gorham   *42*
7. White Mountain School, Littleton   *44*
8. Franconia Inn Cross-Country Ski Center, Franconia   *45*
   Sunset Hill Touring Center, Sugar Hill   *45*
9. Cannon Mountain/Franconia Notch
   State Park, Franconia   *46*
   Pemi Trail, Franconia/Lincoln   *46*
10. Owl's Head Area, Lincoln   *48*
11. Bretton Woods Touring Center, Bretton Woods   *49*
    Zealand Road-Zealand Trail-
    Ethan Pond Trail, Carroll   *49*
12. Mount Willard, Crawford Notch   *50*
13. Wilderness Trail-Carrigain Notch-
    Sawyer River Road, Lincoln   *51*
    Hancock Notch Trail-Sawyer River Trail, Lincoln   *52*
14. Hancock Notch-Cedar Brook-
    Wilderness Loop, Lincoln   *53*
15. Sawyer River Road Area, Hart's Location   *53*
16. Church Pond Loop, Albany   *54*
17. Red Ridge on Middle Moat Mountain, North Conway   *55*
18. Jackson Ski Touring Foundation, Jackson   *56*
19. East Branch Saco River and
    Wild River Valleys, Chatham   *57*
20. Holiday Inn, Intervale   *55*
21. Mount Moosilauke, Warren/Benton   *58*
22. Glover Brook Trail, Woodstock   *58*
    Hubbard Brook Experimental Forest Area,
    West Thornton   *60*
23. Tripoli Road-Russell Pond, Woodstock   *61*
24. Loon Mountain Ski Touring Center, Lincoln   *61*
25. Greeley Ponds Trail, Lincoln/Waterville Valley   *62*
26. Waterville Valley Ski Touring Center,
    Waterville Valley   *62*
27. Guinea Pond Trail to Flat Mountain Pond, Sandwich   *63*
28. Bolles Trail, Mount Chocorua Area, Albany   *64*
29. Foss Mountain Ski Touring, Snowville   *65*

Northern New Hampshire

Northern New Hampshire

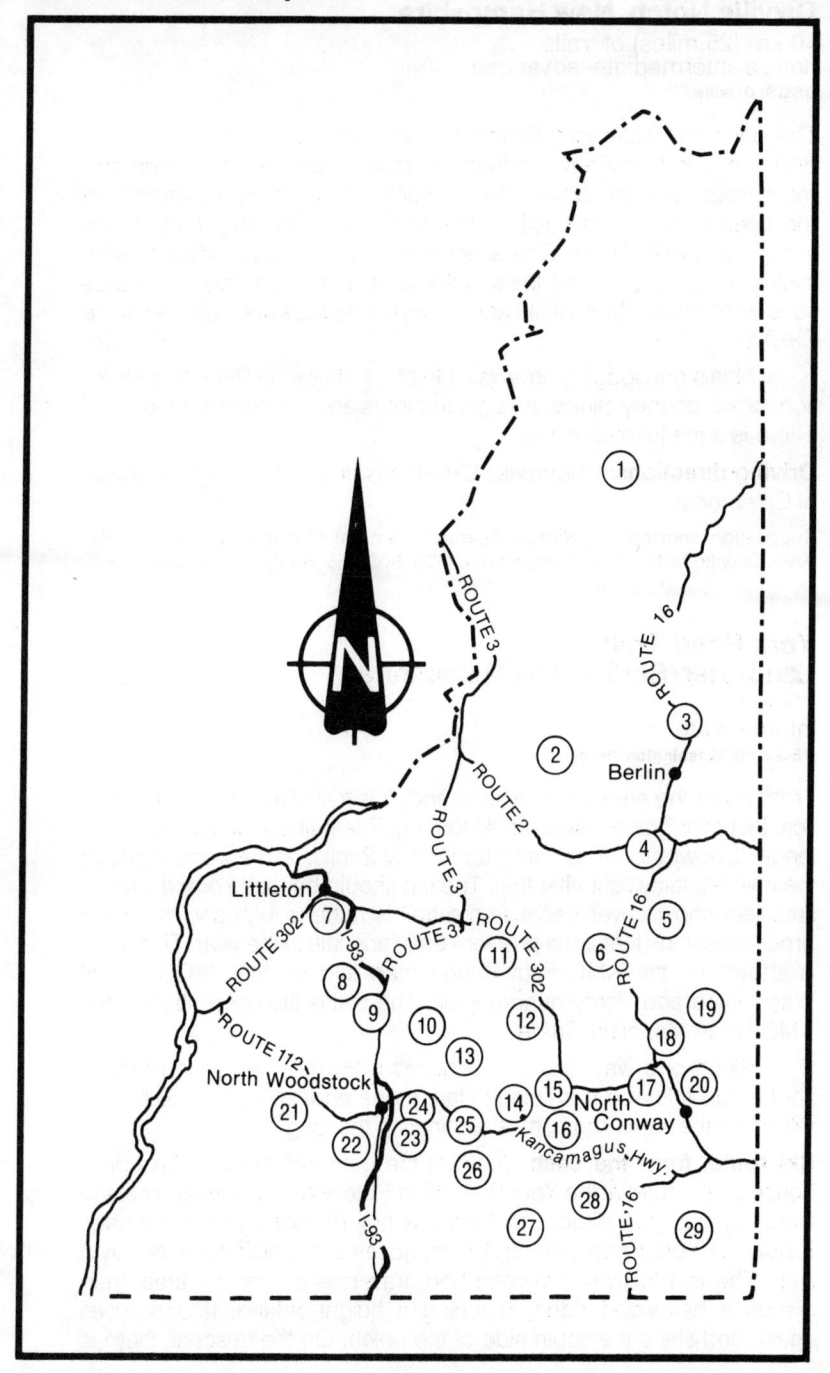

Wilderness Ski Area
Dixville Notch, New Hampshire
40 km (25 miles) of trails
novice-intermediate-advanced
USGS: Dixville

The Balsams/Wilderness Resort has dependable powder snow conditions due to its extreme northern location. There are 14 marked and maintained trails; some have double tracks. Touring is also possible on the open terrain of the golf course and on old logging roads in the vicinity of Dixville Notch. The scenery is beautiful. Snowmobiles use a system of state groomed trails in the area, but share only a few sections with skiers. Maps of ski and snowmobile trails are available at the Ski Area.

Meals and lodging are available at the Balsams. Rentals, instruction, cross-country clinics, and guided tours are offered at the Ski Area. There is a fee for trail use.

Driving directions: Wilderness Ski Area is on Route 26, 11 miles east of Colebrook.

Suggestion courtesy of Warren Pearson, General Manager, Wilderness Ski Area, Dixville Notch, New Hampshire 03576 (603-255-3400).

York Pond Trail
Lancaster/Berlin, New Hampshire
7½ miles
intermediate
USGS: Mt. Washington/Percy

From either the eastern or western end, this trail climbs about 900 vertical feet over grades ideal for ski touring. The trail is wide for most of its length. Snowmobiling is heavy for the first 2 miles at the western end of the trail, but fairly light after that. The trip should be made only if there is sufficient snow cover because the trail is rather rough and there are brook crossings that are a problem early and late in the year. This route is shown on the AMC Pilot Range map and on the USGS Mount Washington and Percy quadrangles. The trail is also described in the AMC *White Mountain Guide*.

Skied one way, this tour requires a 20-mile shuttle in order to spot a car. It is also possible to start at one end, ski to the notch, and return via the same route, thus eliminating the long drive.

Ski route, from the east: Begin at the gate just beyond the upper house on the road at the York Pond Fish Hatchery. The caretaker at the Hatchery can give directions if there is any problem finding the gate. Follow the York Pond Trail for 1 mile; go left at a junction marked by a sign. The trail follows a railroad bed, traverses a swampy area, then climbs a hardwood ridge, reaching a height-of-land. It dips, rises again, and slabs the south side of the notch. On the descent, there is an area of old logging roads where most junctions are marked with arrows or signs. The trail crosses the brook three times, then becomes a main haul road. After 1.3 miles, the trail leaves the road and turns right on another road. This junction is marked by a sign. Continue on this road to the junction with the Bunnell Notch Trail, then turn left for White's Farm.

Driving directions: To approach the western end of the trail, drive west on Route 2 from Jefferson. Turn right on North Road after ¼ mile and go 2.3 miles to Gore Road. Turn right and continue for 1.7 miles. Turn right on Pleasant Valley Road, proceed for 0.8 miles, and continue straight on Arthur White Road. Park at the end of this road where the trail begins. To get to the eastern end of the trail, drive northwest from Berlin on Route 110 for about 8 miles, then turn left at the sign for the York Pond Fish Hatchery. After about 1½ miles, bear right at the fork and continue for about 5 miles to the Fish Hatchery.

Kilkenny Area
Kilkenny/Berlin/Randolph, New Hampshire
55+ miles of trails
intermediate-advanced
USGS: Mt. Washington/Percy

The Pliny and Pilot Ranges, north of the Presidentials, form the southwest border of the section of the White Mountain National Forest known as the Kilkenny wilderness. There are a number of trails in this area, with elevations from 1500 to 3000 feet, that are good for ski touring.

Entry from Berlin at the York Pond Fish Hatchery offers several possibilities for intermediate skiing, including the York Pond Trail (see separate entry). Another, slightly steeper, route with the same end points is the Bunnell Notch Trail. These two can combine to form a loop, for a 1 or 2 day tour that returns to the starting point. From the York Pond Trail, the Mill Brook and Unknown Pond Trails go north and can be skied as a circuit, returning to the Fish Hatchery, or one way to Stark. Skiable trails south of the Hatchery include unplowed sections of Bog Dam Road, the Upper Ammonoosuc Trail, Landing Camp Trail, the Pond of Safety Trail (and an unplowed portion of the road along Stag Hollow Brook), and Vyron D. Lowe's Trail. Using these trails, it is possible to ski from York Pond or Bog Dam to Stag Hollow in Jefferson, or to Randolph. More difficult routes include Cook Path, the Ice Gulch Trail (from Camp 19 to Hunter's Pass), and Carlton Notch Trail. These routes go from the Pond of Safety Trail to Randolph and may be skied in a loop or as part of a longer tour.

Refer to the AMC *White Mountain Guide* for trail descriptions. All trails, except for a couple of short connecting trails near the Fish Hatchery, are shown on the AMC Pilot map.

Driving directions: For directions to the York Pond Fish Hatchery and White Road, see the York Pond Trail entry. To park near Bog Dam, at the start of the Upper Ammonoosuc Trail, go left at the fork on the road to the Fish Hatchery and continue to where the plowed road ends. To ski on the Carlton Notch Trail or Cook Path, take Route 2 west from Gorham and turn right onto Randolph Mountain Road. Park at the end of the road, about ¼ mile west of the Mt. Crescent Hotel. Vyron D. Lowe's Trail begins on Route 2, about 3 miles west of Randolph, at Lowe's Cabins and General Store. To ski Stag Hollow Road to the Pond of Safety Trail, turn onto Ingerson Road from Route 2, just west of the junction with Route 115. Where Ingerson Road goes left, Stag Hollow Road goes straight ahead.

Suggestion courtesy of Jerry Weene, Northern Journeys Ltd., Goshen, Massachusetts.

Nansen Ski Club Touring Trails
Berlin, New Hampshire
19 miles of trails
novice-intermediate-advanced
USGS: Milan

Organized in 1872, Nansen Ski Club is the oldest ski club in America. Nansen maintains an extensive system of trails through soft- and hardwood forests with lovely wilderness scenery. The Beaver Trail passes a beaver pond and lodge. Trails are groomed and are patrolled by a NSPS Nordic Ski Patrol. They are well marked, and trail maps are available. Snowmobiles are prohibited.

Facilities for ski tourers are limited. There is a snack bar next to the parking area, and a warming hut with a fire pit and a grill situated on a trail. Rentals, instruction, and guided tours are available locally. The Ski Club offers citizens' races and fun races, and information on trail conditions and waxing is available every day. Trail use and all Nansen Ski Club activities are free and open to the public.

The Nansen Ski Jump nearby is the site of national and international meets each year.

Driving directions: Parking for Nansen Ski Club trails is off East Milan Road, 3 miles north of Berlin and 5 miles south of Milan.

Suggestion courtesy of Dona Larsen-Denman, Nansen Ski Club, Berlin, New Hampshire

Pine Mountain
Martin's Location, New Hampshire
7.5 miles, round trip
intermediate-advanced
USGS: Carter Dome

This is a gentle, scenic climb to the summit of Pine Mountain. The trail receives heavy snowmobile use. It is shown on the USGS Carter Dome quadrangle and on the AMC Mount Washington Range and Pilot maps. The AMC *White Mountain Guide* contains a detailed trail description.

Ski route: From Route 16, follow Dolly Copp Road west, crossing the bridge over the Peabody River and passing the entrance to the campground to the left. About 1.9 miles west of Route 16, just past the height-of-land and opposite the foot of Pine Link, turn right on a narrow auto road. The road runs east across the col and forks left to ascend the left flank of Pine Mountain. Do not take the right fork: it traverses a cliff on the south side of the mountain. At the summit, leave skis by the building, and walk to the lookout tower.

Driving directions: From North Conway, drive north on Route 16 through Pinkham Notch. Continue for 3½ miles past the Glen House and the beginning of the Mount Washington Auto Road to the unplowed Dolly Copp Road on the left. There is a large sign for the Dolly Copp Campground. Park as far off Route 16 as possible.

Nineteen-Mile Brook Trail to Carter Notch
Pinkham Notch, New Hampshire
3.8 miles
novice (first 2 miles) - intermediate (to Notch)
USGS: Carter Dome

This is a well-graded trail that grows progressively steeper toward the top. It involves a climb of about 2000 vertical feet within less than 4 miles. Snowmobiles generally do not use the trail due to the hillside traverse on the lower section. The trail is shown on the AMC Mount Washington Range map and on the USGS Carter Dome quadrangle. The AMC *White Mountain Guide* includes a trail description.

Ski route: The trail is easy to follow for the first 2 miles. After that it becomes progressively steeper and requires some sidestepping. The notch can be windy and cold; bring warm clothing.

Driving directions: From North Conway, go north on Route 16 through Pinkham Notch. The trail starts on the right; about 1 mile beyond the beginning of the Mount Washington Auto Road. There is a small parking area at the trailhead.

Pinkham Notch Area
Gorham, New Hampshire
17 miles of trails
novice-intermediate-advanced
USGS: Mt. Washington/Crawford Notch/Carter Dome/North Conway

The area around the AMC Pinkham Notch Camp has a number of short trails suitable for ski touring. The terrain is generally steep, with some exciting downhills for advanced skiers, and a couple of trails for novices. Trails are marked with blue diamonds, and maps are available at Pinkham Notch Camp. The trails are also shown on Jackson Ski Touring Foundation maps. Most trails are heavily skied, and snowmobiles are prohibited.

There is a waxing room, an information desk, and a snack bar at Pinkham Notch Camp. The AMC conducts a variety of weekend workshops for ski tourers throughout the season, including beginning and intermediate instruction and a skiing and music weekend in March for chamber music enthusiasts. Send for a current schedule.

Trail descriptions: Old Jackson Road (1.6 miles, intermediate): This trail is often skied in conjunction with the Mount Washington Auto Road. It leaves the Camp from the northwest corner of the Trading Post building near the lower end of the Tuckerman Ravine Trail. It winds through the woods for about 0.2 miles, ascends steeply for about ½ mile, crosses two streams, levels out, then descends slightly. It crosses two more streams, then climbs to the 2-mile marker on the Mount Washington Auto Road. Caution should be used if descending: the trail is steep and narrow. The beginning of the trail is suited for novices.

Blanchard Loop (1 mile, novice): This trail begins with the John Sherburne Ski Trail at the south end of the Pinkham Notch Camp parking lot. The Blanchard Loop Trail bears right from the Sherburne Trail, about 200 feet from the parking lot. Shortly after the junction, it turns sharply left at a staff residence building, continues to the bank of the Cutler River, then joins the Tuckerman Ravine Trail. It follows the Tuckerman Ravine Trail left for about 300 feet, then turns right. The trail descends steeply, then more gradually, to the Old Jackson Road. It crosses a power line and reaches Route 16. To return to Pinkham Notch Camp, turn right at the power line, then left at a marked pole to the north end of the parking lot.

Gulf of Slides Ski Trail (2½ miles, novice to advanced): The bottom section of the trail meanders over gentle terrain through open woods and is suitable for beginners. It gets much steeper, ending in the bowl of the Gulf of Slides. The entire trail may be ascended with light touring equipment, but the descent is quite difficult; ski mountaineering equipment is preferable. This trail offers excellent spring skiing; the upper sections are still good in April and May. From the southern end of the Pinkham Notch parking lot, begin skiing on the John Sherburne Ski Trail. After 100 feet, the Gulf of Slides Trail goes off to the left. Before freezing and after thawing it is possible to avoid a potentially difficult river crossing by continuing on the Sherburne Trail for a short distance, then crossing on a bridge.

Lost Pond Trail (1.2 miles, novice–intermediate): This trail leaves the east side of Route 16, slightly south of Pinkham Notch Camp. In heavy snow, it is possible to ski directly across the swamp and meet the trail on the east bank. Otherwise, the trail crosses a stream on a bridge, then turns sharply to the right. Lost Pond Trail continues straight along the bank of the Ellis River. Caution: do not ski on overhanging snow at the river's edge. The trail ascends slightly and reaches Lost Pond, where there are excellent views. The route south of Lost Pond is difficult and not particularly rewarding.

Pinkham Notch Ski Trail (0.6 miles, novice–intermediate): This is a short, fairly easy route from Pinkham Notch Camp to the Wildcat Ski Area. The trail leaves the east side of Route 16 across from Pinkham Notch Camp, crosses a swamp and a small stream, then enters the woods on a logging road. It ascends gradually to a second stream and soon reaches the base of an old practice slope where the alternate route (see below) joins on the right. The main route climbs another 0.3 miles, then descends steeply to another stream near the base of an old Wildcat racing trail. It ascends briefly and ends at the southernmost Wildcat alpine ski trail.

Pinkham Notch Ski Trail, alternate route (0.4 miles, intermediate): This route bypasses the swamp. It may be reached by taking the Lost Pond Trail from Route 16. Cross a stream on a bridge; turn right, then left. The trail ascends steeply about 300 feet, then flattens out and passes to the east of Ladies Ledge. It crosses the clearing of an old practice slope, turns left, then descends slightly to rejoin the main route. Caution: descent of this trail is not recommended; there is no runout.

Mount Washington Auto Road (4 miles, intermediate–advanced): The section of the Mount Washington Auto Road below timberline provides excellent skiing on minimal snow. (Snow vehicles using the Auto Road for access to the Summit Observatory may cut up the snow cover.) Skiing above the Halfway House is not recommended due to severe conditions. The road is usually reached from Pinkham Notch Camp via the Old Jackson Road.

Avalanche Brook Ski Trail (6.0 miles, advanced): This challenging trail connects Pinkham Notch Camp with the Dana Place Inn to the south. From the south end of the Pinkham Notch parking lot, follow the Gulf of Slides Ski Trail for approximately 0.2 miles to a junction where the Avalanche Brook Trail leaves on the left. The trail climbs about 900 feet in elevation, and drops about 1500 feet, traversing hard- and softwood forests. There are several stream crossings; a number of them have bridges. After about 4.9 miles, the trail follows the Rocky Branch Trail for a short while, then branches right where it ends in a field across the river from the Dana Place Inn. From here, the Highwater Trail goes left to Route 16 or right to connect with the Ellis River Trail from Jackson. Skiers should bear in mind that the Avalanche Brook Trail is quite difficult and should not be attempted alone or in poor conditions.

Driving directions: Pinkham Notch Camp is located on Route 16, 15 miles north of North Conway and 11 miles south of Gorham. There is a parking lot by the camp. Skiers and winter hikers may register their trips at the camp.

Suggestion courtesy of Reuben Rajala, AMC Pinkham Notch Camp, Gorham, New Hampshire 03581 (603-466-2727).

White Mountain School
Littleton, New Hampshire
15-km (9-mile) trail
intermediate
USGS: Littleton

The White Mountain School maintains a trail for race training, which is open to the public. The amount of track set at any given time depends on the weather and racing schedules. Most of the trail is in the woods, although there are also two big fields. The trail is not marked, but maps are available at the school office. Snowmobiles are not permitted. The school occasionally sponsors ESA and citizens' races.

Driving directions: From I-93, take Exit 40 and follow signs to the White Mountain School.

Suggestion courtesy of Alan Watson, Ski Coach, White Mountain School, Littleton, New Hampshire.

Franconia Inn Cross-Country Ski Center
Franconia, New Hampshire
45 miles of trails
novice-intermediate-advanced
USGS: Franconia/Sugar Hill

Franconia Inn maintains an extensive network of trails, from the flat, open airstrip to the NCAA-designed 7.5-km racing trail. In addition to groomed trails, there are 20 miles of primitive trails. All are marked according to NSTOA standards, and maps are free at the Ski Center. Snowmobiles are not permitted. The Franconia Inn system connects several points of interest in the area, including inns and restaurants. These trails also connect with those from Sunset Hill House to the west (see separate entry), and with Cannon Mountain Ski Area (see separate entry) and Mittersill to the east.

The touring center is housed in a barn and offers accessories sales, repairs, rentals, instruction, guided tours, and moonlight tours. Franconia Inn has 29 rooms and a restaurant; reservations are required. There is a $2.00 trail fee.

Driving directions: From Exit 38 off I-93, take Route 116 south for 2 miles to the Inn.

Suggestion courtesy of Karen McKenzie, Franconia Inn Cross-Country Ski Center, Route 116, Franconia, New Hampshire 03580 (603-823-5542).

Sunset Hill Touring Center
Sugar Hill, New Hampshire
50 km (31 miles) of trails
novice-intermediate-advanced
USGS: Sugar Hill/Franconia

Starting at Sunset Hill House, trails wind through the surrounding hills and offer panoramic views of the White Mountains. The area is largely wooded, with an apple orchard, open fields, and stands of hardwoods and pines. Trails are well marked and most are groomed; maps are free at the Touring Center. The Inn Connection Trail joins Sunset Hill trails with those from Franconia Inn (see separate entry). Snowmobiles are prohibited.

The Touring Center includes a unique warming hut with a potbellied stove and homemade soup, a waxing room, and a retail shop. Rentals and instruction are offered. Special activities include citizens' races, guided tours, and winter carnival events. Accommodations are available at Sunset Hill House. A $2.00 trail donation is requested.

Driving directions: Sunset Hill is just off Route 117, 2 miles west of Franconia.

Suggestion courtesy of Douglas A. Reed, Sunset Hill Touring Center, Sugar Hill, New Hampshire 03585 (603-823-5522).

The Pemi Trail
Franconia/Lincoln, New Hampshire
3- or 5-mile trail
intermediate
USGS: Plymouth

This is a sporty trip through the heart of Franconia Notch, with great views of Cannon Mountain Ski Area, Kinsman and Franconia ridges, and the Old Man of the Mountain. The weather can be extreme here; skiers should bring plenty of clothing and a face mask. It is best to ski the trail from north to south so the wind is from behind, and the sun ahead. Since the trail is a little rough, it should be skied only when there is good snow cover.

Ski route: From the parking area at Echo Lake, skirt the western shore of the pond to the base of the ski area. Go south along an unplowed road to the tramway parking area. Walk through this area, and continue south along an unplowed road and trail just west of Route 3 to the "Old Man" area. Skirt the east side of Profile Lake, and pick up the Pemi trail again at the south end. From here the trail follows a brook to Lafayette Campground. Note: do not ski on Profile or Echo lakes. The varying water levels make the ice unsafe.

From Lafayette Campground, there are several possible ski routes. There is a parking lot at the campground, so the tour can end there. The Pemi Trail goes south for another 2 miles to the Basin area and ends at Whitehouse bridge, where there is parking. There is pleasant skiing at the campground, on the campsite access roads, and across Route 3 at the Old Bridal Path and Falling Waters Trail area.

Driving directions: Take I-93 and Route 3 north through Franconia Notch. After Echo Lake, turn left toward Peabody Slopes, go past the lake, and park in the big plowed area on the left. Construction on Route 3 through the Notch may necessitate changes in this route.

Suggestion courtesy of Dr. Ed Cutler, Woodstock Lodge, Woodstock, New Hampshire.

Cannon Mountain/Franconia Notch State Park
Franconia, New Hampshire
5.1 miles of trails
novice–intermediate
USGS: Franconia

Trails from Cannon Mountain Ski Area are gentle and rolling. The main trail to the north runs over the former Route 3; side trails are on old logging roads. Each trail is marked with colored arrows, and maps are available at the Cannon Mountain base lodge. Snowmobiles are not permitted.

Ski tourers may use the facilities of the base lodge. Rentals, instruction, guided tours, and special programs are offered. There is no trail fee.

Pemi Trail

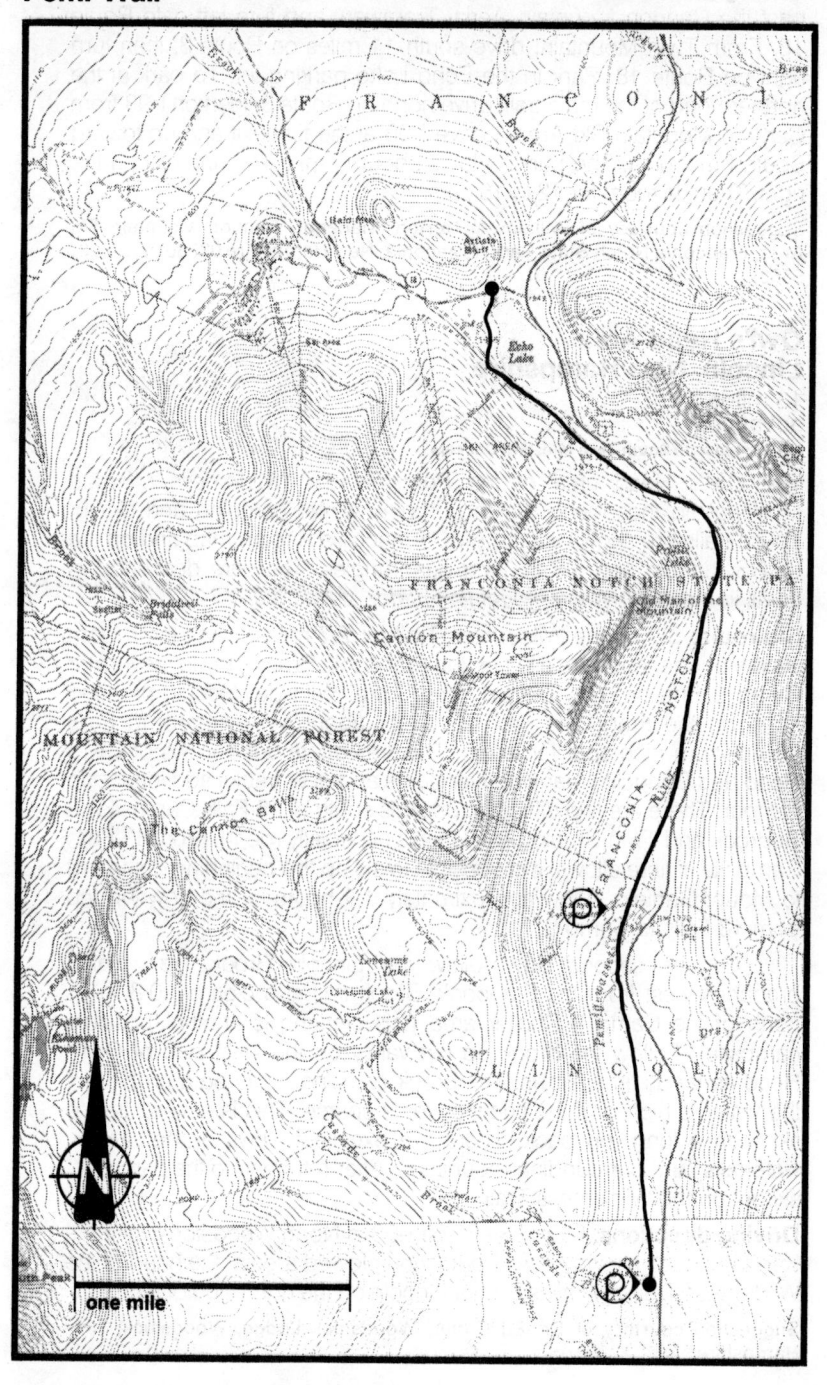

47   Northern New Hampshire

Driving directions: From North Woodstock, drive north on Route 3 past the Cannon Mountain Aerial Tramway, and turn left onto Route 18. From Twin Mountain, drive south 11 miles on Route 3, then turn right on Route 18. Park in the Echo Lake parking lot. To park at the northern end of the main trail, drive north on Route 3, then on I-93 from Cannon Mountain Ski Area. Leave I-93 at the first exit and go toward South Franconia. The parking lot is about ¼ mile from the exit on the right. There is room for 12 to 15 cars.

Suggestion courtesy of William A. Norton, Manager, Cannon Mountain Ski Area, Franconia Notch State Park, Franconia, New Hampshire 03580 (603-823-5563).

Owl's Head Area
Lincoln, New Hampshire
13 miles
advanced
USGS: Lincoln/South Twin Mtn./Mt. Osceola

The Owl's Head area of the Pemigewasset Wilderness offers a challenge to those who like to combine winter camping and skiing. These trails are shown on the AMC Franconia Region map and on the USGS Lincoln and South Twin quadrangles. They are described in detail in the AMC *White Mountain Guide*.

Ski route: Ski up the Wilderness Trail for 2.7 miles, cross the stream via the bridge, and take a left on the Franconia Brook Trail to the former Camp 9 Shelter area. Set up camp here. With day packs, proceed north on the Franconia Brook Trail for about 4¾ miles to 13 Falls Campsite, a nice spot for lunch. This trail offers good views of Owl's Head and Bondcliff; many beaver dams and deer tracks add interest to the tour. There are two difficult crossings south of 13 Falls Campsite, at Redrock and Twin Brooks. The latter is especially rough. From 13 Falls Campsite, if time allows, it is possible to ski up the beginning of the trail to Mount Garfield. Allow approximately 1½ hours for the downhill trip from 13 Falls to Camp 9.

On the second day, follow the Lincoln Brook Trail, which branches west from the Franconia Brook trail at a clearing 0.8 miles north of the Camp 9 Shelter area (this clearing is another possible campsite). Follow the brook up the valley on the west side of Owl's Head as far as time allows. The brook crossings may be a problem if the water is high or if the snow cover is sparse. This is a steep trail to ski, with a long run back. There are excellent views of the stream, waterfalls, and surrounding mountains. After returning to the campsite, ski out on the Wilderness Trail.

Driving directions: From Exit 32 off I-93 in North Woodstock, take the Kancamagus Highway east. Park in the plowed area at the head of the Wilderness Trail, 4.7 miles east of Lincoln on the north side of the road.

Suggestion courtesy of Dr. Ed Cutler, Woodstock Lodge, Woodstock, New Hampshire.

Bretton Woods Touring Center
Bretton Woods, New Hampshire
52 miles of trails
novice–intermediate–advanced
USGS: Mt. Washington/Crawford Notch

Bretton Woods has a newly expanded trail network. Of the 52 miles of trails, over 22 are regularly groomed and maintained. One trail follows an abandoned carriage road, the original route to the Mount Washington Cog Railway. A second trail follows the Ammonoosuc River past Upper Falls. Another leads to the Mount Eisenhower overlook and offers great views of the entire Presidential Range. All trails are well marked, and each intersection is numbered, giving the distance to the Touring Center. Maps are available at the Touring Center. Snowmobiles are not allowed on any of the trails.

The Touring Center has a waxing room, snacks, and a ski shop. It offers rentals, instruction, and guided tours. Races are held regularly, including the Geschmossel Race. There is a rustic shelter, stocked with firewood, about 4 miles out. A trail fee of $3.00 includes a map.

Driving directions: On Route 302, head 5 miles east from Twin Mountain, or 15 miles north from Bartlett. The Touring Center is at the entrance to the Mount Washington Hotel.

Suggestion courtesy of Mike Perlis, Bretton Woods Ski Resort, Route 302, Bretton Woods, New Hampshire 03575 (603-278-5000).

Zealand Road – Zealand Trail – Ethan Pond Trail
Carroll, New Hampshire
14 miles
intermediate (to Zealand Pond)–advanced
   (to Willey House Station)
USGS: Mt. Washington/Crawford Notch

This is a long but exciting trip. It may be skied one way by spotting a car at Willey House Station, or as a round trip from Zealand Campground to Zealand Pond and back. These trails are shown on the AMC Franconia Region map, and on the USGS Mt. Washington and Crawford Notch quadrangles. They are described in detail in the AMC *White Mountain Guide*. It is important to carry a map on this tour, since the trail may be hard to follow in places.

Ski route: From the campground, cross the bridge over the Ammonoosuc River and follow Zealand Road 3.6 miles to its end. There is a sign marking the beginning of Zealand Trail. The trail soon crosses a brook and climbs toward Zealand Notch, for the most part on an old railroad bed. After 2.2 miles, the trail passes the A-Z Trail, skirts the east side of Zealand Pond, and ends at the Ethan Pond Trail. From the campground to this point is about 6 miles. Continue south on the Ethan Pond Trail through Zealand Notch. This necessitates slabbing some steep slide areas: turn back if it is icy and the going is difficult. At the southern end of the notch (2.2 miles from Zealand Pond), turn left where the Thoreau Falls Trail diverges to the right. Continue on Ethan Pond Trail, keeping left at the next two forks where branches of the Shoal Pond Trail enter. From here the trail may be difficult to follow due to the flat terrain and numerous diverging logging roads. Look for the trimmed branches of trees at the edge of the trail. Keep on the south side of the stream that flows from Ethan Pond. There is a shelter on the east shore of the pond. From the height-of-land, the trail descends steadily and turns right where the Willey Range Trail enters from the left. About ½ mile northwest of Willey House Station it is advisable to leave the trail because it becomes too steep to follow. Ski down through the open hardwoods, making long traverses to Willey House Station. Do not ski along the railroad tracks.

Driving directions: From North Conway, follow Route 302 north to the Willey House Station, about 17 miles north of Glen. The station is at the end of a short road leading off to the left. Leave one car here. In a second vehicle, continue north on Route 302, about 10 miles, to Zealand Campground on the left. This is 2.2 miles east of Twin Mountain. There is a parking lot ⅛ mile east of the campground on Route 302.

Mount Willard
Crawford Notch, New Hampshire
3 miles, round trip
intermediate-advanced
USGS: Crawford Notch

This is a short but fairly steep climb to an exposed 2804-foot summit commanding outstanding views of Crawford Notch. There is an old carriage road to the summit; there is also a trail following the carriage road but cutting off the switchbacks. The road is gentler for skiing and is the recommended route. There is usually no problem with snowmobiles. The Mount Willard Trail is shown on the AMC Franconia Region map and on the USGS Crawford Notch quadrangle. The connecting link from the Avalon Trail is not shown on the USGS quadrangle. The AMC *White Mountain Guide* has a detailed description of the Mount Willard Trail.

Ski route: The trail leaves the west side of Route 302 at the Crawford Depot, across from the north end of Saco Lake, together with the Avalon Trail. After 100 yards the Mount Willard Trail turns left. Follow the old carriage road to the summit.

Driving directions: From North Conway, take Route 302 northwest to Glen. Continue north through Crawford Notch and park in the plowed lot, on the west side of 302, next to the Crawford Depot. There is also parking just south of the Crawford Depot across from a state highway garage.

Wilderness Trail – Carrigain Notch – Sawyer River Road
Lincoln, New Hampshire
17 miles
advanced
USGS: Mt. Osceola/Crawford Notch

Advanced skiers who like to combine ski touring with backpacking will find this a challenging trip through the Pemigewasset Wilderness. The Desolation Shelter area can be used for an overnight stop. This trip is best done late in the winter when the days are longer and the snow more settled. These trails are shown on the AMC Franconia Region map and on USGS quadrangles. The USGS map, however, does not show the shelter (about ½ mile southeast of the East Branch of the Pemigewasset, along the Carrigain Branch). Trails are described in detail in the AMC *White Mountain Guide*. It may be necessary to carry a compass, because trails may be covered under fresh snow. Snowmobiles may be encountered south and east of the Pemigewasset River.

Ski route: Ski along the Wilderness Trail from the Kancamagus Highway for about 9 miles to Desolation Shelter. There are two bridges that are difficult to cross on skis, but brook crossings pose no serious problems. Desolation Shelter is in a lovely spot on the bank of a stream, with beautiful views of the surrounding mountains. The shelter may be filled with snow, or occupied, so bring tents. On the second day, continue on the Carrigain Notch Trail as it climbs through the notch. This is one of the prettiest notches in the mountains, with many sheer cliffs on the east wall. There are a few steep places on either side of the notch, and an open crossing of Carrigain Brook that can be very difficult to negotiate. About 2 miles past the notch, the trail joins the Signal Ridge Trail. Follow this trail east to Sawyer River Road; this is a very sporty run with a backpack. Turn left (northeast) on the road and continue for 2 miles to Route 302.

Alternate Route: Another tour in this area begins at Sawyer River Road and runs along the Signal Ridge Trail and Carrigain Notch Trail to Desolation Shelter. On the second day, follow the Shoal Pond Trail north to the Ethan Pond Trail; turn right and go east past Ethan Pond to the Willey House Station on Route 302. The last mile is extremely steep; ski with caution, or make long switchbacks through the woods.

Driving directions: Spot one car at the beginning of Sawyer River Road, about 4 miles west of Bartlett, on Route 302. In a second car, follow Routes 302 and 16 south to Conway. Go west on the Kancamagus Highway for about 32 miles to where the Wilderness Trail leaves the highway (5½ miles west of the hairpin turn, 4.7 miles east of Lincoln). For the Ethan Pond variation, park the first car by Willey House Station, then head south on Route 302, leaving the second car at Sawyer River Road.

Suggestion courtesy of Dr. Ed Cutler, Woodstock Lodge, Woodstock, New Hampshire.

Hancock Notch Trail - Sawyer River Trail
Lincoln, New Hampshire

12 miles
intermediate-advanced
USGS: Mt. Osceola/Crawford Notch

This is a long tour through the Pemigewasset Wilderness. The trip requires approximately 7 hours. These trails are shown on the AMC Franconia Region map and described in detail in the *White Mountain Guide*. They are also shown on the USGS quadrangles; however, the Crawford Notch quadrangle does not show the Kancamagus Highway, so the exact location of the Sawyer River trailhead is not clear (it is 0.3 miles east of Lily Pond).

Ski route: Leave the north side of the highway on the Hancock Notch Trail. It is a steady climb to the notch, and the trail is easy to follow. The descent has some short, steep pitches that should be taken with caution, and there may be some difficult stream crossings in times of high water or sparse snow cover. The last 7 miles are fairly flat. Snowmobiling on the Sawyer River section is common.

Driving directions: From Lincoln, take the Kancamagus Highway east. Spot a car at the beginning of the Sawyer River Trail, about 4 miles east of the highway's hairpin turn. Return to the hairpin turn and park close to the sign for the Hancock Notch Trail (sometimes the parking lot on the hill just above the turn is plowed).

Hancock Notch – Cedar Brook – Wilderness Loop
Lincoln, New Hampshire
13 miles
intermediate
USGS: Mt. Osceola

This is a lovely tour which may be skied in one long day (in good snow conditions) or two. It is best to ski the loop counterclockwise to take advantage of the 1200-feet elevation difference. Snowmobiles use the trails south of the Pemigewasset River.

Ski route: The first 1¾ miles of the Hancock Notch Trail is over old railroad beds and logging roads. There is at least one major brook crossing at a washed-out trestle between the Kancamagus Highway and the Cedar Brook Trail. Turn left on the Cedar Brook Trail, which crosses the height-of-land between Mounts Hancock and Hitchcock. Look for plastic tape marking the trail (the maps may not correctly indicate the route and the location of several brook crossings). The trail descends to the Pemigewasset River over old logging roads and railroad beds with switchbacks, so there are few steep pitches. At the junction with the Wilderness Trail, cross the river and ski west, then south along the Wilderness Trail to the Kancamagus Highway. It is possible to return along an old logging road on the south side of the river, but this trail is heavily snowmobiled.

Driving directions: From Route 3 in North Woodstock, drive east on the Kancamagus Highway. Leave a car at the parking lot for the Wilderness Trail, about 4.7 miles east of Lincoln. Continue east on the highway and park a second car in the lot (usually plowed) on the hill above the hairpin turn. The Hancock Notch Trail leaves the north side of the highway at the hairpin turn.

Sawyer River Road Area
Hart's Location, New Hampshire
novice (Sawyer River Road)–intermediate (other trails)
USGS: Crawford Notch

Sawyer River Road is a flat, wide road with many nice views across the valley. The Sawyer Pond Trail, the Signal Ridge Trail, and the Carrigain Notch Trail are more difficult and provide a nice contrast to the openness of Sawyer River Road. The Carrigain Notch Trail is rocky and requires good snow cover. Trails are shown on the AMC Franconia Region map and on the USGS Crawford Notch quadrangle. They are described in detail in the AMC *White Mountain Guide*. Neither map shows the logging road running from Sawyer River Road up the Carrigain Brook valley, but it wide and easy to follow. All trails are snowmobiled; Sawyer River Road is used heavily but is wide enough that there is usually undisturbed snow for skiing.

Ski route, to Sawyer Pond: Follow Sawyer River Road for 4 miles, and cross the river on the footbridge to the beginning of the Sawyer Pond Trail. Turn left and proceed 1 mile to Sawyer Pond where there is a shelter and 5 tent platforms on the northwest shore. This is a very pretty spot.

Ski route, to Carrigain Notch: Take Sawyer River Road for about 2 miles, then turn right onto the Signal Ridge Trail at the sign just before a concrete bridge. Follow this trail for about 1½ miles to where a main logging road crosses at four corners. Ski north on the logging road, up the Carrigain Brook valley, keeping fairly near the brook. Bear left at the end of the logging road, cross the brook, and turn right on the Carrigain Notch Trail. The last ½ mile of this trail climbs steeply into Carrigain Notch. It is possible to take the Carrigain Notch Trail where it joins the Signal Ridge Trail, but the logging road has nicer views, including a dramatic view of Mount Lowell, one of the steepest in the White Mountains. It is also possible to follow the logging road all the way up the Carrigain Brook valley. It bears right (north) off Sawyer River Road, shortly before the junction with Sawyer Pond Trail.

Driving directions: From North Conway, take Route 302 north through Glen. Sawyer River Road begins about 4 miles west of Bartlett on the left side of Route 302. There is a plowed parking area at the beginning of the road.

Church Pond Loop
Albany, New Hampshire
2½ miles, round trip
novice
USGS: Mt. Chocorua/Crawford Notch

This is an interesting pond surrounded by a ring of high mountains. It is open, so there is opportunity to explore the area around and across the pond. Use caution if venturing out on the ice. The trail is shown on the AMC Franconia Region map and on the USGS Mount Chocorua and Crawford Notch quadrangles. The Crawford Notch map does not show the Kancamagus Highway. The AMC *White Mountain Guide* includes a detailed trail description. There is some snowmobile activity in this area.

Ski route: Leave the highway on the logging road. Cross the bridge over the Swift River, and stay on the logging road for about ½ mile until the Church Pond bog area appears 50 yards to the north. Ski through the bog to the pond.

Driving directions: From Conway, take Route 16 south to the Kancamagus Highway. Go west to the Passaconaway Campground, 2 miles west of Bear Notch Road. Park 0.3 miles west of the campground at the logging road on the right.

Red Ridge on Middle Moat Mountain
North Conway, New Hampshire
8 miles, round trip
advanced
USGS: North Conway

This trip offers above-timberline conditions at lower elevations. The ridge is open and often has beautiful large drifts. Because Red Ridge has been burned over, there are exposed areas that may be bare. The ridge can be seen from North Conway; check to see if there is enough snow before skiing. Trails are shown on the AMC Chocorua-Waterville and Carter-Mahoosuc maps and are described in the AMC *White Mountain Guide;* they are also shown on the USGS North Conway quadrangle.

Ski route: From Diana's Baths, the Moat Mountain Trail leaves the upper end of the clearing on a logging road and follows a brook for ½ mile. At a fork marked by a sign, bear left on Red Ridge Trail. Cross the brook and continue for 1¼ miles up a gentle grade, crossing a government boundary marked with red blazes. After ¼ mile, turn sharply right and follow the brook; this turn is easily missed. After the trail leaves the brook there is a very steep, ½-mile climb through open softwoods. Here the trail crosses a steep ledge. Because of avalanche danger, it is necessary to leave the trail and bushwhack through the woods. Once on the ridge, the going is easier because the terrain is open and not too steep. Drifts may be difficult to negotiate. The summit is steep and windblown, and may be impossible to attempt.

Driving directions: Going north on Routes 16 and 302 in North Conway, turn left just beyond the Eastern Slope Inn onto West Side Road. Continue for 2.2 miles to Lucy's Farm. Turn left on the road to the old inn at Diana's Baths.

Holiday Inn
Intervale, New Hampshire
10 miles of trails
intermediate–advanced
USGS: North Conway

There are a number of trails around Holiday Inn on the slopes of Bartlett Mountain. The area is generally wooded and moderately steep. Trails are well marked, and maps are available at the Inn. Snowmobiles are permitted, although use is limited.

Driving directions: Holiday Inn is on Route 16A, 1½ miles north of the intersection with Route 16. Parking is limited.

Suggestion courtesy of Robert Gregory, Holiday Inn, Route 16A, Intervale, New Hampshire 03845 (603-356-9772).

Jackson Ski Touring Foundation
Jackson, New Hampshire
125 km (78 miles) of trails
novice-intermediate-advanced
USGS: North Conway

The Jackson Ski Touring Foundation maintains an extensive trail system in the upper Mount Washington Valley. The network provides skiing at all levels of ability, ranging from easy touring over a rolling golf course and surrounding woodlands to challenging skiing on the Black Mountain Ski Trail, the Wildcat Valley Trail, and others. The trail system connects most points of interest in the area, including Wildcat Mountain and Tyrol Ski Areas, a covered bridge, and two overnight cabins. Several trails run from the summits of the ski areas into the valleys; single ride tickets are available. Many of the trails are in the White Mountain National Forest.

All trails have signs and are well marked for direction and difficulty. Many are groomed with prepared tracks. Ski trail conditions are posted at the Foundation office, where trail maps and lodging assistance are available. Most of the trails are closed to snowmobiles.

The EMS and Jack Frost shops in town offers retail sales, rentals, and instruction. Meals and accommodations are available in Jackson. There is a trail donation of $3.00 for adults and $1.00 for children 6 to 12. Season memberships are available by joining the Jackson Ski Touring Club.

Driving directions: From North Conway, take Route 16 north for about 7½ miles to the red covered bridge on the right. Cross the bridge and go ¼ mile to the center of Jackson Village where the Foundation office is located. There is parking space in the village, at the alpine ski areas, and at various inns associated with the Foundation's trail system.

Suggestion courtesy of Jackson Ski Touring Foundation, Jackson, New Hampshire 03846 (603-383-9355).

East Branch Saco River and Wild River Valleys
Chatham, New Hampshire
60+ miles of trails
intermediate-advanced
USGS: North Conway

This is a watershed area between two rugged ranges in the White Mountains: The Carter-Moriahs to the west and the Baldface Range to the east. The East Branch of the Saco River and Slippery Brook once had logging railroads that joined the Bartlett line along the Saco River bed. Another lumbering railroad went through the Wild River area, a 35,000-acre tract comprising most of Bean's Purchase, now in the White Mountain National Forest.

It is possible to ski 30 miles from Jackson, New Hampshire, to Hastings, Maine, on Slippery Brook Road and the East Branch and Wild River trails. This can be a 2 or 3 day trip with campsites at No-Ketchum Pond, Spruce Brook Shelter, and the Wild River Campground. These trails follow the valleys and are quite sheltered, with a maximum elevation of about 2500 feet. The trip may be shortened by taking the Wild River and Bog Brook trails west from No-Ketchum Pond, or by taking the Bald Land Trail from the East Branch Trail to the road.

There are also several possible side trips to the east. One short and fairly easy route follows Slippery Brook Trail and a side trail to Mountain Pond, where there is a shelter. It is possible to continue on Slippery Brook Trail along the Baldface Ridge to Eagle Link Trail or the Black Angel Trail; this is a challenging ski mountaineering trip. Trails on the east side of the ridge are steep and difficult, but in an emergency there are several that could be used to exit to Chatham. Another steep side loop follows the Black Angel Trail to Blue Brook Shelter and falls, then the Basin Trail to Wild River Campground. This route is scenic and quite protected.

Another ski trip in the Jackson/Chatham area is a 1 or 2 day circuit over the Province Brook Trail. From Chatham, the trail goes southwest to a shelter at Province Road, then southeast to a road just north of South Chatham. Follow the paved road north to an abandoned road, which leads back to Chatham.

All of these trails are shown on the AMC Carter-Mahoosuc map, and described in the AMC *White Mountain Guide.* Refer to the map and the guide for exact routes and mileages.

Driving directions: Refer to the AMC map and the *White Mountain Guide* for driving and parking information.

Suggestion courtesy of Jerry Weene, Northern Journeys, Ltd. Goshen, Massachusetts.

Mount Moosilauke
Warren/Benton, New Hampshire
6½ miles of trails
novice-intermediate
USGS: Mt. Kineo/Mt. Moosilauke

This snowcapped peak rises prominently above its surroundings. There are two possible trips to the summit; both require intermediate skiing ability due to the length and steady grade over what can be windblown crust. The road to the Ravine Lodge is gentler and suited to novice skiers. Most of the land is owned by Dartmouth College, and camping is prohibited. Snowmobiles are permitted on the Carriage Road to the junction with the Glencliff Trail near South Peak.

Trail descriptions: The Carriage Road (4½ miles) goes up the southern ridge of the mountain. It is a steady climb, but not too steep. Snowmobile use is heavy south of the Glencliff Trail intersection. The road from Route 118 to the Ravine Lodge (1¾ miles) is unplowed. Just south of the Lodge is a fork; take either branch. Explore the Ridge Trail (right), or take the dirt road southwest (left) to the Carriage Road, leading to the summit. With ski mountaineering equipment, it is possible to reach the summit by taking either the Gorge Brook Trail or the Snapper Ski Trail and the Carriage Road.

Driving directions: To reach the beginning of the Carriage Road, take Route 118 west from North Woodstock for about 10½ miles. There is a plowed road on the right that crosses a bridge and leads to Breezy Point. To reach the Ravine Lodge road, take Route 118 west for about 7½ miles from North Woodstock. The beginning of the road is plowed to accommodate several cars.

Glover Brook Trail
Woodstock, New Hampshire
6 miles round trip
intermediate
USGS: Plymouth

This is a scenic trip to a remote area in the White Mountain National Forest, following Glover Brook to its source at Elbow Pond. The little valley is well sheltered from the wind and is very sunny: a good trip for a cold day. The trail is mostly uphill going in and downhill running out. There are some steep and narrow sections that require good control.

Ski route: From the post office parking lot, go past the adjacent red farmhouse. About 400 yards into the woods, take the right fork and go across the stream, then head west, parallel to the stream, along an old road. About 3 miles in, the trail becomes obscure. Bushwhack west about 500 yards to the pond. This is a pretty spot for lunch, with good views.

Mount Moosilauke

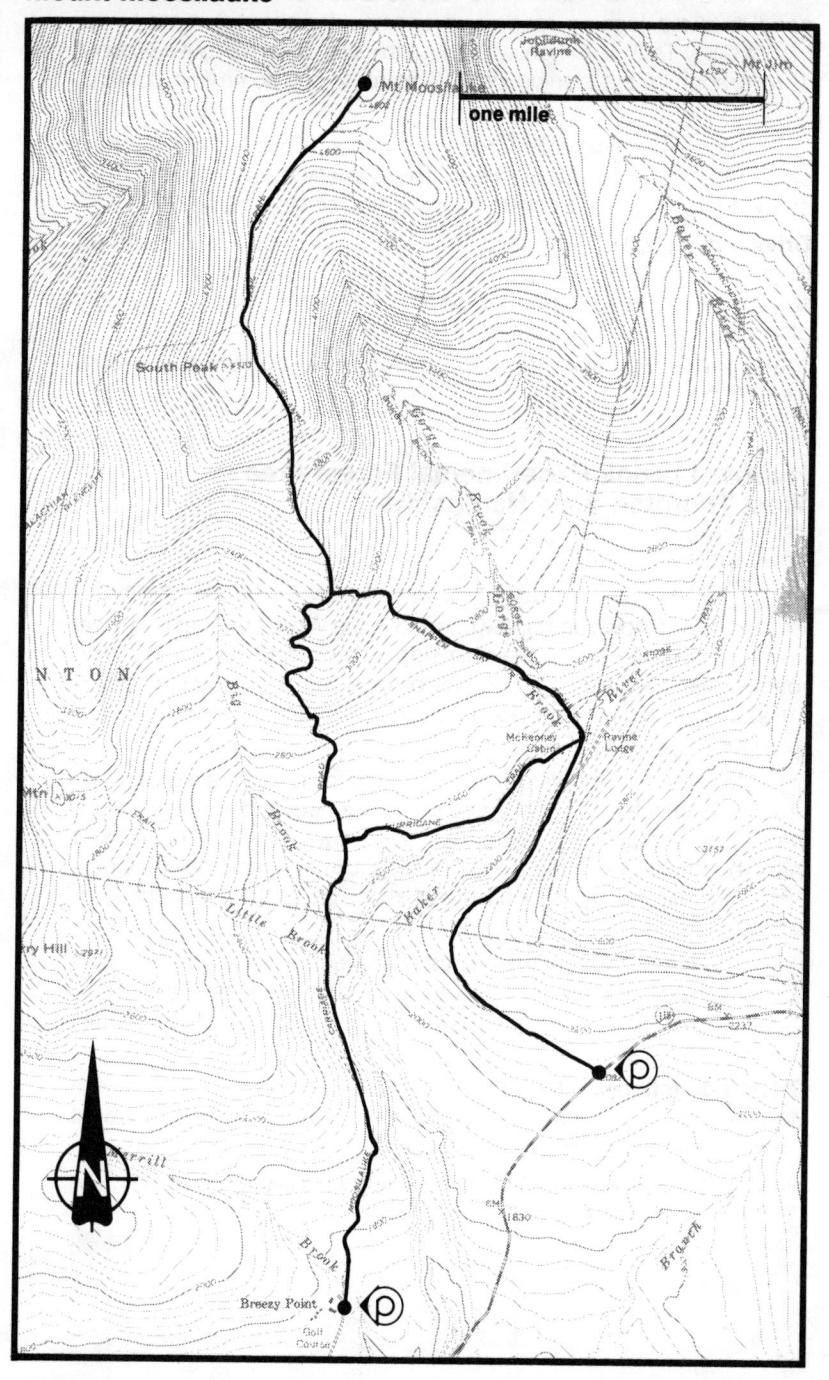

Northern New Hampshire

An alternative return route follows a course northeast from the pond over old logging roads and swamps for about 3 miles to the Mount Cilley Trail. Turn right and follow this trail down to Route 3, about ½ mile north of the starting point. This route has some fine downhill runs.

Another exciting side trip begins about 1 mile in from the post office, near some red-blazed trees. This unmarked trail follows a small brook north for about 1 mile to the east base of Mount Cilley.

Driving directions: From I-93, take Exit 30 to Route 3. Go north on Route 3 for 2 miles to Woodstock. Just past the general store, take a small road to the left for a few yards through the woods to the post office. Park in the plowed area.

Suggestion courtesy of Dr. Ed Cutler, Woodstock Lodge, Woodstock, New Hampshire.

Hubbard Brook Experimental Forest Area
West Thornton, New Hampshire
7600 acres
novice-intermediate
USGS: Plymouth

This ski route follows an unplowed road in the White Mountain National Forest, with a number of possible side trips on connecting trails. The road is skiable on only a few inches of snow and is a good trip early in the season. Detailed maps are available at the administration building if a ranger is present.

The road goes west from the parking lot and is suitable for novices. The side trails offer more of a challenge, and some go all the way up to the ridge road, which has great views. There are no marked trails, but there are many possibilities for climbing and downhill running. The little hill by the parking lot is a nice spot for instruction or practice.

The Experimental Forest Area has been set aside for a study of its regeneration process. Some years ago, large areas on the side of a mountain were clear cut, and the natural regeneration is being carefully watched.

Driving directions: Take Exit 29 or 30 off I-93, and follow Route 3 to West Thornton (a general store). Take Mirror Lake Road west for about 2 miles to the end of the plowed section at the administration building.

Suggestion courtesy of Dr. Ed Cutler, Woodstock Lodge, Woodstock, New Hampshire.

Tripoli Road-Russell Pond
Woodstock, New Hampshire
8 miles, round trip
novice (Tripoli Road)-intermediate (Russell Pond)
USGS: Plymouth/Lincoln

This is a pretty trip in the White Mountain National Forest that is skiable on only a few inches of snow and is usually good quite early in the season. There are impressive views of the large mountains to the east and of local small mountains and ledges. Side trips to Talford Brook and Thornton Gore (both leaving Tripoli Road just east of the Russell Pond turnoff) will offer further skiing opportunities.

Ski Route: Ski east up Tripoli Road for about 2 miles, and turn left onto Russell Pond Road. Here the trail becomes steeper and has some switchbacks. Continue for 2 miles to the campground and pond. This is a scenic and sheltered spot: a good place for lunch. The return is a nice continuous downhill run.

Driving directions: From I-93, take Exit 31 at Tripoli Road. Go east a short way, and park where the plowed section ends.

Suggestion courtesy of Dr. Ed Cutler, Woodstock Lodge, Woodstock, New Hampshire.

Loon Mountain Ski Touring Center
Lincoln, New Hampshire
25 km (15½ miles) of trails
novice-intermediate
USGS: Lincoln/Mt. Osceola

Loon Mountain trails follow a network of old logging roads along the East Branch of the Pemigewasset River. Several abandoned camps make excellent picnic spots. More advanced trails climb ridges that afford excellent views of Mount Moosilauke and Kinsman Notch to the west and the Pemigewasset Wilderness to the east. One trail is being extended to connect with the Wilderness Trail in the Pemigewasset Wilderness. Trails are marked according to NSTOA standards, and maps are distributed at the Touring Center. Snowmobiles are not permitted on Loon Mountain trails.

The Ski Touring Center has a waxing room and a retail shop that sells waxes and accessories. A cafeteria and an inn are located at the base of the alpine ski area. Rentals, instruction, guided tours, and waxing clinics are available. The trail fee is $1.00.

Driving directions: From I-93, take Exit 32 and drive through the village of Lincoln. Continue east for 2 miles to Loon Mountain Ski Area.

Suggestion courtesy of William Corkum, Loon Mountain Ski Touring Center, Lincoln, New Hampshire 03251 (603-745-8111).

Greeley Ponds Trail
Lincoln/Waterville Valley, New Hampshire
5 miles
intermediate
USGS: Mt. Osceola/Plymouth/Mt. Chocorua

This is a very popular trip. It can be skied one way, but this involves a 30-mile shuttle to spot a car; it is usually skied as a round trip. The trail is heavily used by skiers and has a good track. The southern section is used by snowmobiles. The trail is shown on USGS topographic maps, and on the AMC Franconia Region map. The AMC *White Mountain Guide* has a detailed trail description.

Ski route: Beginning at the Kancamagus Highway, follow Greeley Ponds Trail south, making about five stream crossings. Upon reaching the upper pond, ski across it or along the western shore. Use caution if going on the ice. Continue south on the trail, past the lower pond, to Waterville Valley (see separate entry). There are several more stream crossings after the ponds; some may be difficult.

Driving directions: To reach the northern end, take the Kancamagus Highway east from North Woodstock. About 9½ miles east of Lincoln (0.9 miles west of the hairpin turn), the parking area for the Greeley Ponds trailhead is on the south side of the road. It is usually plowed. To get to the southern end, follow directions for Waterville Valley Ski Touring Center.

Waterville Valley Ski Touring Center
Waterville Valley, New Hampshire
26 miles of trails
novice–intermediate–advanced
USGS: Plymouth/Mt. Chocorua/Crawford Notch/Mt. Osceola

Waterville Valley maintains a large network of trails, largely in the White Mountain National Forest, and is in the midst of a major expansion project that will bring the total of groomed and maintained trails to 26 miles. Most present trails are to the east of the valley, in the drainage areas of Drake's, Snow's, Avalanche, and Cascade brooks, and along the Mad River. Eventually, the trail system will provide access to Snow's Mountain, Sandwich Mountain, and Mount Tripyramid. Maps are available at the Touring Center. Other National Forest trails that connect to those from Waterville are Greeley Ponds Trail and Tripoli Road (see separate entries) and Livermore Road. Snowmobiles are not permitted on maintained trails but may be encountered outside the Waterville network.

The Touring Center has a ski shop and offers rentals, EPSTI certified instruction, waxing, repairs, junior and high school racing programs, and a schedule of citizens' races and ESA-sponsored events.

Guided and self-guiding nature tours are available by arrangement from the resident naturalist. There is a charge for trail use. Within the valley are two alpine ski areas, a skating rink, five inns, and a number of restaurants.

Driving directions: From I-93, take Exit 28 for Campton/Waterville Valley, and follow Route 49 north for 11 miles to the Touring Center.

Suggestion courtesy of Chuck Moeser, Director, Waterville Valley Ski Touring Center, Waterville Valley, New Hampshire 03223 (603-236-8311).

Guinea Pond Trail to Flat Mountain Pond
Sandwich, New Hampshire
12 miles, round trip
intermediate
USGS: Mt. Chocorua

This is a long trip through the woods with a gradual ascent to a lovely pond. Most of the trail is over an old logging railroad bed. It is wide, flat, and easy going. There are a couple of stream crossings that are tricky because the banks are steep. At one of the crossings there is a bridge of which very little is now intact. The most difficult part of the trip is the section before the old railroad bed; it is narrow and fairly steep. The trail receives moderate snowmobile use.

These trails are shown on the AMC Chocorua-Waterville map and on the USGS Mt. Chocorua quadrangle. Besides the main route, they show a couple of alternate routes to the Guinea Pond Trail that may be skiable. The Squam Lakes Association trail map covers all but the very northern section of this tour. The AMC *White Mountain Guide* and Squam Lakes Association *Trail Guide* have detailed descriptions of the trails.

Ski route: Ski up the unplowed road to Jose's Bridge. Continue straight past the bridge. Shortly beyond the bridge, there is a sign at a fork; bear left. At the next fork (unmarked) take the steeper trail to the right. The trail joins the Guinea Pond Trail at the top of this stretch. Turn right, and continue all the way to Flat Mountain Pond. Allow plenty of time to explore the pond. Return via the same route.

Driving directions: From I-93, take Exit 23 at New Hampton and drive east on Route 104. Turn left on Route 3. At Meredith, go right on Route 25. Continue to the junction of Route 113, just before South Tamworth; turn left and proceed to North Sandwich. Turn right on Route 113A, and go through Whiteface to Whiteface Intervale. Here the main road turns sharply to the right. Turn left on Bennett Street and take a left at the fork, continuing to a second fork. The left branch is plowed for a short distance for parking. There is also a plowed stretch connecting the two branches; a couple of cars can be parked here.

Suggestion courtesy of Dr. Ed Cutler, Woodstock Lodge, Woodstock, New Hampshire.

Bolles Trail, Mount Chocorua Area
Albany, New Hampshire
7 miles, round trip
novice-intermediate
USGS: Mt. Chocorua

This is one of the loveliest skiing areas in the White Mountains. Open forests, gentle slopes, and a complex of old and current trails make an ideal setting for a day of touring. The Bolles Trail and side trails are shown on the AMC Chocorua-Waterville map and on the USGS Mt. Chocorua quadrangle. Detailed trail descriptions are in the AMC *White Mountain Guide*.

Ski route: From the parking area, go north along Paugus Brook toward the Liberty Trail. Where the Liberty Trail goes right, go straight and cross the stream. The Bolles Trail follows the stream for about 3½ miles to the height-of-land between Mount Chocorua and Mount Paugus. From here north, the trail is not suitable for touring. The Bee Line Trail, which can be followed for a mile or so up Mount Chocorua, and the Whitin Brook Trail, which runs more than 2 miles westward along the southern base of Mount Paugus, are good side trails to explore.

Driving directions: From the junction of Routes 16 and 25, drive west on Route 25 to Whittier. Turn right on Route 113 and go north to the light at Tamworth. From here, follow 113A north. Turn left at the first fork, then right at the next fork to the small parking area near the start of the Liberty Trail on Mount Chocorua.

Suggestion courtesy of Dr. Ed Cutler, Woodstock Lodge, Woodstock, New Hampshire.

Foss Mountain Ski Touring
Snowville, New Hampshire
8 miles of trails
novice-intermediate-advanced
USGS: North Conway

Located at Snow Village Lodge, the touring center has trails through stands of pine and mixed hardwoods, with many views of Mount Chocorua and the White Mountains. Trails are marked with NSTOA blue diamonds, and maps are available. Snowmobiles are not permitted. Uplowed town roads and snowmobile trails in the area provide further skiing possibilities.

The ski hut has a waxing room, a warming area, and a rental shop. Instruction is offered. The Lodge provides lunches and has a bar. There is a fee for area use.

Driving directions: From Conway, take Route 153 south for 5.2 miles and turn left (east) at the sign for Snowville. There is a sign for Snow Village Lodge on the right, about 1 mile beyond the turn; the Lodge is 0.9 mile uphill.

Suggestion courtesy of Igor Wing, Foss Mountain Ski Touring, Snow Village Lodge, Snowville, New Hampshire 03849 (603-447-2818).

Southern New Hampshire Ski Touring Areas

1. Moose Mountain Lodge, Etna 68
2. Mount Cardigan, Alexandria 68
3. Tenney Mountain Ski Area, Plymouth 69
4. White Mountain Country Club, Ashland 70
5. Longwood Ski Touring Center, Center Harbor 71
6. Gunstock Touring Center, Laconia 70
7. The Nordic Skier, Wolfeboro 71
8. Fernald Hill Farm, Cornish 72
9. Gray Ledges Farm, Grantham 72
10. Eastman Ski Touring Center, Grantham 73
11. Norsk Ski Touring Center, New London 73
12. Pemigewasset Valley Ski Touring Center, Franklin 74
13. Mount Sunapee State Park, Sunapee 74
    Dexter's Inn and Nordic Ski Center, Sunapee 75
14. Fox State Forest, Hillsboro 75
15. Pole and Pedal Ski Touring Center, Henniker 76
16. Bear Brook State Park, Allenstown 77
17. Charmingfare Ski Touring Center, Candia 77
18. Mount Pawtuckaway Area, Deerfield 78
19. Sagamore-Hampton Ski Touring Center, North Hampton 78
20. Hyland Hill, Westmoreland 80
21. Road's End Farm, Chesterfield 80
22. Skatutakee and Thumb Mountains, Hancock 82
23. Summer's Ski Touring Center, Dublin 82
24. Human Environment Institute/ Sargent Camp, Peterborough 86
25. Tory Pines Ski Touring Center, Francestown 86
26. Winn and Rose Mountains, Lyndeborough/Greenfield 84
27. Purgatory Falls, Mont Vernon 88
28. New England Center for Outdoor Education at Camp Allen, Bedford 87
29. Gap Mountain, Troy 87
    The Inn at East Hill Farm, Troy 87
30. Monadnock State Park, Jaffrey 90
31. Woodbound Ski Touring Center, Jaffrey 90
32. Temple Mountain Ski Area, Peterborough 91
    Wapack Trail, Ashburnham, Massachusetts, to Greenfield 91
33. Windblown, New Ipswich 93
34. Hollis Hof Ski Touring Center, Hollis 94

Southern New Hampshire

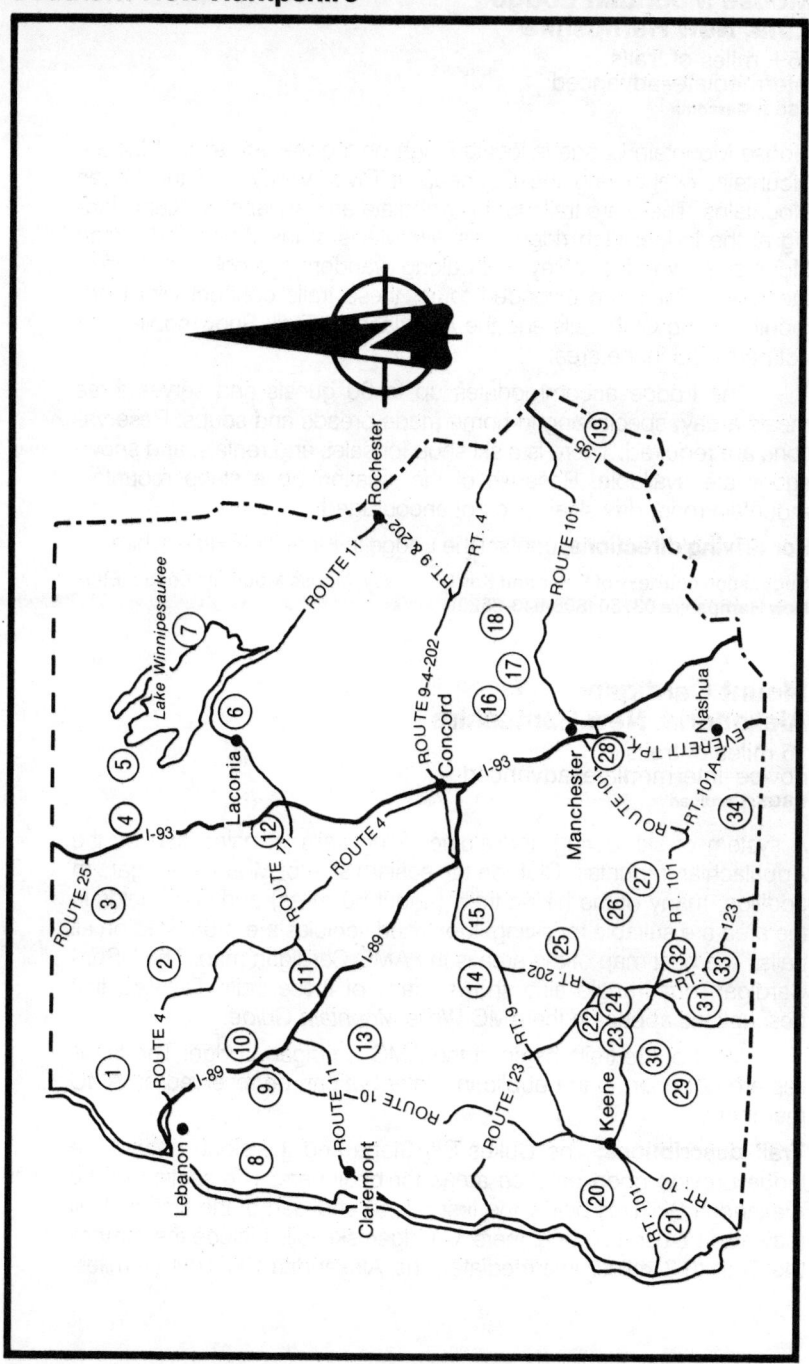

Moose Mountain Lodge
Etna, New Hampshire
25+ miles of trails
intermediate-advanced
USGS: Mascoma

Moose Mountain Lodge is located high on the western side of Moose Mountain, overlooking the Connecticut River Valley and the Green Mountains. There are trails for intermediate and advanced skiers starting at the lodge: high ridge trails with views of the White and Green Mountains, wooded valley trails along wandering brooks, and open meadows. For more extended tours, these trails connect with Dartmouth Outing Club trails and the Appalachian Trail. Snowmobiles are not permitted in the area.

The Lodge accommodates up to 30 guests and serves three meals a day, specializing in home made breads and soups. Reservations are required. There is a ski shop for sales and rentals, and snowshoes are available. Because of the location up a steep mountain mountain road, day skiers are not encouraged.

For driving directions, contact the Lodge in Etna, New Hampshire.

Suggestion courtesy of Peter and Kay Shumway, Moose Mountain Lodge, Etna, New Hampshire 03750 (603-643-3529).

Mount Cardigan
Alexandria, New Hampshire
15 miles of trails
novice-intermediate-advanced
USGS: Cardigan

A system of ski touring and alpine skiing trails is maintained by the Appalachian Mountain Club on the eastern side of Mount Cardigan. In addition, many of the hiking trails (about 50 miles) and open fields in the area are suitable for skiing. Motorized vehicles are prohibited on all trails. The best map of the area is the AMC Cardigan map. The USGS Cardigan quadrangle also shows many of these trails. Detailed trail descriptions appear in the AMC *White Mountain Guide.*

Most of the trails begin at the AMC Cardigan Lodge. The facilities are not open to the public in winter but can be reserved by AMC members.

Trail descriptions: The Dukes Ski Slope and the slope behind the lodge provide good practice areas for beginners. The section of the Alexandria Ski Trail below the first bridge and part of the Nature Trail may also be used by beginners. Cardigan ski trails include the Kimball Ski Trail (0.8 miles, intermediate); the Alexandria Ski Trail (2 miles, novice-intermediate, below Grand Junction; and expert, alpine to the summit); the Dukes Trail (1½ miles); and the Route 93Z Ski Trail (1.3 miles, novice), which is not shown on the AMC map. The Dukes Ski Trail leads to the summit of Firescrew Mountain; the upper portion provides skiing on open ledges for expert skiers. Under favorable conditions, the expert alpine skier can take a round trip over Firescrew and Cardigan on the Dukes Ski Trail, the Mowglis Trail, and the Alexandria Ski Trail. The route along the summits and open ledges may be difficult to find. The 93Z Trail follows an old logging road behind the lodge, joining the Back 80 Trail before the first brook crossing. Hiking trails that are good for skiing are the Skyland Cutoff (novice), the lower portion of the Clark Trail (novice-intermediate), and the Back 80 Trail to the intersection with the 93Z Trail. Above this point, the Back 80 Trail is skiable but can be difficult to follow in winter. The Back-Duke Link Ski Trail (intermediate, not shown on the AMC map) connects the Back 80 Trail to the Dukes Ski Trail and makes a good half-day round trip. It is best skied counterclockwise.

Driving directions: Driving up the valley to the Lodge is very difficult, and local towing is not available. Drivers should be experienced in snow and mud, and cars should be equipped with studded snow tires or chains, shovels, and sand. From I-93; take Route 104 west for 6 miles to Bristol. Take Route 3A north for 2.3 miles, and turn left at the stone church on Newfound Lake. Go west to Alexandria, then follow AMC Cardigan Lodge signs for 9 miles to the Lodge. The last 2.2 miles is over a snowy or muddy gravel road. The parking lot at the lodge is not plowed; shovel a space remembering that others will be coming and leaving. If parking along the road, shovel a space well off the road to allow for passage of a fire truck or snowplow. Sometimes the road is not plowed from the red "schoolhouse" (now the Costin home) to the Lodge.

Tenney Mountain Ski Area
Plymouth, New Hampshire
3 miles
novice-intermediate
USGS: Rumney

Tenney Mountain has one trail that is a ridgetop loop. It is packed by a snowcat and can be reached by chair lift. The Ski Area has rentals, instruction, and retail sales. Inquire at the base lodge for further information.

Driving directions: From Plymouth, take Route 25 north and west. The Ski Area is on the right.

Suggestion courtesy of Tenney Mountain Corporation, Plymouth, New Hampshire 03264.

White Mountain Country Club
Ashland, New Hampshire
500+ acres
novice-intermediate-advanced
USGS: Holderness

Easier trails traverse the golf course, and more challenging runs wind through the surrounding woodlands. There are some nice views of the mountains. Trails are marked with signs and ribbons, and maps are available. Snowmobiles are not permitted in the area. Bridle trails and power lines intersect with trails from the Country Club for further skiing possibilities.

Rentals, instruction, guided tours, and citizens' races are offered. Facilities include a fireplace, a lounge, and a dining area. There is a fee for trail use.

Driving directions: From I-93, take Exit 24 to North Ashland Road.

Suggestion courtesy of Ron Vaillancourt, White Mountain Country Club, Ashland Road, Ashland, New Hampshire 03217 (603-536-2227).

Gunstock Touring Center
Laconia, New Hampshire
9 miles of trails
novice-intermediate-advanced
USGS: Winnepesaukee

Trails begin at the Touring Center and cover varied terrain. One novice trail winds past a 70-meter ski jump, through hemlock forests and along brooks. An expert trail ascends Cobble Mountain for nice views of Lake Winnipesaukee and the White Mountains. Another 450 acres are currently being developed to provide additional trails for ski touring. All trails are marked according to NSTOA standards. Snowmobiles are not permitted on the trails.

The Touring Center is separate from the alpine facilities at Gunstock. It has a waxing area and offers rentals, instruction, and guided tours (including moonlight tours). The alpine base lodge has a cafeteria, restrooms, a nursery, and a lounge. The $2.00 trail fee includes a map.

Driving directions: From Exit 20 off I-93, take Route 3 east to the Route 11 bypass. Gunstock is 7 miles east of Laconia on Route 11A.

Suggestion courtesy of Pamela Weeks Moores, Touring Director, Gunstock Touring Center, Box 336, Laconia, New Hampshire 03246 (603-293-4341).

Longwood Ski Touring Center
Center Harbor, New Hampshire
15 miles of trails
novice-intermediate-advanced
USGS: Winnipesaukee

This is a wooded area with a nice network of groomed trails. All are color coded and marked according to difficulty; maps are distributed at the Touring Center. Snowmobiles are not permitted on the property.

The clubhouse has a snack bar and lounge, a pro shop, a waxing room, and a rental facility. Instruction is available, and there may be citizens' races in the near future. There is a fee for trail use.

Driving directions: Longwood is situated on Route 25 in Center Harbor, 4 miles east of Meredith.

Suggestion courtesy of Shirley Smith, Longwood Ski Touring Center, Box 756, Center Harbor, New Hampshire 03226.

The Nordic Skier
Wolfeboro, New Hampshire
64 km (40 miles) of trails
novice-intermediate-advanced
USGS: Wolfeboro

Trails in Wolfeboro offer many views of nearby mountains and lakes. They are marked according to difficulty and about half of the trails are groomed with a track setter. Some are lighted for night use. Maps are posted at the Nordic Skier and may be purchased for $.50. These trails connect to many other unmarked trails in the vicinity. In addition, there are extensive possibilities for lake skiing (use caution when venturing onto the ice). Snowmobiles are not permitted on groomed trails.

The shop offers instruction, guided tours (including moonlight tours), rental equipment, retail sales, and free waxing clinics on Friday nights. Facilities include a waxing area, restrooms, and a snack bar. A citizens' race is held annually, and benefit tourathons for cancer and cystic fibrosis are held in February and March. The town of Wolfeboro has a number of fine inns, restaurants, and shops. Trail use is free, though donations are welcome.

Driving directions: From Manchester, take Route 3 to Route 28. Follow Route 28 north to Wolfeboro. The Nordic Skier is in the center of town.

Suggestion courtesy of Steve Flagg, The Nordic Skier, Main Street, Wolfeboro, New Hampshire 03894 (603-569-3151).

Fernald Hill Farm
Cornish, New Hampshire
1100 acres
novice-intermediate
USGS: North Hartland

Skiers are welcome to use the woods and fields of Fernald Hill Farm, although there are no developed ski trails. With an average elevation of 1200 feet, there are some nice views, and snow conditions are often good when areas at lower elevations have become crusty or bare.

Driving directions: From Plainfield, take Route 12A north, and turn right onto the Plainfield-Meriden Road. After 2 miles, turn right onto Hell Hollow Road. Keep bearing left for 2 miles, uphill. The farm is at the end of the road. When parking, leave enough room for the milk truck to get by.

Suggestion courtesy of Anne Mausolff, Weston, Vermont.

Gray Ledges Farm
Grantham, New Hampshire
30 miles of trails
novice-intermediate-advanced
USGS: Sunapee/Mascoma

Trails traverse hilly farmland, marked by old stone walls and cellar holes. Much of the land is open hayfields and pastureland, with an orchard, a sugar bush, and several wooded areas. All trails are marked according to NSTOA standards, and maps are posted at each intersection. Excellent waterproof trail maps are available at the touring center. Snowmobiles are not permitted on about 25 miles of trails on and around the farm, but they may use outlying trails. These connect with many other trails in Grantham and Croydon to form a network of over 70 miles of trails.

Gray Ledges has a new ski shop that offers rentals and instruction. There may be races in the near future. Accommodations (motel, lodge, or bunkroom) are available, and The Ledges Restaurant serves beef raised on the farm. Ice skating and snowshoeing are permitted. The trail fee is $2.00.

Driving directions: From Exit 13 off I-89, drive south on Route 10 for 1 mile to Grantham. Turn right at the Mobil station, and continue uphill for 0.7 miles to Gray Ledges.

Suggestion courtesy of the Martin Family, Gray Ledges Farm, Grantham, New Hampshire 03753 (603-863-1002).

Eastman Ski Touring Center
Grantham, New Hampshire
30 km (18½ miles) of trails
novice–intermediate–advanced
USGS: Mascoma

Eastman Ski Touring Center has an extensive network of trails over open and wooden terrain. They are marked with NSTOA blue markers, and trail maps are available.

The Touring Center offers rentals and EPSTI certified instruction. Facilities include a retail shop, a waxing room, a locker room, showers, and Harvey's Ski Cap Lounge for food and beverages. There is also a small alpine ski area. The trail fee is $2.00 and maps are $.75.

Driving directions: Eastman is immediately off I-89, at Exit 13.

Suggestion courtesy of Eastman Ski Touring Center, Box 53, Grantham, New Hampshire 03753 (603-863-4500).

Norsk Ski Touring Center
New London, New Hampshire
30 km (18½ miles) of trails
novice–intermediate–advanced
USGS: Mt. Kearsarge

Norsk Ski Touring Center has 10 km of excellent beginner trails on the 200-acre grounds of Lake Sunapee Country Club, with panoramic views of Mount Kearsage and Ragged Mountain. More advanced trails go through surrounding wooded areas. Trails have colored markers, and maps are available. Snowmobiles are not permitted on groomed trails.

Facilities at the Touring Center include lodging, a restaurant, a waxing room, a snack bar, and a lounge area. Rentals, retail sales, instruction, and guided tours are offered. There is a citizens' race on the last Sunday of each month. The trail fee is $2.50 on weekends, $2.00 weekdays.

Driving directions: From I-89, take Exit 11 and drive east for 2 miles on Route 11.

Suggestion courtesy of John Schlosser, Norsk Ski Touring Center, Route 11, New London, New Hampshire 03257 (603-526-4685).

Pemigewasset Valley Ski Touring Center
Franklin, New Hampshire
300 acres
novice-intermediate
USGS: Penacook

Situated near the flood plain of the Pemigewasset River, this Touring Center has a system of trails plus many other skiing opportunities on snowmobile trails, an old road bed, and government recreation land. Terrain is primarily wooded, with several meadows near the river. Trails are marked with colored signs and are shown on a trail map. Snowmobiles are not allowed on most trails.

The Touring Center includes a waxing room and a snack bar, and offers rentals, instruction, and guided tours. The trail fee is $2.00.

Driving directions: Pemigewasset Valley Ski Touring Center is 3 miles north of Franklin on Route 3A.

Suggestion courtesy of Charles C. Beebe, Jr., Hollis, New Hampshire; and Pemigewasset Valley Ski Touring Center, Route 3A, West Franklin, New Hampshire 03235 (603-934-5614).

Mount Sunapee State Park
Sunapee, New Hampshire
10 miles of trails
novice-intermediate
USGS: Sunapee

Ski touring trails start around the base lodge and parking areas at Mount Sunapee Ski Area. Most go through heavily forested areas with stands of pine, spruce, and hemlock. One set of trails is in the Province Chair area to the west of the lodge and crosses or follows several novice slopes. A larger network to the east includes a mile-long unplowed road that passes an old quarry. Other trails in this area go by a beaver dam and the site of an old hotel. A map of the trails, including a description of each trail, is free at the base lodge. Trails are not groomed or patrolled. Snowmobiles are not allowed in the area.

Though the base lodge of the ski area is open to tourers, there are no separate facilities for ski touring. Rentals are available at the Carroll Reed Shop. There is no charge for trail use.

Driving directions: From I-91, take Exit 8 at Ascutney, Vermont. Take Route 103 east, past Newport, New Hampshire, to Mount Sunapee State Park. From I-89, take Exit 9 to Route 103 west.

Suggestion courtesy of Mount Sunapee State Park, Sunapee, New Hampshire 03772.

Dexter's Inn and Nordic Ski Center
Sunapee, New Hampshire
15 km (9 miles) of trails
novice–intermediate–advanced
USGS: Sunapee

Trails at Dexter's Inn wind over predominantly wooded terrain, with some hilly, open pastureland. There are several small loops for novices behind the Inn; more remote trails traverse a beaver pond and a marsh. All trails are well marked, and maps are distributed at the Nordic Ski Center. Snowmobiles are used only for maintenance and grooming. Trails at Dexter's Inn connect with those in Webb Forest, a 400-acre town recreation area.

Ski touring facilities in the barn include a ski room and a waxing room. Rentals and instruction are offered; guided tours and night skiing may be arranged. Dexter's Inn has 17 rooms, a dining room, and a lounge. Due to the fuel situation, the Inn will only operate during the month of February in 1980. The Touring Center opens in December. There is a fee for trail use.

Driving directions: From Newport, take Route 103 east, and follow signs to the Inn. From Sunapee, go west on Route 11, and follow the signs.

Suggestion courtesy of Frank H. Simpson, Dexter's Inn and Nordic Ski Center, Stage Coach Road, Sunapee, New Hampshire 03782.

Fox State Forest
Hillsboro, New Hampshire
15 miles of trails/1450 acres
intermediate–advanced
USGS: Hillsboro

Located in a transition area between central and northern forests, Fox State Forest has a great diversity of woodland and wildlife. It is used for numerous forest research projects; painted numbers and other strange marking on trees may be found throughout the area. Natural features include a black gum swamp (unusual this far north), a quaking bog around Mud Pond, beaver ponds, and a stand of virgin beech and hemlock. Many stone walls in the forest provide evidence of the fields and pastures that once comprised small hill farms. Other historical points of interest are the cellar holes of the old Gerry Kimball Farm and the Maple Sugar Camp and cemetery nearby.

All trails are well marked. They include the Ridge Trail, which makes a circuit of the forest on high ground, and the shorter Mushroom Nature Trail near the headquarters. A trail guide, including a good map, is available at the State Forest headquarters. Listings of indigenous trees, birds, flowering plants, and ferns may also be found here. Snowmobiles are limited primarily to trails used as access roads in summer. Hiking trails are reserved for snowshoeing and skiing. There is no trail fee, and trails are not groomed.

State Forest headquarters are open during working hours on weekdays. The buildings house offices, research laboratories, a forestry museum, and an environmental center.

Driving directions: From Hillsboro, take Center Road north for about 2 miles to the forest entrance. There are signs in the center of town. Park at the headquarters area.

Suggestion courtesy of Philip Verrier, Fox State Forest, Hillsboro, New Hampshire.

Pole and Pedal Ski Touring Center
Henniker, New Hampshire
32+ miles of trails
novice-intermediate-advanced
USGS: Hillsboro

Pole and Pedal trails leave from the center of town and consist primarily of old trails and logging roads. About 12 miles of trails in the Proctor Hill area and along the Contoocook River are packed and groomed. Others are marked but not maintained. Detailed maps are distributed at the shop. Snowmobiles are not permitted on the maintained trails, but may be encountered elsewhere.

Outlying trails include powerline routes, which lead south to the Quaker Hill district and Totten State Park, and the Mink Hills, 2 miles north of Henniker, with 20 square miles of old logging roads and wilderness skiing.

Rentals, EPSTI certified instruction, and guided tours are available at the Pole and Pedal Shop, which is open seven days a week. There is a warming and waxing hut at the trailhead. Special activities include night skiing on Thursdays and Fridays, NASTAR family races on a lighted course on Thursdays, a Dannon Series race, and the Eastern Spring Race. There is a trail fee.

Driving directions: From I-89, take Exit 5 and follow Routes 9 and 202 west to Henniker. The Pole and Pedal Shop is in the center of town.

Suggestion courtesy of Alan Johnson, Pole and Pedal Shop, Box 327, Henniker, New Hampshire 03242 (603-428-3242).

Bear Brook State Park
Allenstown, New Hampshire
10 miles of trails
novice–intermediate
USGS: Suncook

Bear Brook State Park is one of four state parks in New Hampshire that have set trails aside specifically for ski touring. There is also a large network of snowmobile trails that occasionally cross but do not overlap the ski trails. Signs along the trails distinguish between those for skiing and those for snowmobiling. A map of the major trails is available.

Driving directions: Bear Brook State Park is 5 miles east of Route 28 on Bear Brook Road. Follow cross-country signs. There is adequate parking.

Suggestion courtesy of Bear Brook State Park, Route #1, Suncook, New Hampshire 03275.

Charmingfare Ski Touring Center
Candia, New Hampshire
20 miles of trails/600 acres
novice–intermediate
USGS: Candia

Several trails start at the Charmingfare golf course and run through hardwood and evergreen forests over gentle, rolling terrain. Trails are well marked and patrolled, and 10 of the 20 miles of trails are groomed. Maps are free at the Touring Center. Snowmobiling is not permitted.

Facilities and services include a ski shop, a snack bar, a lounge, a waxing room, rentals, repairs, citizens' races, and EPSTI certified instruction. The trail fee is $2.00, $1.00 for children under 14, and season passes are available. The Touring Center is open Wednesdays through Sundays, and Christmas and Washington's Birthday vacation weeks.

Driving directions: Charmingfare Ski Touring Center is located on South Road, just off Route 101.

Suggestion courtesy of Leonard Chace, Charmingfare Ski Touring Center, Box 146, South Road, Candia, New Hampshire 03034 (603-483-2307).

Mount Pawtuckaway Area
Deerfield, New Hampshire
7½ miles, including side trip
novice
USGS: Mt. Pawtuckaway

In the northwest corner of Mount Pawtuckaway State Park, a summer road loops around the middle peak. A side trail leads to Pawtuckaway Boulders (among the largest in New England) and over a pass to Dead Pond. There are several ups and downs, but none are too difficult for the novice skier. Snowmobile use is heavy; the area is best avoided on weekends or in crusty conditions.

Ski route: Start the clockwise loop by skiing north on the unplowed road. Bear right at every fork except one: a short side trail leading steeply uphill. The side trail to the boulders and to the pond branches off to the left at the northern end of the loop. The beginning of the trail runs downhill to the boulders; from there it goes uphill to a pass. This part of the trail is marked in red, but it is sometimes hard to find. On the left side of the pass there is a high vertical cliff forming the east face of the north peak. Continue north to the pond, which is an interesting place to explore. Return to the loop road and turn left. Upon reaching the road, turn right and ski along the road back to the car.

Driving directions: From I-93 in Manchester, go east on Route 101 through the village of Bean Island, then north on Route 107. Continue for 3.3 miles to a side road on the right. There is a post here that supports the State Park sign in the summer. Turn right and follow this road for 2.5 miles. Park at the corner of the second unplowed road going off to the left. It may require a little digging to get a car safely off the road.

Sagamore-Hampton Ski Touring Center
North Hampton, New Hampshire
30 km (18½ miles) of trails
novice–intermediate
USGS: Hampton/Portsmouth

Sagamore-Hampton has a fine network of novice and intermediate trails, with one 1.5-km loop for advanced skiers. One third of the trails are on the open, rolling terrain of a golf course. The remainder wind through stands of red pine, hemlock, and beech in the adjacent wildlife sanctuary. Trails are well marked; about half are groomed and tracked, and the rest are packed when necessary. Maps are distributed at the clubhouse. Snowmobiles are not allowed in the area. Rentals and refreshments are available in the clubhouse, and there is an area set aside for waxing. Picnic tables are situated along the trails. There is a trail fee. The area is open from 9:00 AM to 4:00 PM.

Driving directions: The Ski Touring Center is located on North Road in North Hampton, between Routes 1 and 151. There is ample parking.

Suggestion courtesy of R. D. Luff, Sagamore-Hampton Ski Touring Center, 101 North Road, North Hampton, New Hampshire 03862 (603-964-5341).

Mount Pawtuckaway Area

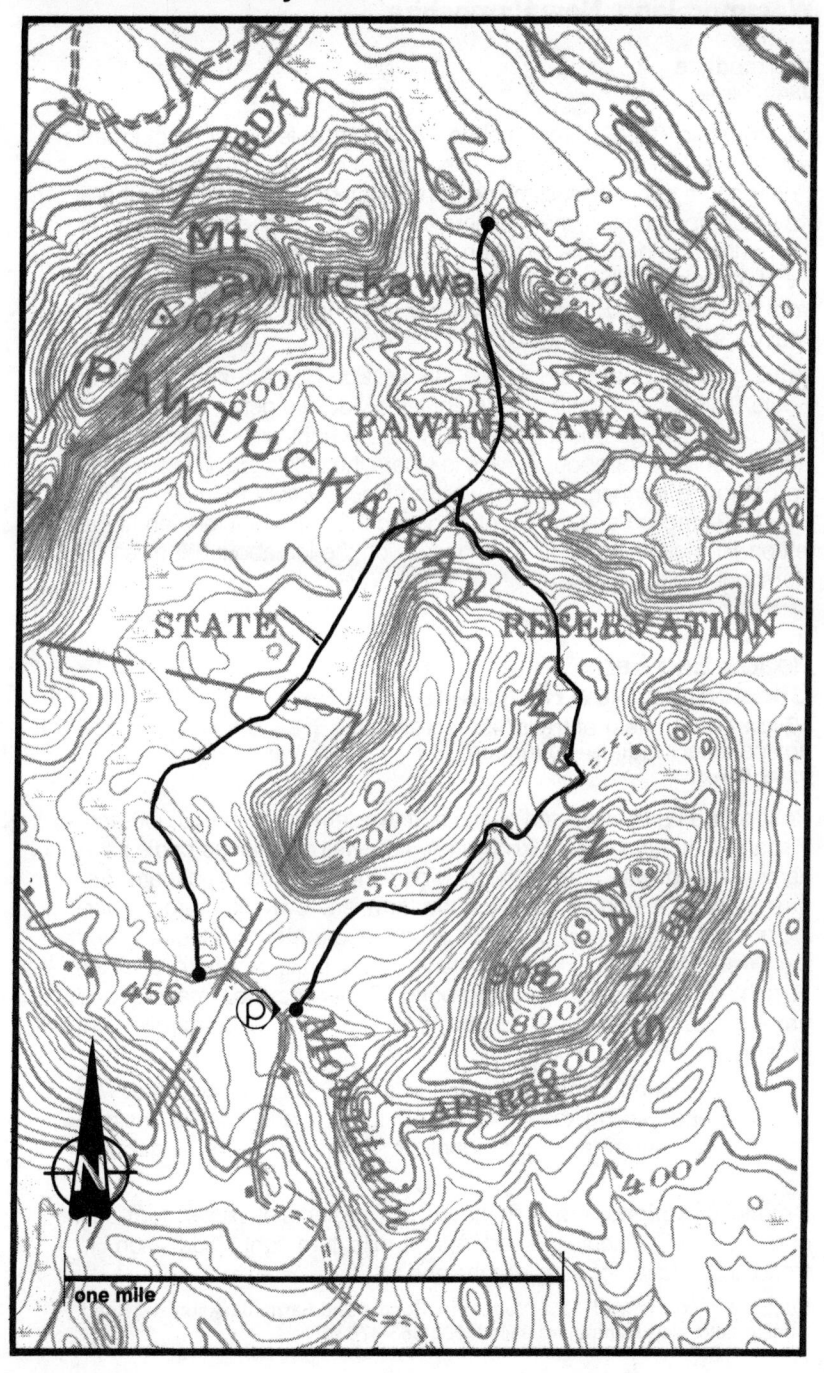

Southern New Hampshire

Hyland Hill
Westmoreland, New Hampshire
2 miles
intermediate
USGS: Keene

This tour is a steady climb of almost 800 vertical feet over an old road with a side trail to the summit. There is a fire tower on top of the hill. Under some conditions, climbing skins might be necessary. For a one-way tour, spot a car at the southern end of the trail and begin skiing at the northern end. In this direction, the longest part of the trail is downhill. If returning to the starting spot, it is preferable to ski to the summit from the south and to return over the same trail. Snowmobile use is heavy.

Driving directions: From Keene, go west on Route 9 and 12, taking Route 9 to the left where the two routes divide. To get to the southern end of the trail, go about 7½ miles and turn right onto Westmoreland Road. Continue for about 2 miles to where the trail takes off to the right. To get to the northern end, go west on Route 9 about 1 mile past the Route 12 junction and turn right. Proceed 0.2 miles to a fork, and bear left on Hurricane Road. The trail leaves on the left about 3½ miles up Hurricane Road.

Road's End Farm
Chesterfield, New Hampshire
17 km (10½ miles) of trails/450 acres
novice-intermediate-advanced
USGS: Keene

Road's End Farm is located on the northwestern rim of the 13,000-acre Pisgah Wilderness Area. Skiing is on wide, well maintained bridle trails, across meadows, and through woodlands. Some fields are frequented by the horses for which the farm is known. Numerous overlooks offer lovely views of Mount Monadnock, Mount Ascutney, and the Green Mountains in the distance, and Lake Spofford and the Pisgah Wilderness in the foreground. Trails are well marked and groomed, and maps are distributed at the farm. Snowmobiles are prohibited.

The Touring Center is located in a 1750 Cape Cod house, with warming and waxing rooms, rental equipment, and snacks. Instruction is offered informally, and moonlight skiing is available by appointment.

Driving directions: From Route 63 in Chesterfield Center, turn east onto the Old Chesterfield Road. After 1 mile, turn right on Jackson Hill Road and follow it for ½ mile to the end.

Suggestion courtesy of Tom Woodman, Road's End Farm, Jackson Hill Road, Chesterfield, New Hampshire 03443 (603-363-4703).

Hyland Hill

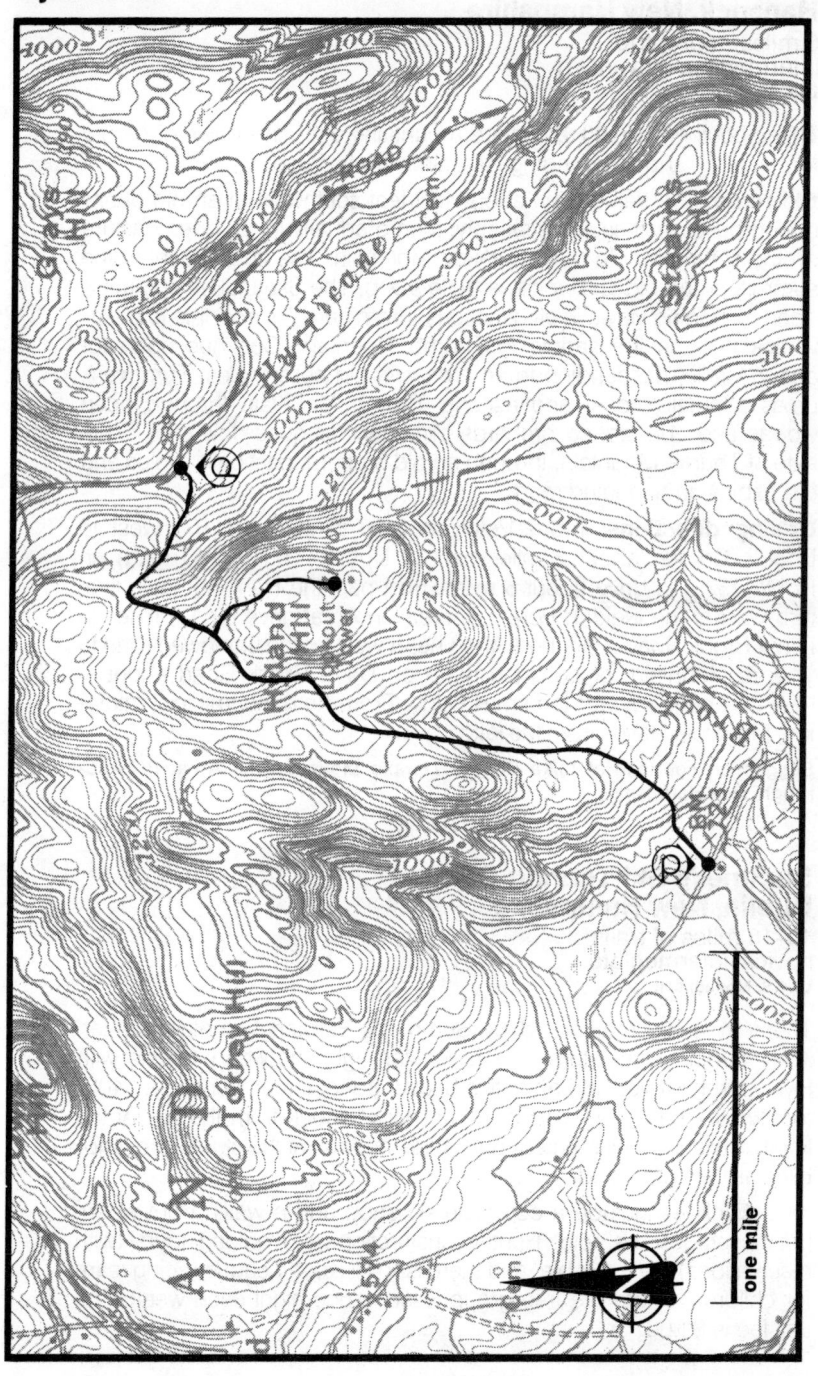

Southern New Hampshire

Skatutakee and Thumb Mountains
Hancock, New Hampshire
5 miles, round trip
intermediate-advanced
USGS: Monadnock

These southern New Hampshire mountains offer fine views of Mount Monadnock and surrounding hills. Snowmobile use is light.

Ski route: The trail begins about 100 feet southwest of an old abandoned building. It ascends steeply, then gradually, to an open pasture on the southern side of Skatutakee Mountain. The final ascent to the summit, on an old jeep road, is quite steep. The Skatutakee summit is open, providing views in all directions. From here it is possible to bushwhack through the saddle to Thumb Mountain. Continue north for about 1 mile, descending to an area with old cellar holes. Turn west, cross a small brook, and ascend Thumb Mountain through open woods and abandoned orchards. Another trail goes down the south side of Thumb Mountain, through an old orchard, past cellar holes and old cabins, to a logging road.

Driving directions: From Peterborough, take Route 101 west to Bond's Corner, about 2 miles east of Dublin. Turn right (north) on Route 137 and drive about 5 miles. Just past the Hancock town line, turn west at the Field 'n Forest Recreation Area; drive for 1¾ miles to Davis Brook Road. Park here, then head west on the unplowed road to Thumb Mountain, or continue north on Davis Brook Road about ¾ mile and park beyond the small fields. From here the trail to Skatutakee Mountain leaves from the left.

Suggestion courtesy of Mike Beebe, Temple Mountain Ski Area, Peterborough, New Hampshire.

Summer's Ski Touring Center
Dublin, New Hampshire
10-15 miles of trails
novice-intermediate
USGS: Monadnock

These trails are maintained by Summer's Ski and Mountain Center. They begin at the store and range through hardwood forests with lovely birch groves and an active beaver pond, circumventing a 1400-foot knoll. There are views of Mount Monadnock from the top of the knoll. Trails are well marked, and maps are free at the store. Snowmobiles are not permitted.

Facilities include a complete ski shop and a waxing hut where hot beverages are sold. Rentals, instruction, and guided tours (with reservations) are available, and there is a Bill Koch League racing team for children. There are free group lessons one night each week. The trail fee is $1.00.

Skatutakee and Thumb Mountains

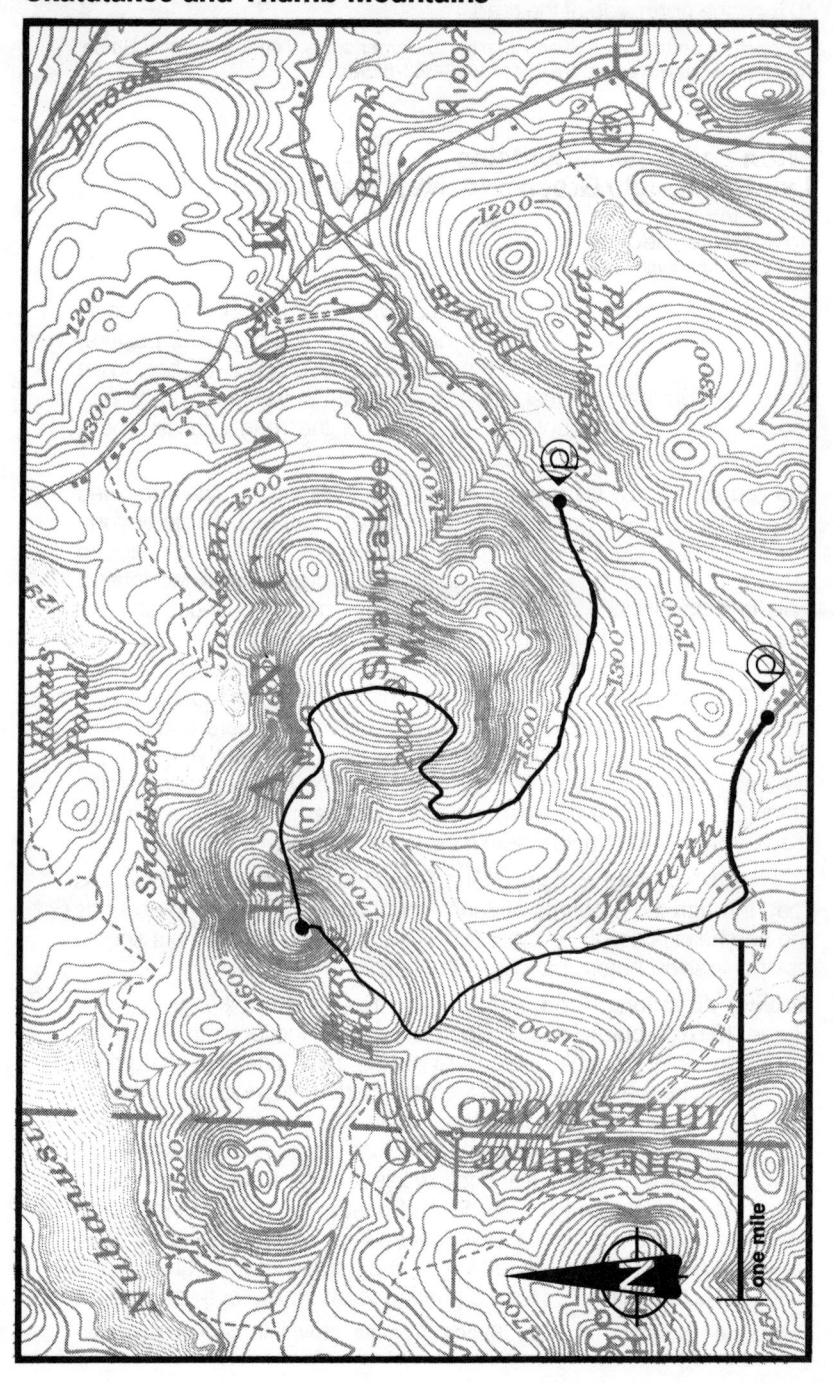

Southern New Hampshire

Driving directions: The Touring Center is east of Dublin, on Route 101, on the north side of the road.

Suggestion courtesy of Susan Martin, Summer's Ski Touring Center, Route 101, Dublin, New Hampshire 03444 (603-563-8556).

Winn and Rose Mountains
Lyndeborough/Greenfield, New Hampshire
5-6 miles
novice-intermediate
USGS: Peterborough

This is a touring trail over a wood road with two side trips to summits that command excellent views. Winn Mountain is a blueberry pasture; the summits of Rose and Lyndeborough are also open. It is best to ski the route from east to west, spotting a car at the western end. Snowmobiles may be encountered. Jeep use of the road can also be a problem.

Ski route: The trail starts at an elevation of 1080 feet on the unplowed road. After ½ mile it passes through a col at 1350 feet. A little beyond the col, a road on the right, marked by a piece of chrome wrapped around a tree, leads ¾ mile to Rose and Lyndeborough Mountains. This is a good place to eat lunch. The main road continues straight, reaches a height-of-land, descends, then crosses another rise. After passing a swamp on the right, a road branches left, leading to a large open field and the summit of Winn Mountain. When not too crusty, this field is good for some real alpine skiing. Leave skis here and walk to the summit. Winn Mountain, at 1675 feet, has excellent views and is also a good lunch spot. The main trail can be followed back to the starting point or followed westward along a stream. From here, the road leads downhill for 1 mile where it becomes plowed.

Another good route up Winn Mountain is on the summit access road through the orchards of Winn Mountain Farm. This road ascends the southeast side of the mountain to the open summit. Skiers should ask permission before parking at the farm.

Driving directions: From Exit 7 off the Everett Turnpike, go west on Route 101A through Milford. Continue to the junction with Route 31, and turn right through Wilton. About ½ mile past South Lyndeborough, take a side road off to the right marked "Lyndeborough Center." After about 1½ miles, look for a green sign that says "Winn Mountain Orchard" (the sign is located 50 feet up a side road to the left and is not seen easily). Turn left and follow this road for a short distance to a fork; take the right fork up the hill and past a "pavement ends" sign. The road reaches its highest point near a farm with a yellow barn, then turns right and goes steeply downhill. The unplowed road going uphill to the left is the ski route. There is parking room for two or three cars.

Suggestion courtesy of Mike Beebe, Temple Mountain Ski Area, Peterborough, New Hampshire.

Winn and Rose Mountains

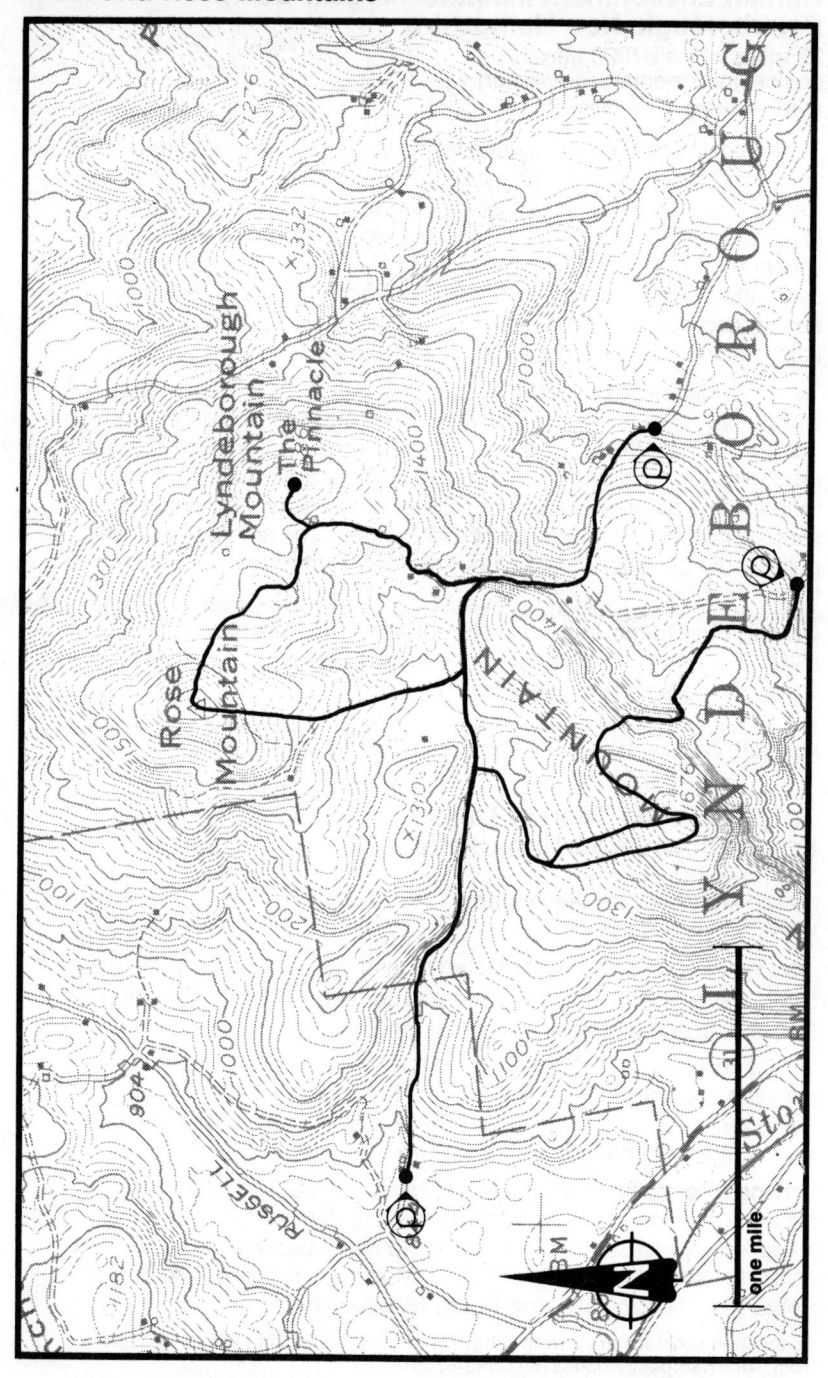

Southern New Hampshire

Human Environment Institute/Sargent Camp
Peterborough, New Hampshire
22 miles of trails/900 acres
novice–intermediate–advanced
USGS: Monadnock/Peterborough

Trails from Sargent Camp cover a varied landscape that includes a 56-acre pond, marshes, a 17-acre meadow, and small, forested hills with stands of mature hardwoods and mixed second growth. In addition, there are trails set aside for snowshoeing. All trails are well marked and shown on a map available at the Camp. Skiers should sign in before using the trails. Sargent Camp trails connect to others in the vicinity: abandoned roads, railroad rights-of-way, and a number of private trails. Snowmobiles are not allowed on the property.

Facilities include a heated building with hot beverages, and a waxing area. Rentals and instruction are available, and group accommodations may be arranged in advance. The Human Environment Institute is a part of Boston University, so there are a number of environmental education programs offered, including weekend workshops, environmental tours, and credit courses. The area is open to the public only on weekends and during New Hampshire school vacations.

Driving directions: Take Union Street west from Peterborough for 1½ miles. Turn right on Windy Row and continue 3½ miles to Sargent Camp. There is parking space for over 60 cars.

Suggestion courtesy of Human Environment Institute, Sargent Camp, Windy Row, RFD #2, Peterborough, New Hampshire 03458 (603-525-3311).

Tory Pines Ski Touring Center
Francestown, New Hampshire
30 miles of trails
novice–intermediate–advanced
USGS: Peterborough/Hillsboro

Tory Pines has a network of marked touring trails, plus open fields with lovely views of Crotched Mountain and surrounding areas. The terrain is varied, accommodating skiers of all abilities.

The resort offers rentals, instruction, and guided tours, and is planning a children's racing program. The 1799 Colonial Clubhouse has a restaurant and lounge, and there is a 30-room luxury hotel for overnight accommodations. There is a $3.00 trail fee.

Driving directions: From Route 3 in Nashua, take Route 101A west to Milford. Go north on Route 13 through Mont Vernon, and take a left at the fork to Francestown. Continue on Route 47 past Francestown and watch for signs to Tory Pines. From Manchester, take Route 114 to Route 13 at Goffstown. Follow Route 13 to New Boston.

Suggestion courtesy of LouAnn King, Tory Pines Ski Touring Center, Francestown, New Hampshire 03043 (603-588-6345).

New England Center for Outdoor Education at Camp Allen
Bedford, New Hampshire
10 km (6 miles) of trails
novice-intermediate-advanced
USGS: Manchester South

Most trails wind through heavily wooded areas, with 2 or 3 km of trails through open fields. They are well marked, and trail maps are available. Snowmobiles use some adjoining trails, but use is fairly light.

Facilities include a heated lounge with a fireplace, a dining room, and a snack bar. Instruction, guided tours, and moonlight tours are offered. There is a trail fee.

Driving directions: From the Manchester area, take Route 101 west to Route 3. Go south about ½ mile, and turn right by the Texaco Station onto Back River Road. Continue for 1.5 miles, and turn left onto a dirt road at the Camp Allen sign.

Suggestion courtesy of Gary M. Robb, New England Center for Outdoor Education, Camp Allen, RFD #5, Bedford, New Hampshire 03102 (603-622-8471).

Gap Mountain
Troy, New Hampshire
intermediate
USGS: Jaffrey

Gap Mountain offers great views of Mount Monadnock to the north. Starting from open pastures, it is a fairly steep, though largely open, climb to the summit.

Driving directions: From Keene, go southeast on Route 12. About halfway between Fitzwilliam and Troy, turn northeast on Fern Hill Road. Take the right fork at the first intersection, turn right at the next, and turn left about ¼ mile later. Park at the end of the road.

Suggestion courtesy of Mike Beebe, Temple Mountain Ski Area, Peterborough, New Hampshire.

The Inn at East Hill Farm
Troy, New Hampshire
150 acres
novice-intermediate-advanced
USGS: Monadnock

East Hill ski trails traverse wooded areas and circle a pond at the base of Mount Monadnock. Most are suitable for novices. Trails have colored markers and are shown on a map. Snowmobiles are not permitted on cross-country trails.

Ski rentals, meals, and lodging are available at East Hill Farm. There is also a small rope tow for alpine skiing. Trail use is free for guests at the Inn.

Driving directions: East Hill Farm is situated on Mountain Road, off Route 12 in Troy.

Suggestion courtesy of Dave Adams, The Inn at East Hill Farm, Troy, New Hampshire 03465 (603-242-6495).

Purgatory Falls
Mont Vernon, New Hampshire
3 miles
novice–intermediate
USGS: New Boston

This is a short run with several fairly steep ups and downs, which may be skied either one way or as a round trip. A side trail leads to a spectacular frozen waterfall. Snowmobile use can be heavy.

Ski route: Ski up the unplowed portion of Upton Road. At the top of the rise there are side trails to the left and right; proceed downhill, passing Purgatory Road on the left. At the bottom of the run is a side trail to the left, on the near bank of Purgatory Brook. Follow this trail, and after about 500 feet, bushwhack through the woods to the right. A little searching will probably be necessary in order to find a spot at which to leave the trail. This will lead to a deep, narrow, short canyon where the stream drops into a horseshoe-shaped, cliff-walled amphitheater. In cold weather, the stream freezes into strange ice formations with icicle curtains hanging from the cliff. The spot was formerly a tourist attraction, and a few iron posts, part of an old guardrail, can still be seen in rocks along the canyon. This is a good place to eat lunch. Bushwhack back to the trail, then back upstream to the bridge. If a car has been spotted at Johnson Corner, cross the bridge and continue west. Otherwise, return east toward Mont Vernon. On the way back, it is pleasant to take a side trip south along Purgatory Road. It is almost 1 mile each way and includes a fairly long but gentle downhill run. Turn around when the road emerges at a farm and return over the same route to the main trail. From here back to Mont Vernon is another good downhill run.

Driving directions: From Exit 7 off the Everett Turnpike, go west on Route 101A to Milford. From Milford, go north on Route 13 through the center of Mont Vernon. After passing the town cemetery, take a sharp left onto Wilton Road (poorly marked) at the three-way fork. After about ½ mile, take Upton Road on the right. This road is poorly plowed. Park where the plowed section ends. For a one-way tour, spot a car at Johnson Corner.

Purgatory Falls

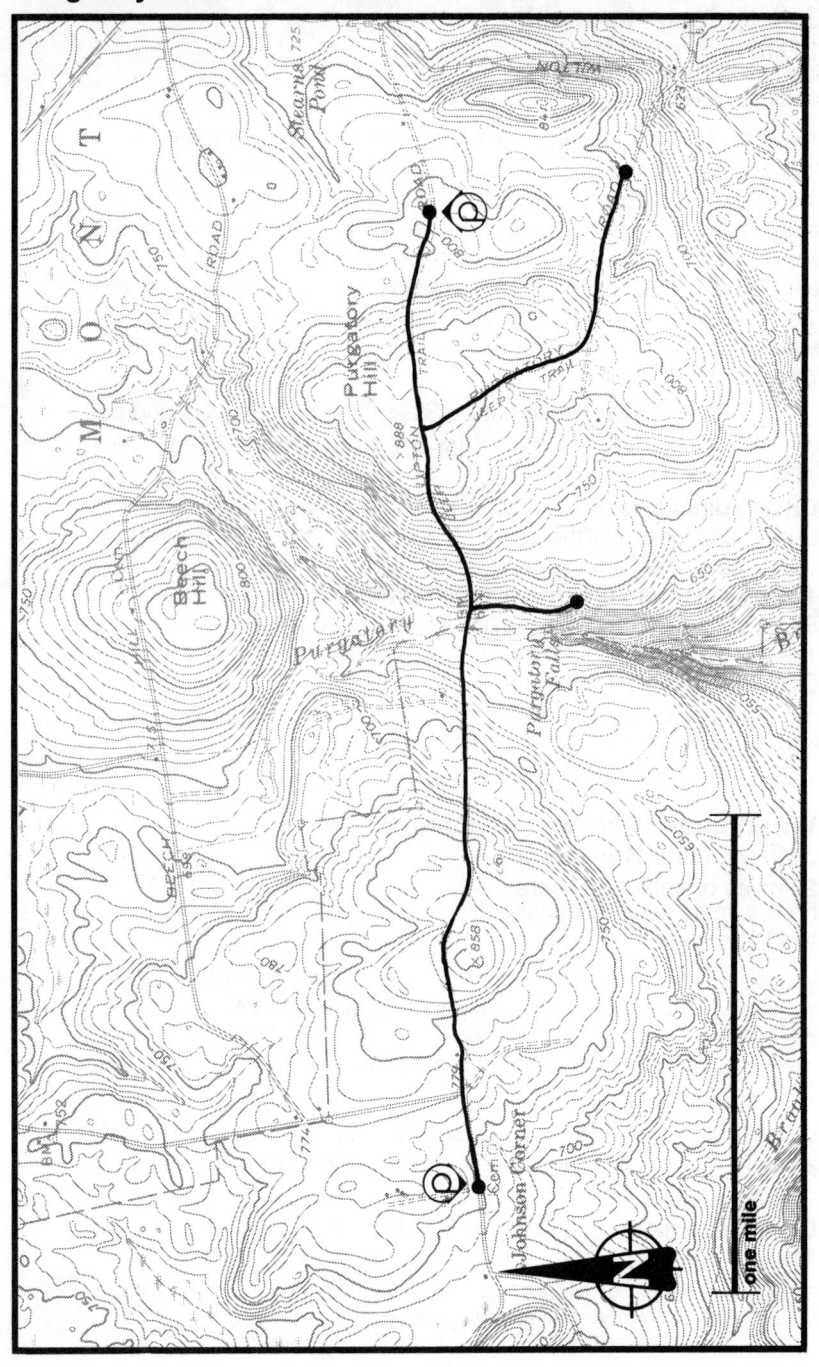

Southern New Hampshire

Monadnock State Park
Jaffrey, New Hampshire
15 km (9 miles) of trails
intermediate-advanced
USGS: Monadnock

There is good ski touring over hiking trails and logging roads on the lower slopes of Mount Monadnock. This is a wooded area, mostly a mature, second growth forest of mixed hard- and softwoods. There are a few open areas with a couple of nice views of the mountain. Skiers should carry a map and compass, since trails are not marked for difficulty or direction. Trail maps are available from a dispenser box near the parking lot. Snowmobiles presently share one section of trail with skiers: from Ballou City to the Monadnock Bible Conference Center via Wesselhoeft Pond.

The only winter facilities at the State Park are outhouses and picnic tables. The Park Manager is usually in the area to answer questions or to help in emergencies.

Driving directions: From Peterborough, take Route 101 west through Dublin, and turn left at the sign for Monadnock State Park. Continue for 5½ miles to the Park entrance on the right. From Jaffrey, take Route 124 west, and turn right onto Dublin Road where there is a sign for the State Park. After 1½ miles, turn left into the Park. There is plowed parking at the Park headquarters. Do not park on the road near the Bible Conference Center (the Ark) or at Bacon's Sugar House.

Suggestion courtesy of Mike Beebe, Temple Mountain Ski Area, Peterborough, New Hampshire; and Monadnock State Park, Jaffrey, New Hampshire.

Woodbound Ski Touring Center
Jaffrey, New Hampshire
22 miles of trails/1000 acres
novice-intermediate-advanced
USGS: Monadnock

Woodbound trails cover varied terrain, mostly through evergreen woodland. They connect to state park trails and Windblown and Temple Mountain Touring Centers (see separate entries). Snowmobiles are not permitted on Woodbound trails. Maps are available free of charge.

Rentals, instruction, and guided tours are available at Woodbound Inn. There is also alpine skiing, skating, and tobogganing at the area. Trail use is free for guests at the Inn; for others there is a $2.00 charge.

Driving directions: The Inn is on Woodbound Road, 2 miles off Route 119.

Suggestion courtesy of Jed Brummer, Woodbound Ski Touring Center, Woodbound Road, Jaffrey, New Hampshire 03452 (603-532-8341).

Temple Mountain Ski Area
Peterborough, New Hampshire
35 miles of trails
novice-intermediate-advanced
USGS: Peterborough

Situated in a southern New Hampshire snow belt, Temple Mountain has a long touring season on trails at elevations from 1000 to 2200 feet. The terrain is varied and includes many areas of open hardwoods and mountain ridges with excellent views. Trails are well marked and maintained, and maps are available and posted at the Ski Area. Maps for a number of other interesting tours in the Monadnock Region are also available. Temple Mountain connects to Windblown and Mount Watatic (in Ashby, Massachusetts) ski touring centers via the Wapack Trail to the south (see separate entries). Snowmobiles are not permitted on most trails; on some outlying trails there is limited use.

Facilities include two base lodges, a snack bar, a cross-country waxing hut, and lean-tos for camping. Rentals, instruction, and free monthly touring clinics are offered. Guided tours and group programs may be arranged. The annual Souhegan Lions Fun Race is held in January, the Robbins Run from Windblown to Temple Mountain in February, and the annual Wapack Tour (Temple Mountain to Mount Watatic) in March. Snowshoeing is permitted, and there is skating nearby. The $3.00 trail fee includes use of the T-bars. Register at the ski shop before using the trails.

Driving directions: Temple Mountain Ski Area is on Route 101, 4 miles east of Peterborough, 23 miles west of Nashua.

Suggestion courtesy of Mike Beebe, Owner, Temple Mountain Ski Area, Route 101, Peterborough, New Hampshire 03458 (603-924-6946).

Wapack Trail
Ashburnham, Massachusetts to Greenfield, New Hampshire
21 miles
advanced
USGS: Ashburnham/Peterborough

The Wapack Trail is a challenging route for experienced skiers. It traverses the Wapack Range, which includes Mount Watatic, Barrett Mountain, Temple Mountain, and South and North Pack Monadnock. The trail runs through northern spruce forest and along many open ledges with fine panoramic views. Some sections are steep. The trail is narrow and poorly maintained. Although it it marked with bright yellow blazes, the trail may be hard to follow and difficult to negotiate, especially if snow cover is inadequate. The Wapack Trail is shown on USGS topographic maps. A map and trail description are included in the AMC *White Mountain Guide*. Rough terrain discourages snowmobile use.

Ski route, southern section: The trail from Route 119 up the south side of Mount Watatic is too steep for skiing. Join the trail by ascending an alpine ski trail at Mount Watatic Ski Area or by following a touring trail from Mount Watatic Ski Touring Center (see separate entry). From the summit of Mount Watatic, the Wapack Trail heads north just beyond the ski lift terminal (look for the yellow blazes). It descends through spruce forest, crosses pastures, and ascends Nutting Hill, where there are good views. The trail continues north through beech woods, then, after ½ mile, crosses a wall that marks the state line. After another ¼ mile, the trail bears left and heads downhill for ⅓ mile, then turns right and reaches Binney Hill Road after ½ mile. It follows Binney Hill Road west for about 1000 feet, then turns right (north), crosses a small brook, and skirts the western shore of Binney Pond. The trail then climbs Barrett Mountain, nearly 3 miles long, with four open summits affording good views. This is a difficult section of the trail. Ski touring trails from Windblown (see separate entry) intersect the Wapack Trail on the north end of Barrett Mountain. The trail ascends an outlying knoll on Barrett Mountain before descending steeply to the Wapack Lodge on Route 123. After crossing Route 123, the trail enters the woods opposite the Lodge driveway, then crosses the western slopes of Kidder Mountain. About ½ mile from Route 123, an obscure trail diverges right to the summit of Kidder Mountain. The main trail bears left and gradually descends along an old logging road bordered by a stone wall. It passes a pond outlet and soon reaches Nashua Road.

Ski route, central section: The trail follows the road toward Sharon for about 0.4 miles, bears right at the fork, then turns right onto a paved road. It ascends the southern end of Temple Mountain and traverses an open ridge over several summits. The highest summit is wooded, but others are bare and offer good views. From the northern summit, the trail descends through Temple Mountain Ski Area (see separate entry) to Route 101 in Peterborough.

Ski route, northern section: Walk or ski the auto road to Miller State Park at the summit of South Pack Monadnock. The trail leaves the north side of the summit and descends steeply along rocky ledges for 1 mile to the open saddle between the peaks. The trail traverses open pastures and stands of spruce for 1¾ miles, then climbs steeply 600 feet to the bare summit of North Pack. From North Pack, it leads north 1¼ miles, descending steeply, then gradually, to the Peterborough-Russell Road. This section is marked infrequently with blazes and blue and yellow ribbons.

Driving directions: To reach the southern end of the trail, see directions for Mount Watatic Ski Touring Center. The trail starts 100 yards west of the Touring Center, beyond a field. To reach the Wapack Lodge crossing, take Routes 123 and 124 northwest from New Ipswich for 3 miles. There is a sign where the trail crosses the road, but there is no sign for the Lodge. To get to the Nashua Road crossing, continue northwest from the Lodge and fork right on Route 123. Drive 1 mile, and turn right onto Nashua Road. The trail crosses the road in ½ mile. Park by the side of the road. To reach Temple Mountain, see directions under the separate entry. Park at the Ski Area or across the road in the Miller State Park parking lot. The access road to the State Park is plowed in winter. To get to the northern end of the trail, take Route 101 west from Temple Mountain and turn right onto Old Mountain Road just after the pond. Continue on this road for 3 miles; turn right at the first intersection, then right again at the next. The trail leaves the right (south) side of the road ½ mile from the last turn at the height-of-land. There is a sign nailed to a tree.

Suggestion courtesy of Mike Beebe, Temple Mountain Ski Area, Peterborough, New Hampshire.

Windblown
New Ipswich, New Hampshire
20 miles of trails/300 acres
novice-intermediate-advanced
USGS: Peterborough

This is a small, rustic area with trails covering varied terrain, mostly at higher elevations. Trails traverse Barrett Mountain (1853 feet), a stream valley, a frozen bog, a beaver pond, and hillside fields with excellent views of the Monadnock region to the north and west. About 10 miles of trails are groomed with a track sled; snowmobiles are used for trail maintenance but are not otherwise permitted.

Trails are well marked, and maps are provided at no cost. The Wapack Trail, part of which is too steep for skiing, traverses this area and is marked differently. Windblown trails connect with those from Temple Mountain, and Mount Watatic Ski Touring Center in Ashby, Massachusetts (see separate entries).

Facilities include a ski shop with a snack bar and a wood stove, a waxing shed, a warming hut in the woods, and a sugar house in operation in the spring. The warming hut may be reserved for overnight use. Wood stoves, water, and sleeping mats are provided; sleeping bags and food must be brought in. Windblown rents ski equipment and snowshoes and provides instruction. Trail fees are $2.50 for adults and $1.50 for those 10 to 18 years old. Children under 10 are admitted free.

Driving directions: From I-495, take Route 19 to West Townsend, Massachusetts. Take Route 124 to New Ipswich and continue past town for another 2 miles. Turn left at the sign for Windblown. If coming from the north on Route 124, the sign is ¼ mile past the junction with Route 123. There is a plowed parking area below the ski shop for about 40 cars. Additional cars may park alongside the road.

Suggestion courtesy of Al Jenks, Windblown, Turnpike Road, New Ipswich, New Hampshire 03071 (603-878-2869).

Hollis Hof Ski Touring Center
Hollis, New Hampshire
30+ miles of trails
novice-intermediate
USGS: Pepperell/South Merrimack

Hollis Hof has 10 miles of marked and groomed trails, plus access to over 20 miles of unmarked trails and many open fields. Rental equipment, instruction, guided tours, and a snack bar are available. The Touring Center is affiliated with Temple Mountain Ski Area, where there is a ski shop. The trail fee is $2.00.

Driving directions: Take Route 130 from Nashua to the center of Hollis, and bear left by the Town Hall, on Depot Road. Take the first left off Depot Road onto Richardson Road; the Touring Center is at the second house on the right.

Suggestion courtesy of Charles C. Beebe, Jr., Hollis Hof Ski Touring Center, 53 Richardson Road, Hollis, New Hampshire 03049 (603-465-2633).

Ski Touring Vermont
CHAPTER 3

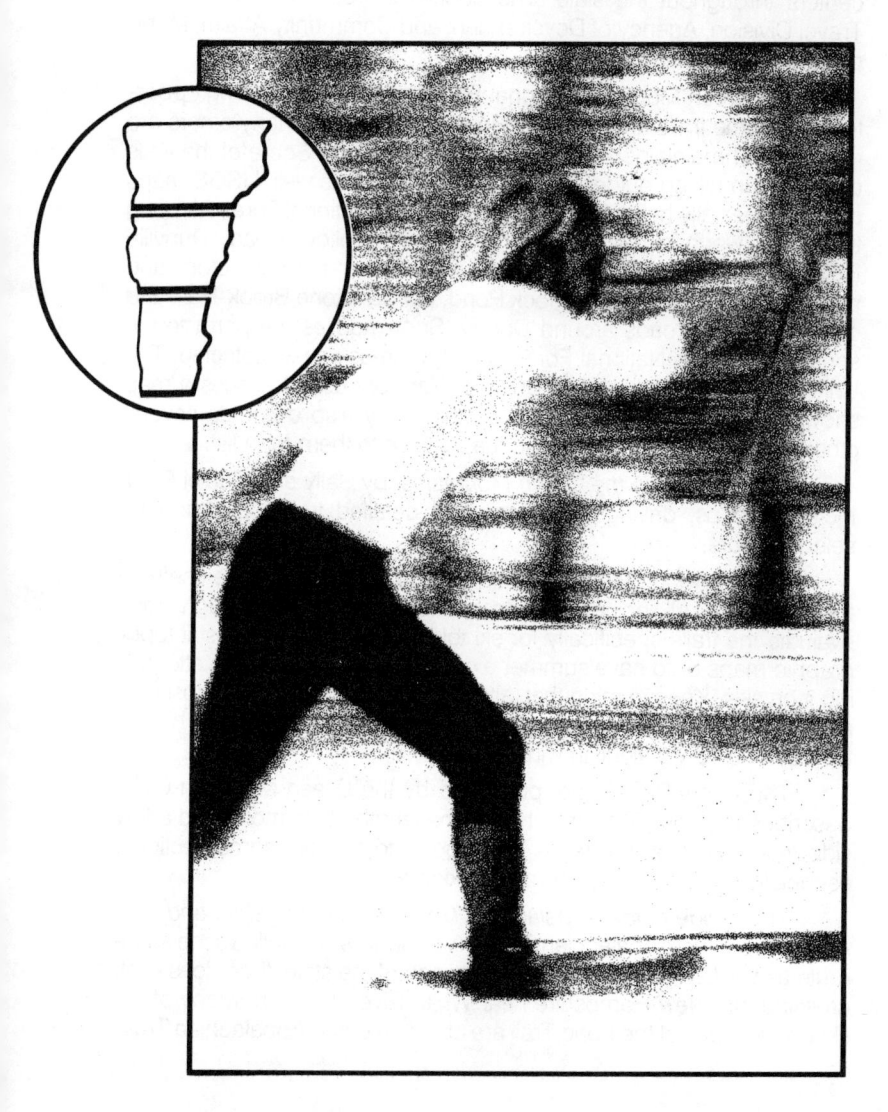

Vermont has a large number of ski touring centers, including several affiliated with inns. Because of the large number of privately maintained trails, the state has not developed public lands for ski touring, with the exception of the Puddledock Trails (see separate entry). Many state parks and forests, however, have trails suitable for ski touring. Among them are Gifford Woods State Park in Sherburne, Putnam State Forest in Worcester, and Camel's Hump State Park in Waterbury and Duxbury.

The state of Vermont issues an annual booklet, the "Vermont Winter Vacation Guide," which lists alpine ski areas and ski touring centers throughout the state. The booklet is free from the Vermont Travel Division, Agency of Development and Community Affairs, Montpelier, Vermont 05602.

The Green Mountain National Forest offers many striking opportunities. Some trails are described in this *Guide,* and many others are marked and maintained by various touring centers. Some of the trails described in hiking guides are suitable for skiing as well. USGS maps can be especially helpful for finding trails in the National Forest. Among the areas worth exploring are the Dunville Hollow Road, Dunville Hollow Trail, Burgess Road, and Sucker Pond in Bennington; and parts of the Long Trail, Little Rock Pond, Homer Stone Brook Trail, and other unplowed roads around Danby. Snowmobiles are permitted in some parts of the National Forest; in other areas use is restricted. The United States Forest Service, Rutland, Vermont 05701, issues a map showing designated snowmobile routes. They also distribute several other recreation and topographic maps; write to them for a list.

25 Ski Tours in the Green Mountains, by Sally and Daniel Ford, includes maps, driving directions, and detailed trail information for selected tours.

The following guides to hiking trails in Vermont may be useful to the ski tourer. All include trail descriptions and maps, though none evaluate the trails specifically for ski touring. It is best to consult topographic maps or to have summer experience on a trail before attempting it on skis. Keep in mind that, although negotiating stream crossings and finding parking areas may not pose problems for summer hikers, they can be very difficult in winter.

The *Long Trail Guide,* published by the Green Mountain Club, describes the Long Trail, which runs the length of Vermont, and a few side trails. Most of the trail is too rugged to ski, but some sections, especially in southern Vermont, are skiable.

The *Guide to the Appalachian Trail in New Hampshire and Vermont* covers the Appalachian Trail in Vermont, which follows the same route as the Long Trail in the southern part of the state, then goes east, crossing into New Hampshire near White River Junction. Many of the skiable sections of the Long Trail are also part of the Appalachian Trail.

Fifty Hikes in Vermont, by Paul and Ruth Sadlier, includes several hikes that would also be good ski tours. Among the best possibilities are Pine Hill Park, Somerset Reservoir, The Pinnacle, Harmon Hill, Merck Forest, Mt. Antone, Slack Hill, Quechee Gorge, Abbey Pond, Osmore Pond/Little Deer Mountain, Big Deer Mountain, and Blake Pond. Refer to *Fifty Hikes* for trail information, maps, and driving directions.

The *Day Hiker's Guide to Vermont,* published by the Green Mountain Club, has many trails with ski touring potential, although none are evaluated for that purpose. The book includes excellent maps and detailed trail descriptions.

Northern Vermont Ski Touring Areas

1. Missisquoi National Wildlife Refuge, Swanton *100*
2. Northland Ski Touring Center, North Hero *100*
3. Hazen's Notch Ski Touring Center,
    Montgomery Center *101*
4. Jay Peak Touring Center, Jay *101*
5. Stark Farm Ski Touring Center, Westford *102*
6. Horsford Ski Touring, Charlotte *102*
7. Village of Smugglers' Notch, Jeffersonville *103*
8. The Farm Resort, Morrisville *104*
9. Trapp Family Lodge, Stowe *104*
    Edson Hill Ski Touring Center, Stowe *105*
    Topnotch Ski Touring Area, Stowe *105*
    Mount Mansfield Ski Touring Center, Stowe *106*
10. Bolton Valley Ski Resort, Bolton *106*
11. Ski Hostel Lodge, Waterbury Center *107*
12. Craftsbury Nordic Ski Center,
    Craftsbury Common *107*
13. Highland Lodge Ski Touring Center, Greensboro *108*
14. Burklyn Ski Touring Center, East Burke *108*
    Burke Mountain Recreation, Inc. Touring Center
        East Burke *109*
15. Rabbit Hill Inn Ski Touring Center,
    Lower Waterford *109*

Northern Vermont

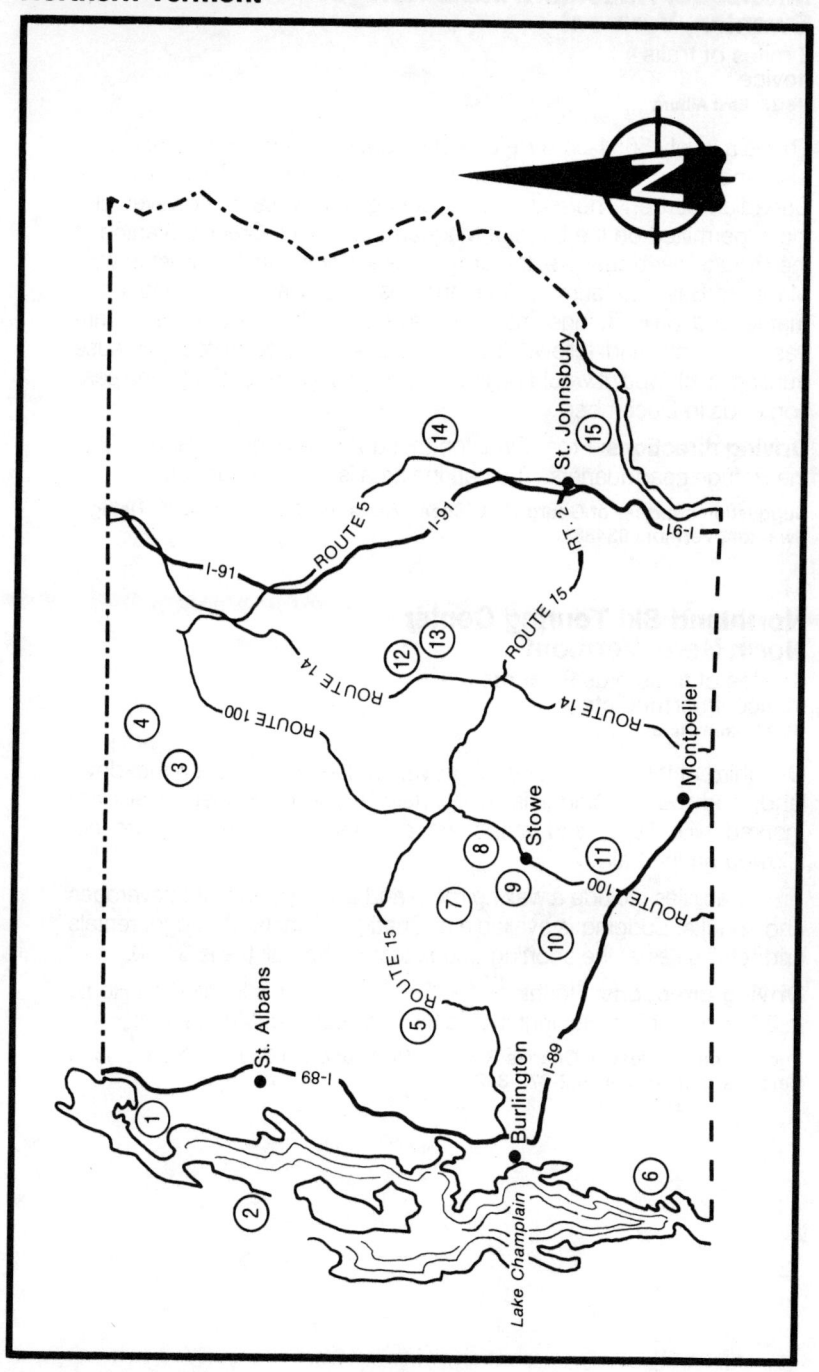

Missisquoi National Wildlife Refuge
Swanton, Vermont
3 miles of trails
novice
USGS: East Alburg

This is a lovely 5651-acre Refuge of meadows, marshland, brush, timber, and open bays located on the Missisquoi River Delta near the Canadian border. There are no ski touring trails as such; however, skiing is permitted on the beds of Maquam and Black Creeks. Starting at the Refuge headquarters, the creeks meander south and west toward Maquam Bay. The surrounding terrain is brushy marsh with stands of maple and oak. Refuge maps are available, though the creeks are easy to locate and follow. Snowmobiles are not permitted. Because hunting is allowed, it would be inadvisable to ski here until after the season ends in December.

Driving directions: From Swanton, head 2 miles west on Route 78 to the Refuge headquarters. The parking area is at the headquarters.

Suggestion courtesy of George F. O'Shea, Missisquoi National Wildlife Refuge, Swanton, Vermont 05488.

Northland Ski Touring Center
North Hero, Vermont
8 miles of trails plus 90 acres
novice-intermediate
USGS: North Hero

One third of this area is a cedar grove, another third is open meadowland, and the remainder is moderately hilly and wooded. Trails are marked with flags, and maps are available. Snowmobiles are not allowed on the trails.

Facilities include a waxing room and a lounge with hot beverages and snacks. Lodging is available at Charlie's Northland Lodge, rentals and retail sales at the sporting goods store. The trail fee is $1.00.

Driving directions: Northland Ski Touring Center is located on Route 2, 32 miles north of Burlington and 65 miles south of Montreal.

Suggestion courtesy of Charles R. Clark, Northland Ski Touring Center, North Hero, Vermont 05474 (802-372-8822).

Hazen's Notch Ski Touring Center
Montgomery Center, Vermont
20+ miles of trails
novice-intermediate-advanced
USGS: Jay Peak

Set in an area known for its long and reliable ski season, Hazen's Notch Ski Touring Center has a large network of trails through mountain meadows and spruce and hardwood forests. There are excellent views of the Jay Mountains, historic Hazen's Notch, and several other mountain ranges. Points of interest include a beaver pond, working sugar houses, large free-standing boulders, and a log cabin. Trails are marked with colored ribbons and shown on a map distributed at the Touring Center. The Hazen's Notch trails connect with unplowed roads that lead to Hazen's Notch State Forest and other trails in Lowell and Westfield.

The ski house has a day room, rental shop, rest rooms, snack bar, and waxing area. Rentals and instruction are available. Special activities include guided tours, Wednesday night tours with head lamps, a couple race in February, and the Hazen's Notch annual cross-country race and pig roast at the end of March. There is a $2.00 trail fee.

Driving directions: Take Route 118 or Route 242 to Montgomery Center, then go east on Route 58 for 1½ miles to the Touring Center. (Route 58 through the notch is closed in winter.)

Suggestion courtesy of Val Schadinger, Hazen's Notch Ski Touring Center, RFD #1, Montgomery Center, Vermont 05471 (802-326-4708).

Jay Peak Touring Center
Jay, Vermont
20 km (12½ miles) of trails
novice-intermediate-advanced
USGS: Jay Peak

Part of the Jay Peak Ski Area, the Touring Center is at an elevation of 1,600 feet. It offers excellent views of Jay Peak and other peaks in the Jay Mountains, which line the Vermont-Quebec border. The system of groomed trails winds through open beech, maple, and birch forest, where rabbit, grouse, and deer are abundant. Novice and intermediate trails connect the Touring Center with all other facilities at Jay: the hotel, restaurants, and condominiums. Intermediate and advanced trails cross the various tributaries of Jay Branch Brook, which drains a high plateau at the base of a circle of peaks. Many of these trails are groomed; others are suitable for backcountry skiing. Trails are well marked, and maps are distributed at the Touring Center. Snowmobiles are not permitted on the trails.

Ski touring facilities include a warming hut with a fireplace and a wood stove, a sport shop, a waxing area, and a sun deck. Soup and sandwiches are available. Rentals, instruction, guided tours, waxing clinics, and citizens' races are offered. There is a $1.50 trail fee.

Driving directions: Jay Peak is west of Jay on Route 242.

Suggestion courtesy of Johanne Moore, Jay Peak Touring Center, Jay, Vermont 05859 (802-988-2611).

Stark Farm Ski Touring Center
Westford, Vermont
25 km (15½ miles) of trails
novice–intermediate–advanced
USGS: Essex Center

Based in a rustic farmhouse near Brown's River, Stark Farm maintains trails on more than 400 acres of rolling meadows and woods. There are trails along Brown's River and Morgan's Brook, affording some lovely views of the surrounding countryside and a 30-foot waterfall. Many trails are suitable for novices, with a few challenging runs for more experienced skiers. Trails are marked with NSTOA standard signs, and most are groomed. Maps are available at the Touring Center. Snowmobiles are not permitted on the trails, except for maintenance purposes.

The warming hut is attached to the century-old farmhouse, with a wood stove, hot beverages and snacks, and a repair center. Rentals and instruction are offered. Special activities include ladies' day on Wednesdays, guided night tours, citizens' races, a sugar-on-snow party in early spring, and other group programs. The trail fee is $2.00 for adults and $1.00 for children.

Driving directions: Stark Farm is located on Route 128 in Westford, south of Route 104 and north of Route 15.

Suggestion courtesy of William A. Stark, Stark Farm Ski Touring Center, Route 128, Westford, Vermont 05494 (802-878-2282).

Horsford Ski Touring
Charlotte, Vermont
12.5 km (8 miles) of trails
novice–intermediate
USGS: Willsboro

Trails from the Horsford Nursery go through meadows and woods, with views of Lake Champlain and the Adirondacks. They are marked according to difficulty, and maps are available. Snowmobiles are not permitted on the trails.

There is a warming/waxing room in the farmhouse, with complimentary hot chocolate and cider. Rentals and instruction are offered. The trail fee is $2.00. Horsford Ski Touring is open only on weekends and holiday vacation weeks.

Driving directions: From Route 7 in Charlotte, drive 4½ miles south of the Shelburne Museum and turn west at the blinking light. Take the first right and continue for ¾ mile to the entrance of the Horsford Nursery.

Suggestion courtesy of Tony Pascal, Horsford Ski Touring, Route 7, Charlotte, Vermont 05445 (802-425-2811).

Village of Smugglers' Notch
Jeffersonville, Vermont
32 miles of trails
novice-intermediate-advanced
USGS: Hyde Park/Mt. Mansfield

This alpine ski area maintains a trail system originating in the Village on the north face of the Sterling Range. Trails wind through hardwood and pine forests and across meadows, over greatly varied terrain, and boast excellent views of the surrounding mountains. Most trails interconnect to form several loops. All trails are well marked and color coded to indicate degrees of difficulty. A brochure, including a trail map, is available throughout the Village. Snowmobiles are not permitted in the area. The 24-kilometer Madonna VASA Trail to Underhill, the Smugglers' Notch Trail, and the network of trails in the Mount Mansfield area all connect to the Smugglers' Notch system.

Rental equipment is available at the ski touring center, and the Village Ski Shop carries equipment, clothing, and supplies. Instruction, guided tours, and clinics are available through the cross-country ski school. Other facilities in the Village include lodging, dining, grocery store, nursery, pool, sauna, and tennis courts. There is no charge for trail use or for maps.

Driving directions: From I-89 in Waterbury, go north on Route 100, through Morrisville, to Route 15. Go west on Route 15 to Jeffersonville, then take Route 108 south 4½ miles to the Village of Smugglers' Notch. Route 108 through the notch from Stowe is closed at the first snowfall, necessitating the longer northern approach.

Suggestion courtesy of Kathryn Warren, Cross-Country Director, Village of Smugglers' Notch, Jeffersonville, Vermont 05464 (802-644-2932).

The Farm Resort
Morrisville, Vermont
6-7 miles of trails
novice-intermediate
USGS: Hyde Park

Trails in this area are over old logging roads. They wind through a mixed evergreen and hardwood forest and over a maple-covered ridge. The gently rolling golf course provides good skiing for novices and offers views of the Worcester Mountains. All trails are marked, and a map is available at the Resort.

Meals, motel rooms, and housekeeping units are available at the Inn. The trail fee is $2.00 per day or $5.00 per year.

Driving directions: The Farm Resort is on the west side of Route 100, 5 miles north of Stowe.

Suggestion courtesy of the Farm Resort, Stowe Road, Morrisville, Vermont 05661.

Trapp Family Lodge
Stowe, Vermont
100 km (62 miles) of trails
novice-intermediate-advanced
USGS: Montpelier/Hyde Park/Mt. Mansfield/Bolton Mtn.

The Trapp Family Lodge has a network of trails on 1200 acres in the Green Mountains. They meander through woods and fields, offering lovely views of the mountains. These trails are groomed and patrolled every day, and most are suitable for novice and intermediate skiers. Farther out, there is a series of wilderness trails for more experienced skiers; these are shown on the trail map, but are not groomed.

The ski touring center, adjacent to the Lodge, offers retail sales, rentals, instruction, and guided tours. There is a heated cabin 6 km into the woods, which serves lunch. The trail fee is $2.00.

Driving directions: From Stowe, take Route 108 north. Turn left after passing The Shed and stay on the main road. Park on the right after passing the ski touring building.

Suggestion courtesy of the Trapp Family Lodge, Stowe, Vermont 05672 (802-253-8511).

Edson Hill Ski Touring Center
Stowe, Vermont
2000 acres
novice-intermediate
USGS: Hyde Park/Mt. Mansfield

This is a large area of undulating woodlands and fields offering good views of the Green Mountains. It is laced with a large network of trails, most of which are sheltered from the wind. Trails are marked with red plastic rectangles and, in open areas, by red flags. Maps are available at the Touring Center. The Trapp Family Lodge and other Stowe area trails can be reached on skis from Edson Hill. Snowmobiling is prohibited.

Edson Hill Manor offers lodging, meals, a ski shop, Nordic Ski Patrol, and instruction. There is a $2.00 per person per day trail fee.

Driving directions: From I-89, take Route 100 north to Stowe. Turn left on Route 108 and continue north for 3 miles. Immediately after the Buccaneer Motel, take a right fork and drive 1.7 miles. Follow the signs to Edson Hill Manor

Suggestion courtesy of Elizabeth Turner, Edson Hill Manor, RR #1, Stowe, Vermont 05672 (802-253-8954).

Topnotch Ski Touring Area
Stowe, Vermont
30 miles of trails
novice-intermediate-advanced
USGS: Mt. Mansfield

Novice trails go through meadows and wooded areas in the vicinity of Topnotch at Stowe. Advanced skiing is in the foothills of Mount Mansfield. The area is mostly wooded, with several streams, and affords excellent views of Mount Mansfield and the surrounding hills. Most trails are groomed regularly; a few are left as wilderness trails. All trails have red plastic markers and signs at intersections. Maps are $1.50 at the Touring Area. Trails from Topnotch connect with those from the Trapp Family Lodge and Edson Hill and Mount Mansfield Ski Touring Centers (see separate entries) to provide a vast ski touring network in the Stowe area.

Rentals, instruction, retail sales, hot spiced cider, and snacks are offered. Guided tours are available upon request, and there are special citizens' races during the season. The Touring Area is affiliated with Topnotch Lodge. There is a $2.00 trail fee.

Driving directions: From Stowe, drive west on Route 108 (the Mountain Road) for approximately 4 miles.

Suggestion courtesy of Lewis Coty, Topnotch Ski Touring Area, Stowe, Vermont 05672 (802-253-7794).

Mount Mansfield Ski Touring Center
Stowe, Vermont
35 km (22 miles) of trails
novice–intermediate–advanced
USGS: Mt. Mansfield

Trails follow logging roads and streams through the Ranch Valley area at Mount Mansfield. These connect with trails from other ski touring centers in the Stowe area, offering over 150 km of trails in all. Mount Mansfield trails are well marked, and maps are sold at the Touring Center. Snowmobiles are not allowed.

The Touring Center has a complete ski shop with equipment, clothing, accessories, rental equipment, hot food, and beverages. Instruction, guided tours, and citizens' races are offered. There is a trail fee.

Driving directions: From Stowe, drive north on Route 108 (the Mountain Road) for approximately 5 miles. The Touring Center is on the left.

Suggestion courtesy of Peter Ruschp, Mount Mansfield Ski Touring Center, RFD #1, Stowe Vermont 05672 (802-253-7311).

Bolton Valley Ski Resort
Bolton, Vermont
22 miles of trails/6000 acres
novice–intermediate–advanced
USGS: Bolton Mtn.

The Bolton Valley trail system includes old logging roads, footpaths, and hiking trails, including part of the Long Trail. One 14-mile expert trail goes to the Trapp Family Lodge in Stowe (see separate entry). All trails are well marked, and a map is available at the ski area. Snowmobiling is not allowed.

Bryant Lodge, built in 1931, was the original Bolton Valley Lodge. It is situated on a cross-country trail and, with its woodburning stove, serves as a warming shelter. All of the resort facilities (base lodge, meals, accommodations, nursery, shops) are available to ski tourers. Rentals and instruction are offered. Trail use is $2.00 on weekdays, and $3.00 on weekends.

Driving directions: From I-89 heading north, take Exit 10 and follow Route 2 west. From I-89 heading south, take Exit 11 and follow Route 2 east. The Bolton Valley access road is about 7 miles from each exit.

Suggestion courtesy of Maralyn Moore, Bolton Valley Corporation, Bolton Valley, Vermont 05477 (802-434-2131).

Ski Hostel Lodge
Waterbury Center, Vermont
5½ miles of trails
novice-intermediate
USGS: Middlesex/Stowe/Bolton Mtn.

Ski Hostel Lodge trails wind over gently rolling country in a very scenic area with open views of Mount Mansfield, Mount Hunger, Bolton Mountain, Camel's Hump, White Rock, Pinnacle, and the Worcester Mountain range. One loop leaves across the road from the Lodge and climbs upward to a sugar bush. Another trail climbs toward the Worcester Mountain range and returns along the same route. There is a trail through Middlesex Gap that travels over a beaver dam and through rock cliffs. Trails across the Waterbury Dam connect to Stowe area trails (see separate entries); they also travel upward through the old roads on Ricker Mountain, past farm and mill sites displaced by the dam. Snowmobiles are used on some trails.

Dorm and private room accommodations, breakfast, and dinner are available at the Lodge. Rental equipment is available in the area; instruction is offered at the Lodge. There is a small charge for trail maps, but use of the trails is free.

Driving directions: From I-89, take Exit 10 north to Route 100 and travel 4 miles north. Follow the Ski Hotel sign to the Lodge, ½ mile off Route 100.

Suggestion courtesy of Martha Guthridge, Ski Hostel Lodge, Waterbury Center, Vermont 05677 (802-244-8859).

Craftsbury Nordic Ski Center
Craftsbury Common, Vermont
30 km of trails (18½ miles) plus 140 acres wilderness trails
novice-intermediate-advanced
USGS: Hardwick

Trails from Craftsbury Center pass through hard- and softwood forests, crossing open pastures with views of Mount Mansfield and the surrounding area. In addition to the 30 km of groomed trails, there are numerous wilderness trails in the system. All trails are marked according to level of difficulty, and maps are available at the Ski Center. Snowmobiles are not permitted on the maintained ski tracks. Craftsbury Center trails connect with those from Highland Lodge in Greensboro (see separate entry), and there are many other unplowed roads and non-maintained trails in the area suitable for skiing.

The Ski Center has a shop and waxing room, sauna and showers. Meals and lodging are available. Rentals, instruction, and guided wilderness trips are offered, and other special outings may be arranged. Craftsbury Center includes a Nordic race training facility for serious racers of all ages and abilities. The trail fee is $2.00.

Driving directions: From Hardwick, take Route 14 north to Craftsbury Common, then go 2 miles east to the Ski Center.

Suggestion courtesy of Russell M. Spring, Craftsbury Nordic Ski Center, P.O. Box 56, Craftsbury Common, Vermont 05827 (802-586-2514).

Highland Lodge Ski Touring Center
Greensboro, Vermont
30 miles of trails
novice-intermediate
USGS: Hardwick

These trails range over rolling hills and open fields, and through hard- and softwood forests, often on old logging and sugaring roads. Some overlook Caspian Lake. Trails vary in elevation from 1500 to 2000 feet, and higher spots command good views of the northern Green Mountains. All trails are well marked, and a map is available at the Lodge.

Accommodations are available at Highland Lodge. The ski touring shop offers sales, rentals, instruction, and guided tours. Other facilities include a waxing area and soup-and-sandwich bar. There are facilities for snowshoeing, sledding, and ice fishing. There is a fee for trail use.

Driving directions: Highland Lodge is on the main road from Greensboro to East Craftsbury, overlooking Caspian Lake, 7 miles north of Hardwick.

Suggestion courtesy of David B. Smith, Highland Lodge Ski Touring Center, Greensboro, Vermont 05841 (802-533-2647).

Burklyn Ski Touring Center
East Burke, Vermont
50+ km of trails
novice-intermediate-advanced
USGS: Burke

Burklyn Ski Touring Center is located in the heart of Vermont's Northeast Kingdom. What was once the Elmer Darling Estate has been transformed into a new winter resort. In general, trails parallel Bemis Ridge and wind through the adjacent valleys. All are marked with a new sign system and maps under glass. Trail maps are free at the Touring Center. All trails are machine groomed, and snowmobiles are not permitted.

The ski shop offers rentals, retail sales, service, and instruction. There is a waxing table and hot, spiced cider on the wood stove. Special activities include full moon tours, the Burklyn Stampede (a USSA Nordic qualifying race), and the Burklyn Cup series. There is a $3.00 trail fee on weekends, $2.00 weekdays. Also available at Burklyn are a restaurant and tavern, lodging, stables, and a redwood hot tub.

Driving directions: From I-91, take Exit 23 and go north on Route 5 through Lyndonville. Bear right onto Route 114 and continue for 5 miles to East Burke. Turn left just past the Exxon station. Keep left up the hill 1 mile to Burklyn.

Suggestion courtesy of Jim Griffiths, Burklyn Ski Touring Center, Darling Hill Road, East Burke, Vermont 05832 (800-451-4163; in Canada and Vermont, 802-626-9332).

Burke Mountain Recreation, Inc., Touring Center
East Burke, Vermont
32 miles of trails
novice-intermediate-advanced
USGS: Burke

Burke Mountain Ski Area offers good touring over a large network of trails. Trails run over rolling terrain, through hard- and softwood forests with several nice birch groves. Open fields provide views of Willoughby Gap, Victory Bog, Burke Mountain, and the White Mountains. All trails are marked, and maps are available at the Touring Center. Snowmobiles are prohibited.

The Touring Center offers rentals, sales, EPSTI certified instruction, and guided tours by reservation. Ski tourers may use the base lodge facilities at the ski area; meals and lodging are available at Burke Mountain and the Old Cutter Inn. There is a fee for trail use.

Driving directions: From I-93 in Littleton, take Route 18 west to St. Johnsbury. Travel north on I-91 to Lyndonville. Take Route 114 northeast through East Burke and follow signs to Burke Mountain.

Suggestion courtesy of Burke Mountain Recreation, Inc., Touring Center, East Burke, Vermont 05832 (802-626-3305).

Rabbit Hill Inn Ski Touring Center
Lower Waterford, Vermont
10+ miles of trails
novice-intermediate-advanced
USGS: Lower Waterford

Rabbit Hill Inn is situated along the Connecticut River, in the heart of the famous White Village of Vermont, with views of the White Mountains. Trails go over open fields, through wooded areas, and along an exposed ridgeline with a 1000-foot drop to the river. They are marked with NSTOA blue diamonds and survey tapes. Nearby is an extensive trail network maintained by the local snowmobile club.

The Touring Center has a waxing room, and offers rentals, EPSTI certified instruction, and guided tours. There is a lounge and a dining room next door at Rabbit Hill Inn. Trail maps are $1.00; there is no fee for trail use.

Driving directions: Rabbit Hill Inn is between Littleton, New Hampshire, and St. Johnsbury, Vermont, just off Route 18.

Suggestion courtesy of Kirk Bryant, Director of Skiing, Rabbit Hill Inn Ski Touring Center, Route 18, Lower Waterford, Vermont 05848 (802-748-5168).

Central Vermont Ski Touring Areas

1. Tucker Hill Ski Touring Center, Waitsfield   *112*
2. Battell Trail, Lincoln   *112*
3. Sugarbush Inn/Rossignol Ski Touring Center, Warren   *113*
4. Ole's Cross-Country, Warren   *113*
5. Paine Mountain Trails, Northfield   *114*
6. Puddledock Ski Touring Trails, Granville   *114*
7. Cram Hill, Brookfield   *115*
8. Green Trails Ski Touring Center, Brookfield   *115*
   Allis State Park, Brookfield   *116*
9. Churchill House Ski Touring Center, Brandon   *116*
10. Blueberry Hill Ski Touring Center, Goshen   *117*
11. Breadloaf Touring Center, Ripton   *118*
12. Green Mountain Touring Center, Randolph   *118*
13. Riverbend Cross-Country Ski Shop, South Newbury   *119*
14. Tulip Tree Inn, Chittenden   *119*
    Mountain Top Ski Touring Center, Chittenden   *120*
15. Cortina Inn Ski Touring Center, Killington   *120*
16. Mountain Meadows Ski Touring Center, Killington   *121*
17. Sky Line Trail, Barnard/Pomfret   *121*
    Amity Pond Natural Area, Pomfret   *125*
18. Turnpike Road, Thetford   *126*
19. The Plymouth Village Ski Touring Center, Plymouth Union   *126*
20. Woodstock Ski Touring Center, Woodstock   *127*

Central Vermont

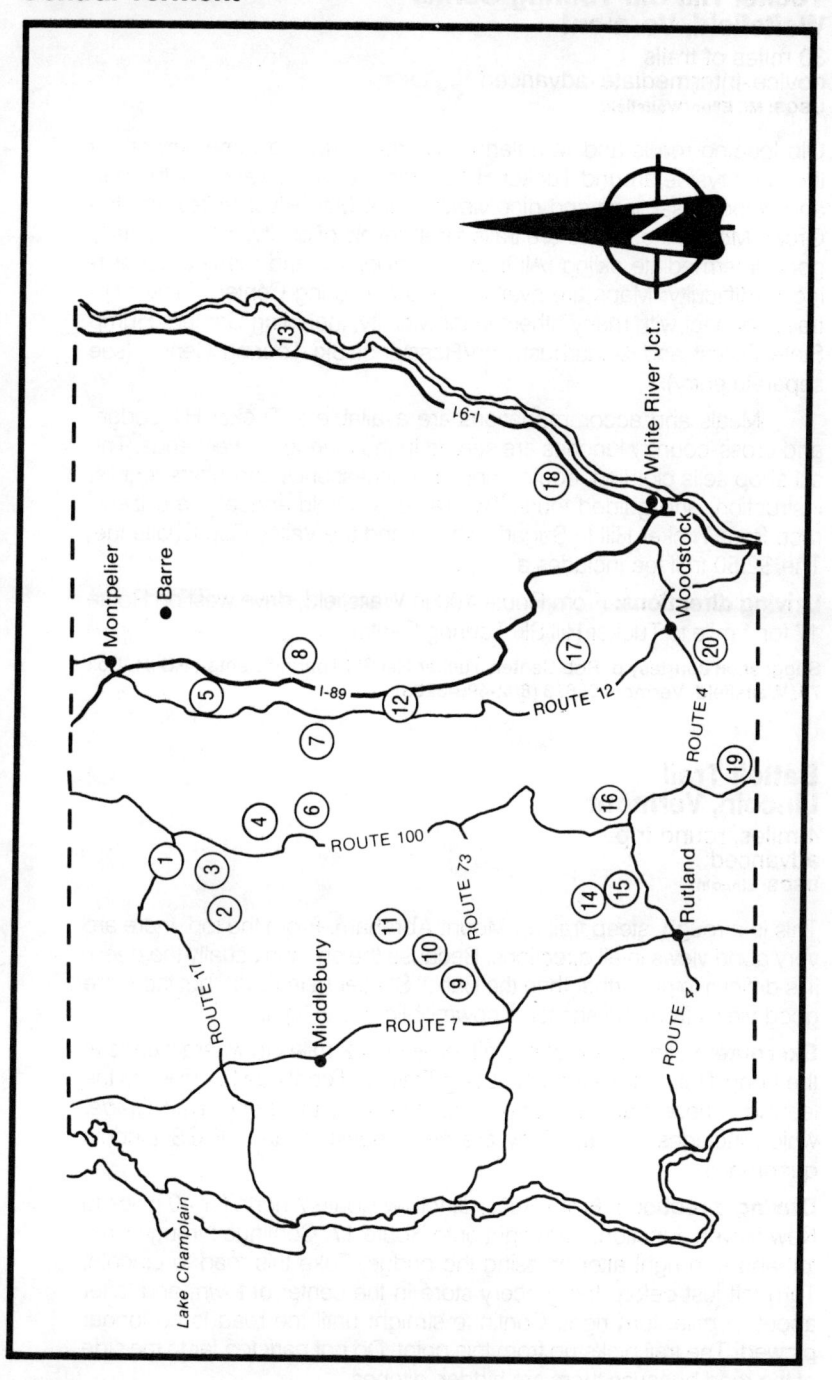

Tucker Hill Ski Touring Center
Waitsfield, Vermont
30 miles of trails
novice-intermediate-advanced
USGS: Mt. Ellen/Waitsfield

Old logging roads and woodland trails make up a diverse network in the countryside around Tucker Hill Lodge. Terrain is varied, with open and wooded sections and nice views of the Mad River Valley and the Green Mountains. There are trails for all levels of ability, with especially good intermediate skiing. All trails are groomed and marked according to difficulty. Maps are available at the Touring Center. Tucker Hill trails connect with many others in the vicinity, including Camel's Hump State Forest and Sugarbush Inn/Rossignol Ski Touring Center (see separate entry).

Meals and accommodations are available at Tucker Hill Lodge, and cross-country lunches are served in the lounge on weekends. The ski shop sells clothing, equipment, and accessories and offers rentals, instruction, and guided tours. Two races are held annually: a citizens' race from Tucker Hill to Sugarbush Inn and the Valley Cup Challenge. The $2.50 trail fee includes a map.

Driving directions: From Route 100 in Waitsfield, drive west on Route 17 for 1 mile to Tucker Hill Ski Touring Center.

Suggestion courtesy of Rob Center, Tucker Hill Ski Touring Center, RD #1, Box 74, Waitsfield, Vermont 05673 (802-496-3203).

Battell Trail
Lincoln, Vermont
4 miles, round trip
advanced
USGS: Lincoln

This is a rough, steep trail up Mount Abraham. From the top, there are very good views in all directions. Because the snow is usually too deep, it is difficult to go further than the Battell Shelter (a lean-to), but there are good views from the shelter. Snowmobile use is light.

Ski route: Follow the Battell Trail for almost 2 miles to where it ends at the Long Trail. Turn left on the Long Trail, and continue 0.1 miles to the lean-to. These trails are described briefly in the *Long Trail Guide*, which includes a map. They are also shown on the USGS Lincoln quadrangle.

Driving directions: From Rutland, follow Route 7 north for 40 miles to New Haven Junction. Turn right onto Route 17. Continue through Bristol, and turn right after crossing the bridge. Take this road to Lincoln. Turn left just before the grocery store in the center of town, and, after about ½ mile, turn right. Continue straight until the road is no longer plowed. The trail picks up from this point. Do not park too far to the side of the road because there are hidden ditches.

Sugarbush Inn/Rossignol Ski Touring Center
Warren, Vermont
35 miles of trails
novice-intermediate-advanced
USGS: Warren/Waitsfield/Mt. Ellen/Lincoln

Sugarbush Inn maintains a series of well-marked trails in the valley, including 20 miles that are machine tracked. There are also a few unmaintained trails nearby that connect with those from Sugarbush. Two trails connect with Tucker Hill Ski Touring Center in Waitsfield (see separate entry). Maps are available at the Inn. Snowmobiles are not permitted.

The ski shop is located across from the Inn and offers rentals, and instruction. Lunches are available. There is a trail fee. Season passes are available for individuals and families, including cooperative passes with Tucker Hill Ski Touring Center.

Driving directions: From White River Junction, take I-89 north to the Bethel area, then take Route 107 west for 9 miles to the junction with Route 100. Turn right and continue to Warren. Turn left onto the road leading to Sugarbush Valley Ski Area. The Sugarbush Inn is on the right, 3 miles from Route 100.

Suggestion courtesy of Rick Hale, Sugarbush Inn/Rossignol Ski Touring Center, Warren, Vermont 05674 (802-583-2605).

Ole's Cross-Country
Warren, Vermont
30 miles of trails
novice-intermediate
USGS: Warren

Many of Ole's trails are suited to novices. Some traverse the open fields of Sugarbush Airport, with excellent views of the Mad River Valley. Other, longer trails go through wooded areas, including the 16-km Folsom Brook Trail. All are well marked, and maps are distributed at the Touring Center. Snowmobiles are not permitted.

Ole's Cross-Country offers rentals, instruction, guided tours, and two or three races each season. Facilities include a rental shop, retail shop, and waxing room. There is a trail fee.

Driving directions: From Route 100 in Warren, drive east on Brook Road. Turn left after 2 miles, then left again onto Roxbury Gap Road. After ½ mile, turn right onto Airport Road.

Suggestion courtesy of Ole Mosesen, Ole's Cross-Country, Warren, Vermont 05674 (802-496-3430).

Paine Mountain Trails
Northfield, Vermont
15 miles of trails
novice-intermediate-advanced
USGS: Barre

These trails wind around the lower slopes of Paine Mountain, through mixed hard- and softwoods crossed by several beautiful brooks and streams. The area is dotted with abandoned, overgrown slate quarries which boast striking, high cliffs and ice falls. It is possible to ski into some of the quarries. The area is marked for conservation, and many logging trails lead from the Paine Mountain trail system into nearby acreage. From the higher elevations, there are beautiful views of Hunger Mountain to the north and of Berlin Pond to the east.

The Paine Mountain Touring Center is no longer in operation, but trail maps and rentals are available at the Vermont North Ski Shop in Northfield.

Driving directions: From I-89, take Exit 5, and follow signs to Northfield and Route 12 North. Take Route 12 into Northfield, and turn right to the Norwich University Ski Area.

Suggestion courtesy of Michael Cerulli-Billingsley, Northfield, Vermont.

Puddledock Ski Touring Trails
Granville Gulf State Reservation
Granville, Vermont
4+ miles of trails
novice-intermediate
USGS: Warren

This area provides loops of various lengths through a scenic river valley between the Green and Northfield Mountain ranges. The terrain is fairly gentle but requires good snow cover for skiing. Trails are marked with red metal rectangles and arrows. When necessary, there are signs marked "easier," "more difficult," and "caution." Brochures with a map are available at the Reservation. Please register at the brochure distribution box.

Driving directions: From I-89, take Route 107 west to Route 100. Follow Route 100 north to Granville. Puddledock Road branches sharply right 3 miles north of Granville. The plowed area accommodates six cars.

Suggestion courtesy of Russell S. Reay, State Land Forester, Department of Forests, Parks, and Recreation, Rutland, Vermont.

Cram Hill
Brookfield, Vermont
9 miles
intermediate
USGS: Barre

This is an unmarked loop on unplowed forest roads with good views from Cram Hill. Roads are shown on the USGS Barre quadrangle.

Ski route: From the West Brookfield church, walk south on an unplowed road approximately ½ mile. Start skiing down the first road (which may be plowed a short way) on the right. Follow this road west along Cold Brook for about 3 miles to a road junction at elevation 1371. Turn right and take the unplowed road north over the shoulder of Cram Hill for about 2 miles. At another junction near elevation 1734, turn right again and follow another unplowed road east for about 3 miles, downhill, to the West Brookfield church.

Driving directions: From I-89, take Exit 4 and proceed west to Randolph. Turn right onto Route 12 and continue north for about 6½ miles. Take the left fork at the cemetery, which leads into West Brookfield. Park at the church.

Suggestion courtesy of Chris Williams, Green Trails Inn, Brookfield, Vermont.

Green Trails Ski Touring Center
Brookfield, Vermont
25 miles of trails
novice–intermediate–advanced
USGS: Barre

The hills surrounding Green Trails Inn offer a broad range of trails varying in slope and type. They are well marked and often well tracked. Because many trails pass over private property, skiers are asked to treat the land with respect and not to enter buildings on these properties without permission. Snowmobiles are prohibited. Trail maps are available at the Touring Center.

Cram Hill and Allis State Park, with other ski touring trails, are nearby (see separate entries). There is also good skiing in Roxbury State Forest.

Equipment and accessories are available at the Pond Village Store. Green Trails Inn offers meals and lodging (including efficiency apartments). Reservations are recommended. The Ski Touring Center supplies a waxing room and rentals; instruction and guided tours may be arranged. Snowshoeing is permitted. A $1.00 per person trail donation is suggested.

Driving directions: From Exit 4 off I-89, take Route 66 east to Randolph Center. Turn left and proceed north for 8 miles, following signs to Brookfield. Green Trails Inn is in the village near the floating bridge. Park at the Inn or along the road.

Suggestion courtesy of Chris Williams, Green Trails Inn, By the Floating Bridge, Brookfield, Vermont 05036 (802-276-2012).

Allis State Park
Brookfield, Vermont
2½ miles of trails/487 acres
intermediate
USGS: Barre

This small park affords fine views and good skiing on unplowed roads and footpaths. It can be reached on skis from Green Trails Inn (see separate entry). There is moderate snowmobile use on weekends.

Driving directions: Take Exit 4 from I-89, and follow Route 66 east to Randolph Center. Turn left and head north, following signs to Brookfield. Continue north through the village, bear left at the fork, and drive beneath the I-89 overpass. Turn left at the first intersection and continue for 1 mile to the first road on the right. Turn here and follow signs to the Park.

Suggestion courtesy of Chris Williams, Green Trails Inn, Brookfield, Vermont.

Churchill House Ski Touring Center
Brandon, Vermont
40 km (22 miles) of trails
novice-intermediate-advanced
USGS: Brandon

Trails follow ridge lines to the east and west of Leicester Hollow, from Churchill House Inn to Silver Lake. They are well marked with NSTOA blue diamonds. They connect to Blueberry Hill Farm trails to the north and with Mountain Top Inn (via Puss and Kill Gap) to the south (see separate entries). Churchill House is at the 50 km point on the 60 km American Marathon Trail.

The Inn accommodates fourteen people. Other facilities include a restaurant, bar, lunch room, ski shop, and waxing room; rentals and instruction are available. The $2.00 trail fee includes a map. Day tours are scheduled every Sunday, mostly on routes outside the Churchill House trail system. Overnight guided tours go from Inn to Inn. Races include the 15-km Blueberry-Churchill Race on the second Sunday in January; the Brandon Scramble, a 5-km family fun race on the last Saturday in February; a triathalon in late March; and Bill Koch League races.

Driving directions: From Route 7 in Brandon, take Route 73 east for 4 miles to the Touring Center. From Route 100 near Rochester, take Route 73 west.

Suggestion courtesy of Mike Shonstrom, Churchill House Ski Touring Center, RFD #3, Brandon, Vermont 05733 (802-247-3300).

Blueberry Hill Ski Touring Center
Goshen, Vermont
40 km (25 miles) of trails
novice-intermediate
USGS: Breadloaf/Brandon/East Middlebury

Trails from Blueberry Hill Farm go through private lands and sections of the Green Mountain National Forest. They wind through open wooded areas with views of Middlebury Snow Bowl and Romance Mountain, past Silver Lake and several beaver ponds. All trails are marked with NSTOA blue diamonds, and detailed maps are available for $3.00 at the Farm. There is snowmobiling on a few trails, but it is generally confined to the Sugar Hill area north of the Farm. Blueberry Hill trails connect with those from Churchill House to the south and to Breadloaf Touring Center to the north (see separate entries).

The Touring Center is housed in a new ski touring complex with a shop and warming and waxing area. It is heated by pot bellied stoves and is known for the kettles of hot soup usually bubbling on a back burner. Rentals, EPSTI certified instruction, guided tours (including ecology tours and night tours), and junior olympics are offered; and the annual Pig Race is held in March. Other special activities include the Blueberry Hill-Churchill House time trial and the Hennessy Marathon. There is an area use fee of $3.00. Blueberry Hill Inn has lodging for a small number of people; reservations are required.

Driving directions: From Rutland, take Route 7 to Brandon and turn right (east) on Route 73. Follow Route 73 for about 4¼ miles, past Churchill House and fork left at the sign for Blueberry Hill. From here there are signs. The Touring Center is about 4 miles past the fork. There is parking space for about 100 cars.

Suggestion courtesy of Tony Clark, Blueberry Hill Farm, Route 73, Goshen, Vermont 05733 (802-247-6735).

Breadloaf Touring Center
Ripton, Vermont
50 km (31 miles) of trails
novice-intermediate
USGS: Bread Loaf/East Middlebury

Located at the Breadloaf Campus of Middlebury College, the Touring Center grooms about 30 km of trails in and around hills at the base of the Green Mountains. Other trails go to the Snow Bowl, the Robert Frost Historic Site, and Blueberry Hill Ski Touring Center (see separate entry). This is basically an intermediate area, with some novice trails provided. Trails vary in length from ½ km to 15 km, and all are marked and posted with signs.

The Touring Center includes a warming hut, where rentals, instruction, waxes, and accessories are available. No trail fee is required, but donations of $1.00 or more are requested.

Driving directions: Breadloaf Touring Center is located on Route 125 in Ripton.

Suggestion courtesy of Ward Mann, Director, Breadloaf Touring Center, Ripton, Vermont 05766 (802-388-4356).

Green Mountain Touring Center
Randolph, Vermont
30 miles of trails
novice-intermediate-advanced
USGS: Randolph

The 1200 acres of the Green Mountain Stock Farm include rolling riverside meadows, wooded sidehills, and high open pastures. Of the 30 miles of trails, over 20 miles are groomed; others are left unbroken for a more primitive skiing experience. One trail is lighted for night skiing. Trails are well marked, and maps are posted. Snowmobiles are not permitted.

Ski touring facilities include a waxing and warming room with free hot cider. Rentals, instruction, and guided tours are offered. Meals and lodging are available at the Inn, a 19th century farmhouse (reservations required). There is a $2.00 trail fee.

Driving directions: The Touring Center is located between Randolph and I-89 on Stock Farm Road, just south of Route 66.

Suggestion courtesy of Bob Gray, Green Mountain Touring Center, Green Mountain Stock Farm, Randolph, Vermont 05060 (802-728-5575).

Riverbend Cross-Country Ski Shop
South Newbury, Vermont
15 miles of trails
novice–intermediate–advanced
USGS: Newbury

Trails go through open fields and hilly, wooded areas, with excellent views of the Connecticut River Valley and the White Mountains. Maps are available at the ski shop.

Riverbend offers rentals, instruction, and retail sales. There is no trail fee.

Driving directions: From I-91, take Exit 16 (Bradford) and drive north 6 miles on Route 5; or take Exit 17 (Wells River) and drive south 7 miles on Route 5.

Suggestion courtesy of Michael Thomas, Riverbend Cross-Country Ski Shop, South Newbury, Vermont 05066 (802-866-5921).

Tulip Tree Inn
Chittenden, Vermont
USGS: Chittenden

Trails near the Inn cover varied terrain and provide easy access to logging roads and snowmobile trails in the Green Mountain National Forest. One trail goes to Mountain Top Ski Touring Center (see separate entry) only 2 miles away.

The Inn is open almost all year and offers ten bedrooms and gourmet cooking. Reservations are required. There is a waxing room, and rentals are available at Mountain Top.

Driving directions: From Rutland, take Route 7 north. Fork right at the power station and continue on this road. Tulip Tree Inn is 6.6 miles from the intersection with Route 7. From Route 4, turn north opposite Mendon Church on Meadow Lake Drive. At the end of the road, go right and continue straight to the Inn.

Suggestion courtesy of Barbara and Gerry Liebert, Tulip Tree Inn, Chittenden, Vermont 05737 (802-483-6213).

Mountain Top Ski Touring Center
Chittenden, Vermont
55 miles of trails/500 acres
novice-intermediate-advanced
USGS: Chittenden/Carmel

Mountain Top's 2000-foot elevation assures a long ski season. Scenic trails wind through hardwood forests and open meadows, over mountains, and around a lake. There has been an increase in development of novice and intermediate trails, with emphasis on the first-time tourer. Three large fields with some short loop trails provide a good practice area for beginners. Fifteen of the 55 miles of trails are groomed with set tracks. All are well marked and color coded to a map available at the Touring Center. A couple of trails are shared with a local snowmobile club, but they are not heavily used.

The Touring Center has a ski shop, rental equipment, and EPSTI certified instruction; meals and lodging are within walking distance at Mountain Top Inn. Overnight and all-day tours may be arranged. Moonlight tours, citizens' races, sleigh rides, and tobogganing are also offered. There is an area fee of $3.50.

Driving directions: From Route 4 near Killington, head west toward Rutland. Turn right (north) in Mendon at the Mountain Top sign, then follow signs for 6 miles to the Center. From Rutland, go north about 8 miles on Route 7 and turn right at the sign for Mountain Top Inn.

Suggestion courtesy of Don Cochrane, Mountain Top Ski Touring Center, Chittenden, Vermont 05737 (802-483-2311).

Cortina Inn Ski Touring Center
Killington, Vermont
40-45 km (25+ miles of trails)
novice-intermediate-advanced
USGS: Pico Peak

The Cortina Inn trail network covers varied terrain, from flat to hill, with views of Pico Peak. The woods are predominantly pine, maple, and birch, and beaver ponds are abundant. Some trails are located in the Rutland City Forest and others are in the Green Mountain National Forest. They are marked with NSTOA blue diamonds, and maps are available at the Touring Center. Snowmobiles are not allowed on the trails. Cortina Inn trails connect with those from Mountain Top Ski Touring Center and Mountain Meadows Ski Touring Center (see separate entries).

Rentals, certified instruction, and guided tours are available at the Touring Center. There is a special ladies' day program on Tuesdays. Facilities at the Inn include an indoor pool, sauna, ski shop, lounge, and tennis courts. Trail use and maps are free for guests at the Inn; for others there is a $2.00 trail fee and a $2.00 charge for maps.

Driving directions: Cortina Inn is located on Route 4, 7 miles east of Rutland and 4 miles west of Route 100.

Suggestion courtesy of Cortina Inn Ski Touring Center, Route 4, Killington, Vermont 05751 (802-773-3331).

Mountain Meadows Ski Touring Center
Killington, Vermont
40 miles of trails
novice–intermediate–advanced
USGS: Pico Peak

Located by 100-acre Kent Lake, the Touring Center commands views of hills and mountains, including the upper slopes of Pico Peak. Ski trails go around the lake and through the surrounding hills, with some sections designed specifically for novice skiers. Fifteen miles of trails are extensively groomed and are closed to snowmobiles; many other trails in the area are connected to these and are marked on the Mountain Meadows map.

The Lodge and Ski Touring Center occupy a Colonial farmhouse and huge converted barn. Mountain Meadows Lodge has winter accommodations for 90 people, including family rooms and small dorms. Lunches are also available. The Touring Center has a complete retail shop. EPSTI certified ski school, guided tours by arrangement, moonlight tours on Wednesday and Saturday nights, and an annual Heart Fund race on the second Saturday in March. There is a $3.50 trail fee. Maps are free.

Driving directions: From White River Junction, take Route 4 west for 35 miles to Sherburne Center. Continue on Route 4 for 1¼ miles to the right turn for Mountain Meadows Lodge. Coming from the west, turn left ¼ mile east of the Killington access road.

Suggestion courtesy of John Tidd, Mountain Meadows Ski Touring Center, Thundering Brook Road, Killington, Vermont 05751 (802-755-7077).

Sky Line Trail
Barnard/Pomfret, Vermont
about 20 miles
intermediate–advanced
USGS: Woodstock North/Randolph

Most of the Sky Line Trail follows a ridge, commanding good views of the Vermont countryside. It offers fine ungroomed skiing, yet due to its popularity there are almost always tracks left by other skiers. Killington, Pico, Ascutney, the Rochester Mountains, and occasionally the White Mountains are all in view from the ridge. The trail was designed to follow a constant contour, but due to irregular terrain there are several drops and climbs. Some sections are quite difficult, and others are easy. The trail crosses several roads, and may be skied in sections.

There are a series of loops, some of which avoid the steeper pitches, providing further possibilities for shorter tours. Most of the route is on private land; skiers must stay on the marked trail. The Sky Line Trail is marked with orange and blue squares: heading north, the top half of the markers is orange; heading south the top half is blue. At abrupt turns, the signs are rotated 90 degrees to point in the direction of the turn. Trail maps are available at the shelter near the entrance to Amity Pond and at the Woodstock Ski Touring Center (see separate entries).

Trail descriptions: Hawk's Hill to Wooley Place (1¼ miles): This section of the trail is a partial loop on Hawk's Hill. From the guest house, ski west about 100 yards, then turn north across a brook. Head east at the cabin. The trail skirts a small pond and goes gently uphill. A short loop can be made by returning to Hawk's Hill; otherwise, follow the trail downhill through a pasture and across a pond to the Wooley Place.

Wooley Place to Campbell House (½ mile): The trail marker is at the entrance of a lane southeast of the Wooley house. The lane becomes an abandoned road leading to the Campbell House. Watch for the turn marker on a large maple just north of the house. From here the trail heads north and descends an open slope to Broad Brook Road.

Campbell House to Amity Pond Junction (2 miles): The trail marker is across Broad Brook Road at the entrance to the Amity Pond Natural Area. If the brook is frozen, ski across it and pick up the trail on the other side. If it is not frozen, go north and cross the bridge, then bushwhack back to the trail. This section climbs steadily and traverses the hillside. It makes several abrupt turns but heads generally northeast, crossing a power line, re-entering the woods, and then following a road on the side of a gully. The trail ascends the side of the gully and comes out on a flat area with large birches. There is a junction here. To continue on the trail to Harvey Farm, follow the signs with blue on top; to go to Amity Pond, look for signs with orange on top. Skiing this section from east to west, starting at the Amity Pond entrance, makes for a long downhill run. For a more detailed description of the Amity Pond Area, see separate entry.

Pail Trail, Amity Pond to Broad Brook Road: This is a new trail that makes a loop from Amity Pond back to Broad Brook Road, north of the main trail. From the Amity Pond junction, continue toward the pond, and turn left (west) at the large elm stump in the field. Follow the blue discs past a shelter to the south and across the power line. This loop ends in an open field across from the Broad Brook Fire Station. Follow the road back to the west entrance to Amity Pond Natural Area, or cross the bridge to the Chang House and continue on the trail that heads south toward the Campbell House. Here the loop rejoins the main trail and returns to the Wooley Place.

Amity Pond to Webster Hill and the Harvey Farm (3 miles): This section of the trail starts at a fence opening on the west side of the Mail Route. There is a shelter at the entrance with a register book and pamphlets. The trail goes northwest across an open field to a stone wall, then turns south, passing Amity Pond and the Pail Trail loop. It arrives at the junction with the Campbell House–Amity Pond section in a clump of birches. From here the trail heads southeast, descending to a gully and a small swamp, then climbing uphill to an open field. After a jog to the east, it heads south again, now on the ridge. Pass below the Allen log house and continue southeast to the Haydock House where the trail joins the road for a brief stretch. This section is exposed and can be cold and icy. About 75 yards south of the Haydock House, the trail turns onto a private road that proceeds roughly parallel to the Mail Route. It wanders through a partially overgrown pasture, crosses a large pond, and follows another plowed public road for a very short distance. From here, it turns abruptly south up a steep grade used by snowmobiles. The snowmobile trail turns away at the height-of-land, and the ski trail continues downhill through a sugar bush to a sugar road. Follow this almost to the Brooks House, but, before reaching the driveway, turn onto the old trail for a short distance, then go through a field to the Webster Hill crossing. Cross Webster Hill Road and follow the power line to an opening in the woods. The trail follows a private wood road. At the meadow, turn west, where the trail joins the unplowed Poor Farm Road running east and west.

Here, the trail continues south, and there is a loop back to Webster Hill Road following the trail markers with orange on top. To loop back, follow the Poor Farm Road to the Mail Route, crossing to the Jones' land. This section heads north, through woods to the height-of-land, then down to Webster Hill crossing. The Webster Hill loop is especially nice when run counterclockwise, returning north on the main trail. To continue south, follow the trail another ½ mile to open fields and the Harvey Farm.

Harvey Farm to Suicide Six (3 miles): The trail now climbs a short open hill, and then heads south along a ridge that offers fine views to the east. Descending through a sugar maple stand, the trail then bears left through overgrown fields and continues for ¼ mile until it turns right onto an unplowed road. After ¾ mile, there is a short spur to the right that ascends Totman Hill, which commands fine views but is exposed to strong winds. From the point where the spur turns off, the main trail drops a rather rapid 800 vertical feet in the next 1½ miles. At the bottom, the trail turns right just prior to the Churchill House, crosses a small field, and descends through a sugar bush and a final steep field to the parking lot at Suicide Six Ski Area.

Suicide Six to River Street in Woodstock (5½ miles): At the Suicide Six parking lot, cross the brook to the lodge and proceed south below the beginner J-bar lift. Cross a small field and enter the woods just above the brook. The trail continues in and out of fields for the next mile, then it ascends through an old field in a saddle between two small hills. Here the trail descends steeply to Route 12, an especially difficult descent even with the open fields available for traverses.

Skiers must walk up Route 12 for 75 yards and then cross a bridge that provides access to several homes across from the Woodstock Veterinary Clinic. Walk up the driveway for 100 yards, and watch for the markers that leave on the right. The trail then climbs 250 feet in the next mile to a small parking lot located on the Prosper Road to West Woodstock. Here the trail cuts back sharply and ascends through red pines for nearly a mile. In the second red pine stand, the trail joins the groomed trails operated by the Woodstock Ski Touring Center. From here, turn left and then immediately right. After a 200-yard descent, turn right again to a small lake. Bear left around the lake, turn left at the junction at the lake's outlet, and continue straight for ⅔ mile. At this point the trails fork. Take the right fork, and continue for ¼ mile. Keeping the pasture to the left, ski through a gate and then bear sharply right, keeping spruces and pines to the right. The trail continues for ¼ mile through another gate, where the trail turns left near a woodland cabin. The final ¼ mile to River Street and the cemetery offers a descent with five hairpin turns.

Driving directions: From Woodstock, go north on Route 12 to Thompson's Garage and take the right fork. At the Teago Store in South Pomfret take another right fork. Turn left (north) on Webster Hill Road just before reaching the Town Hall, a large white building on the left. Continue north to a wide place in the road at the top of Webster Hill. The Sky Line Trail crosses the road at this point. To go to Hawk's Hill, continue down Webster Hill. At the foot of the hill, turn right (north) to East Barnard. Turn left at the store and, after crossing the concrete bridge, take the next left. Hawk's Hill is at the end of this road and is the beginning of the Sky Line Trail.

Suggestion courtesy of Richard M. Brett, Woodstock, Vermont and John Wiggin, Woodstock Ski Touring Center, Woodstock, Vermont.

Amity Pond Natural Area
Pomfret, Vermont
2¾ miles of trails
novice–intermediate
USGS: Woodstock North

This area was given to the state of Vermont so that many people could enjoy camping, hiking, skiing, and snowshoeing in a natural environment away from the unpleasant aspects of a hectic world. The area was once heavily timber harvested and overgrazed but has since recovered. A very interesting pamphlet, available from the Vermont Department of Forests and Parks, includes a map and explains the natural features and history of the area.

The main entrance to Amity Pond is at the eastern end of the area along the Mail Route. There are two main trails traversing the area in an east-west direction. The southern trail is a segment of the Sky Line Trail (see separate entry). The northern trail goes by Amity Pond and has excellent views of the surrounding mountains; skied east to west, it includes a long downhill run to Broad Brook Road. Two short sections of trail connect the northern and southern trails. One crosses the open field in the vicinity of Amity Pond; the other is about 1 mile from the main entrance, crossing a footbridge over a brook.

There are two shelters that may be used for picnics or overnight camping: the Amity Pond Shelter is near the main entrance; the Sugar Arch Shelter is along the northern trail where the western connecting trail heads south. There is a register book and pamphlets (which include maps) in the Amity Pond shelter. All motor vehicles are prohibited.

Driving directions: From Woodstock, go north on Route 12 to Thompson's Garage, then take a right fork. At the Teago Store in South Pomfret take the right fork to Hewett's Corners (a stone wall marks the Moore Farm, selling farm produce). Take a sharp left and the next left also. This is the Mail Route. At the height-of-land, the entrance to Amity Pond Natural Area is on the left, with trail markers visible from the road. To go to Hawk's Hill, continue north to East Barnard. From here follow the directions for the Sky Line Trail entry.

Suggestion courtesy of Richard M. Brett, Woodstock, Vermont.

Turnpike Road
Thetford, Vermont
3 miles, one way
intermediate
USGS: Mt. Cube

This is a nice downhill run on an unplowed road, from the hills above Lake Fairlee to the Connecticut River Valley. It may be skied as a round trip, starting from North Thetford, or one way, starting at Five Corners. From the end of the plowed road above Five Corners, the trail goes uphill to a small notch, then descends along a stream. One short section may be plowed, where another road takes off to the right. This route is used by snowmobiles and is best avoided in icy or crusty conditions.

Driving directions: To leave a car at the bottom, go north from Route 113 onto Latham Road (just east of I-91). Drive about 2 miles and turn left. After this road goes under I-91, go straight and park where the plowed road ends. To get to the upper end, take Route 113 west to Post Mills, and turn right onto Route 244. Fork right and continue uphill to a five-way intersection. Turn right, then immediately left. Follow this road about 1 mile and park where the plowing ends. The trail follows the road straight ahead.

The Plymouth Village Ski Touring Center
Plymouth Union, Vermont
10 miles of trails/75 acres
novice-intermediate
USGS: Plymouth

Plymouth Village trails run along the Black River and through surrounding woodlands. Novice trails are primarily over open meadows; intermediate trails go through wooded areas with some hilly terrain. Points of interest include a beaver dam, several brooks, and an old lime kiln. Trails are marked with colored surveyor's tape and shown on a map that is available at the Touring Center. They connect with trails in the Coolidge State Forest to the west, which offers further skiing opportunities. Snowmobiles are permitted in the area; dogs are not allowed.

    The Touring Center has indoor and outdoor picnic facilities, with hot chocolate and coffee, and a ski shop. Rentals, instruction, and guided tours are available. The trail donation is $1.00.

Driving directions: Plymouth Village is located on Route 100, 6 miles south of Killington.

Suggestion courtesy of Rick Harootunian, The Plymouth Village Ski Touring Center, Plymouth Union, Vermont 05056 (802-672-3708).

Woodstock Ski Touring Center
Woodstock, Vermont
75 km (47 miles) of trails
novice-intermediate-advanced
USGS: Woodstock North/Woodstock South

Starting from the Touring Center and the village of Woodstock, the trails wind through scenic woods and pastures, ascending to 550 m (1800 feet) from a base elevation of 215 m (700 feet). All trails are marked according to NSTOA standards, and over 35 km of trails are groomed. There is also a trail for snowshoers and a 5-km racing loop. One trail connects with Suicide Six Ski Area, where the Skyline Trail heads north (see separate entry). Maps are included with the $3.00 trail fee.

Rentals, equipment and clothing sales, EPSTI certified instruction, and guided tours are available. Facilities at the Touring Center include a fireside lounge and restaurant, a warming area, locker rooms and showers, and paddle tennis courts. Special activities include sleigh rides, sugaring (in season), citizens' races and lodging packages with the Woodstock Inn.

Driving directions: From Exit 1 off I-89, take Route 4 west to Woodstock. Go around the green to the Woodstock Inn and take Route 106 south. The Touring Center is on the left, 1 km (about ½ mile) from the Woodstock Inn.

Suggestion courtesy of John Wiggin, Woodstock Ski Touring Center, Woodstock, Vermont 05091 (802-457-2114; Woodstock Inn, 802-457-1100).

Southern Vermont Ski Touring Areas

1. Okemo Mountain, Inc., Ludlow   *130*
2. Fox Run Resort, Ludlow   *130*
3. Mount Ascutney Ski Area, Brownsville   *131*
4. Barrows House Ski Touring Center, Dorset   *131*
5. Peru Outdoor Recreation Commission, Peru/Landgrove   *132*
   Wild Wings Ski Touring Center, Peru   *132*
   Nordic Inn Ski Touring Center, Londonderry   *133*
6. Viking Ski Touring Center, Londonderry   *133*
7. West Mountain Inn, Arlington   *134*
8. Long Trail to Stratton Pond, Stratton   *134*
   Lye Brook Wilderness, Manchester   *135*
9. Stratton Ski Touring Center, Stratton   *135*
10. Crackerbarrel Ski Shop, Rawsonville   *136*
11. Cross-Country Ski Shop and Trail System at Grafton, Grafton   *136*
12. Dome Trail, Pownal   *137*
    Broad Brook Trail, Pownal   *138*
13. Timberlane Touring Trails, Woodford   *137*
14. Country Club Cross-Country Touring Center, West Dover   *138*
    Hermitage Ski Touring Center, Wilmington   *140*
    Haystack Mountain Ski Touring Center, Wilmington   *140*
15. White House Touring Center, Wilmington   *141*
16. Sitzmark Ski Touring Center, Wilmington   *142*
17. Living Memorial Park Cross-Country Trail, Brattleboro   *142*
18. Brattleboro Country Club Ski Touring Center, Brattleboro   *143*
19. West Hill Ski Touring Center, Putney   *143*

Southern Vermont

Southern Vermont

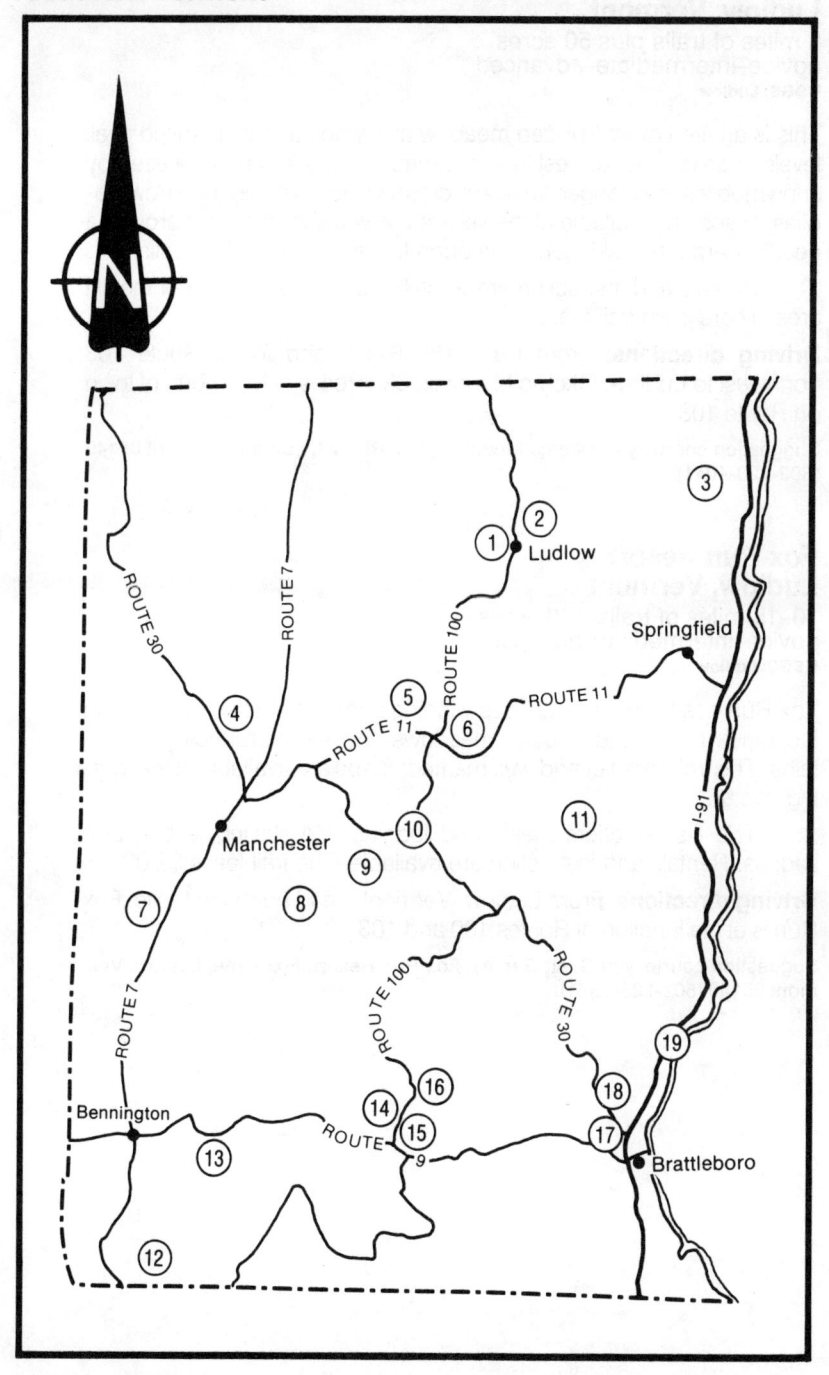

Okemo Mountain, Inc.
Ludlow, Vermont
8 miles of trails plus 50 acres
novice-intermediate-advanced
USGS: Ludlow

This is an area of well-blazed meadow and woodland trails suited to all levels of ability. The easiest trails are machine-packed and not used by snowmobiles; the longer trails are crossed occasionally by snowmobiles. Maps are available at the ski area. A watershed project around a nearby dam offers ski touring on open fields and unmarked trails.

Rentals and instruction are available at the base lodge of the ski area. There is no trail fee.

Driving directions: From I-91, take Exit 6 and follow Route 103 northwest to Ludlow. Okemo Mountain Ski Area is ½ mile north of town on Route 103.

Suggestion courtesy of Okemo Mountain, Inc. RFD #1, Ludlow, Vermont 05149 (802-228-4041).

Fox Run Resort
Ludlow, Vermont
10-15 miles of trails/180 acres
novice-intermediate-advanced
USGS: Ludlow

Fox Run has trails for all abilities winding across the golf course, along the Black River, and through meadows and the surrounding mountains. The trails are set and well marked; maps are available at the touring center.

The Resort offers meals and lodging, ice skating, a bar, and saunas. Rentals and instruction are available. The trail fee is $2.00.

Driving directions: From Ludlow, Vermont, head north for 1 mile. Fox Run is at the junction of Routes 100 and 103.

Suggestion courtesy of Scott Garvey, Fox Run Resort, Fox Lane, Ludlow, Vermont 05149 (802-228-8871).

Mount Ascutney Ski Area
Brownsville, Vermont
5-6 miles of trails
novice-intermediate-advanced
USGS: Claremont

This alpine ski area has several ski touring trails: short loops near the base lodge and parking area for the novice, and a longer trail west of the Ski Area for the more advanced skier. This trail runs over terrain ranging from flat to quite steep and from open fields to dense woods. All trails are well marked and shown on a map available free at the base lodge. Snowmobiles use is very light.

Ski tourers may use the facilities of the base lodge, which include rest rooms, double cafeteria, lounge, and nursery. Rentals and instruction are also offered. There is no charge for trail use.

Driving directions: From I-91 heading north, take Exit 8. Turn left (north) at the light onto Route 5. After 1 mile, turn left and continue 3 miles to Route 44; turn left and continue for 2 miles to the Ski Area. From I-91 heading south, take Exit 9 and go west on Route 44 for 6 miles to Mount Ascutney.

Suggestion courtesy of Mount Ascutney Ski Area, Box 29, Brownsville, Vermont 05037 (802-484-7711).

Barrows House Ski Touring Center
Dorset, Vermont
15 miles of trails
novice-intermediate-advanced
USGS: Dorset/Pawlet

From Barrows House Inn, trails extend into the countryside over moderately hilly terrain. Some wind through the woods over logging roads, others traverse beautiful streams, and some cross open country offering lovely views. The trails connect to those in the Merck Forest, which greatly expands the ski touring possibilities. Maps are posted at the Touring Center. Because many of the Barrows House trails cross private property, snowmobiles may be encountered. They are not permitted in the Merck Forest.

The ski shop is heated by a wood stove and offers rental equipment (including snowshoes), instruction, and guided tours. Rooms, meals, and a tavern are available at the Inn. There is no charge for trail use.

Driving directions: From Manchester, Vermont, take Route 30 north for 6 miles to Dorset. Barrows House is on the right, heading into town.

Suggestion courtesy of Charles Schubert, Barrows House Ski Touring Center, Dorset, Vermont 05251 (802-867-4455).

Peru Outdoor Recreation Commission
Peru/Landgrove, Vermont
12 miles of trails
intermediate–advanced
USGS: Wallingford

These trails are for more experienced skiers and are primarily in the Green Mountain National Forest. Most are over logging roads and skid trails, and skiers may encounter active timber operations. Several sections go through deer wintering areas. Trails are marked with blue diamonds; an excellent trail map is available at The Village Inn in Landgrove. Register at The Village Inn or at registration boxes near the trailheads before skiing. These trails are also used by snowshoers and snowmobilers.

There are limited rentals, a waxing area, and a lounge at The Village Inn. Meals and lodging are available, but reservations are advisable. Trail maps cost $1.00; there is no trail fee.

Driving directions: From I-91, take Exit 6 at Rockingham and go west on Routes 103 and 11 to Londonderry. About ½ mile west of the shopping center, turn right onto Landgrove Road. Continue for 4 miles to the village of Landgrove and bear left after crossing the bridge. The Village Inn is 1 mile north of Landgrove on the right.

Suggestion courtesy of D. Jay Snyder, The Village Inn, RFD, Landgrove, Vermont 05148 (802-824-6673).

Wild Wings Ski Touring Center
Peru, Vermont
10 miles of trails
novice–intermediate–advanced
USGS: Wallingford

Most trails are suited to novice and intermediate skiers. They traverse rolling terrain with mixed hardwood forest. There is also a two-acre open field for instruction and practice. Most trails are groomed, though about 3 miles are left primitive. All are marked according to NSTOA standards and are closed to snowmobiles, except for trail maintenance. Maps are available at the Touring Center. Wild Wings trails connect with those of the Peru Outdoor Recreation Commission (see separate entry) in the Green Mountain National Forest.

Housed in a modified horse barn, Wild Wings has a small rental shop and a warming room with free hot bouillon; instruction is available. There is an area use fee.

Driving directions: Wild Wings is located 2½ miles north of Peru: Maps are available at the local store. There is limited parking.

Suggestion courtesy of Angus C. Black, Jr., Wild Wings Ski Touring Center, P.O. Box 132E, Peru, Vermont 05152 (802-824-6793).

Nordic Inn Ski Touring Center
Londonderry, Vermont
30 km (18½ miles) of trails
novice-intermediate-advanced
USGS: Londonderry

Nordic Inn trails cover varied terrain in the Green Mountain National Forest, from mountain ridges to gentle open fields. Much of the area is forested, with stands of red pine and sugar maples, and several brooks and beaver ponds. One trail passes an old colonial cemetery on a hilltop. Trails are marked with NSTOA signs and patrolled by a Nordic Ski Patrol. Maps are distributed at the Inn. Snowmobiles are not allowed, except to groom trails.

The Touring Center includes a ski shop and a pub that serves lunches and snacks. Rentals, EPSTI certified instruction, guided tours, and night tours with headlamps are offered. Nordic Inn has meals and lodging, and offers "learn to cross-country ski" weekly packages. Ski touring films are shown on weekends. There is a $3.00 trail fee.

Driving directions: Nordic Inn is on Route 11, 14 miles east of Manchester and 3 miles west of Londonderry.

Suggestion courtesy of Filippo Pagano, Nordic Inn Ski Touring Center, Route 11, Londonderry, Vermont 05148 (802-824-6444).

Viking Ski Touring Center
Londonderry, Vermont
20+ miles of trails
novice-intermediate
USGS: Londonderry/Wallingford

These trails wind over gently rolling terrain through open fields and forests of hardwood and conifer. There are excellent views of the surrounding mountains. Trail maps are free at the Touring Center. The Green Mountain National Forest, which has a great number of skiable trails, is only 5 miles away; the Lye Brook Wilderness, 10 miles away, also offers excellent skiing (see separate entry). The Touring Center has a retail shop, cafeteria, bar, and a small deli. Rentals, repairs, and EPSTI certified instruction are offered. There is a separate waxing hut heated by a wood stove. Special activities include guided tours, night tours, and races; a full schedule and brochure are available. The trail fee is $3.50, and season passes are available.

Driving directions: From the Bellows Falls exit off I-91, take Route 103 to Chester. Then take Route 11 west for about 10 or 12 miles, past Magic Mountain Ski Area. Turn right onto Little Pond Road about 1 mile past the ski area. Continue for ½ mile to the Touring Center. There is plowed parking for 80-90 cars; do not park on the road. Parking can be a problem on holidays such as Christmas and Washington's Birthday.

Suggestion courtesy of Stan Allaben, Viking Ski Touring Center, Little Pond Road, Londonderry, Vermont 05248 (802-824-3933).

West Mountain Inn
Arlington, Vermont
14 miles of trails
novice-intermediate-advanced
USGS: Arlington

There are 14 miles of scenic horse, jeep, and hiking trails at West Mountain Inn. They are not marked. Snowmobiles are prohibited. The Inn offers meals and lodging (reservations requested), plus ice skating, tobogganing, and snowshoeing. At present there are no ski touring programs; however, nearby there are three excellent touring centers.

Driving directions: The Inn is ½ mile west of Route 7 on Route 313.

Suggestion courtesy of Wes and Mary Ann Carlson, Innkeepers, West Mountain Inn, Route 313, Arlington, Vermont 05250 (802-375-6516).

Long Trail to Stratton Pond
Stratton, Vermont
6½ miles, round trip
novice
USGS: Londonderry

This is the old route of the Long Trail. The new route goes over Stratton Mountain and is too steep to ski. Because of the change, the old trail may not be maintained or blazed as it used to be. It is shown clearly on the USGS Londonderry quadrangle; however, the guidebooks to the Long Trail and Appalachian Trail show the new route.

This is a very pleasant and easy trip. The beginning of the trail follows a stream that swirls around mounds of snow. The trail is wide, and the woods are not dense, making it very sunny on good days. Snowmobile use is light.

Driving directions: From Brattleboro, go west on Route 9 and turn north on Route 100 in Wilmington. Continue on Route 100 to West Wardsboro. After passing Brown's Store on the right, turn left and continue through the town of Stratton. About 2¾ miles west of Stratton, there is a junction; go straight. This road is private and used for logging; beware of trucks. There is a plowed parking area on the right, next to a house that sits back from the road. Almost immediately past the parking area, the road crosses a bridge over the stream. The trail starts at the corner of the parking lot closest to the house. There is a sign, and the trail is blazed in white.

Lye Brook Wilderness
Manchester, Vermont
14,300 acres
advanced
USGS: Londonderry/Equinox/Sunderland

This wilderness area is a part of the Green Mountain National Forest. Trails suitable for skiing include the Branch Pond Trail to Bourn Pond from the Arlington-West Wardsboro Road, and the old route of the Long Trail from Stratton Pond to Swezey Shelter, via Bourn Pond. Other trails have not been field checked but may be skiable; consult a topographic map for possibilities. Snowmobiles are not permitted.

Skiers and hikers must have a permit before entering the Lye Brook Wilderness. The permit is free and may be obtained from the U.S. Forest Service at any of the following addresses: Catamount National Bank Building, Manchester Center 05255; Rochester Company Building, Rochester 05767; P.O. Box 568, Middlebury 05753; Federal Building, Rutland 05701. The Forest Service also has maps of the area.

Driving directions: The Branch Pond Trail leaves the Arlington-West Wardsboro Road about 1½ miles west of the old route of the Long Trail (see entry for Long Trail to Stratton Pond). Other trails leave Manchester and Manchester Depot. USGS maps show road access more clearly than the Forest Service map. Park with caution; there are no developed parking facilities.

Suggestion courtesy of Jerry Weene, Goshen, Massachusetts.

Stratton Ski Touring Center
Stratton Mountain, Vermont
7+ miles of trails
novice-intermediate-advanced
USGS: Londonderry

Trails cover rolling terrain on the Stratton Mountain golf course and adjacent wooded land to the east. In addition to groomed trails, there are about 15 miles of ungroomed trails east of the alpine complex. Snowmobiles are used only for maintenance and emergencies. Trail maps are available.

The Touring Center includes a ski shop, waxing room, cocktail lounge, and snack bar. Rentals, repairs, Nordic Ski Patrol, and EPSTI certified instruction are offered. Other activities include races and Wednesday evening guided tours. There is a $2.00 trail fee.

Driving directions: From I-91 going north, take the second Brattleboro exit to Route 30. Follow Route 30 west to the signs for Stratton Mountain Ski Area.

Suggestion courtesy of John Eckhardt, Stratton Ski Touring Center, Stratton Mountain, Vermont 05155 (802-297-1880).

Crackerbarrel Ski Shop
Rawsonville, Vermont
12 miles of trails
novice–intermediate
USGS: Londonderry

Trails from the Crackerbarrel go through heavily wooded areas, with several streams and signs of deer and other wildlife. About half the trails are groomed; all are well marked and shown on a map that is distributed at the shop. Snowmobiles are not permitted, except to set tracks.

The Crackerbarrel has a complete retail shop, with rentals and instruction, a cheese and wine shop, and plenty of heated space for waxing. Special activities include guided trips (by special arrangement) and an annual Lincoln's birthday weekend race. There is no trail fee.

Driving directions: The Ski Shop is at the junction of Routes 30 and 100 in Rawsonville.

Suggestion courtesy of John Marona, Crackerbarrel Ski Shop, Box 263, Bondville, Vermont 05340 (802-297-1200).

Cross-Country Ski Shop and Trail System at Grafton
Grafton, Vermont
30+ km (18+ miles) of trails
novice–intermediate–advanced
USGS: Saxton's River

This is a small touring center with an extensive and diverse network of marked trails. Some are on large tracts of flat, open land along Saxton's River. One trail leads to the summit of Bear Hill (elevation 1724 feet), and others circle around the far side of the hill. Some of the outlying trails pass through very wild country, with excellent views of the surrounding area. The forest is primarily hardwood with some stands of evergreen. These trails connect with many old roads in Grafton State Forest to the south, and with Haywire Farm Ski Touring Center in Townshend. There are occasional snowmobiles on a few of the trails. Maps cost 25¢ at the Ski Shop.

The Shop is set in a rustic log cabin with a large fireplace and kerosene lights (there is no electricity). There is a waxing area on the porch, and hot drinks are served indoors. Rentals, instruction, and guided tours are offered. Lodging is available nearby at the Old Tavern at Grafton. There is a $2.00 area use charge.

Driving directions: From I-91, take the Bellows Falls exit and follow Route 121 west for 15 miles to Grafton. At the Old Tavern, turn left (south) onto Townshend Road (Route 35), and continue ½ mile to the Cross-Country Ski Shop.

Suggestion courtesy of Jud and Gretchen Hartmann, Cross-Country Ski Shop and Trail System at Grafton, Townshend Road, Grafton, Vermont 05146 (802-843-2234).

Dome Trail
Pownal, Vermont
6 miles, round trip
intermediate-advanced
USGS: Williamstown/Pownal

The view from the summit of The Dome makes this a unique trip: the Greylock, Taconic, and Hoosac Ranges, the Berkshires, and the Green Mountains are all visible. The descent from the top is rather steep. Snowmobile use is light.

Ski route: The Dome Trail begins as a wood road and leads north into a field, It passes through woods and fields, runs under a power line, then ascends for 1 3/8 miles to the Agawon Trail on the right. Meetinghouse Rock, just beyond the Agawon Trail, is the halfway point of the trail. From here the Dome Trail follows an even grade, growing steeper near the top. At the intersection with two old roads, follow white paint blazes and make a sharp right turn. From this point to the top, the trail must be followed carefully. Continue skiing below the crest of the ridge, through open woods. Many skiers tend to head for the top of the ridge, which is heavily wooded and difficult to ski. Follow the blazes for 1/2 mile before heading to the top. The approach to the summit is covered by a growth of birch, beech, maple, and scrub oak. This cover gives way at the summit to a plateau of stunted spruce and balsams often coated with frost and snow.

Driving directions: From Williamstown, Massachusetts, take Route 7 north about 1 mile and turn right onto North Hoosac Road (the first right after crossing the river). Take the first left onto White Oaks Road and drive north past the White Oaks School and Chapel. Cross the Broad Brook Bridge about 100 yards past the state line. Park in the plowed lot on the right, 0.3 miles past the bridge.

Timberlane Touring Trails
Woodford, Vermont
25 km (15 1/2 miles) of trails
novice-intermediate-advanced
USGS: Woodford/Stamford

Situated high in the Green Mountains, Timberlane trails traverse lovely areas and boast excellent snow conditions. There is a variety of groomed and wilderness ski trails.

Housed in a chalet, Timberlane offers rentals, EPSTI certified instruction, wilderness camping, trail lunches, and many fun programs. Contact the Touring Center for information on special events, races, and other programs.

Driving directions: From Bennington, drive east 8 miles on Route 9 to Timberlane Touring Trails at Prospect Mountain Ski Area.

Suggestion courtesy of Richard Taylor, Timberlane Touring Trails, Inc., Woodford, Vermont 05201 (802-442-5791).

Broad Brook Trail
Pownal, Vermont
8 miles, round trip
novice-intermediate
USGS: Williamstown/Pownal

This is a beautiful trip up a valley between The Dome and a southern spur of the Green Mountains. The first 1½ miles of the trail are suited to novices; the remainder is more difficult. Few snowmobiles should be encountered.

Ski route: The trail follows Broad Brook northeast, over several crossings. It begins in a field alongside the brook, then crosses a sluiceway and enters the woods. At 1 mile, the trail crosses to the north side of the stream. At 1½ miles the Agawon Trail branches off to the left and ascends to the Dome Trail. Just beyond the intersection, the Broad Brook Trail makes a diagonal, upstream crossing. At 1⅞ miles, a wood road comes in on the right. The trail crosses the stream again just above an old ridge and continues on the north bank. At 2¼ miles it leaves the road and descends a small bank; shortly beyond, it crosses a small stream, climbs a short distance, descends to the valley floor, and picks up another wood road. At 2⅞ miles, the trail crosses the brook to the south side, then crosses a tributary. On the northwest side of the tributary, the trail ascends, passes through a hemlock grove, and emerges on the north bank. Finally, it descends the bank, crosses the stream, and meets the Long Trail 0.2 miles south of the Seth Warner Shelter.

Driving directions: See entry for the Dome Trail. The Broad Brook Trail begins to the right (east), just south of the bridge.

Country Club Cross-Country Touring Center
Wilmington, Vermont
250 acres
novice-intermediate-advanced
USGS: Wilmington

Trails extend over the open hills of the Mount Snow Country Club golf course and continue through surrounding wooded areas, with outstanding views of the Mount Snow valley. They are marked according to NSTOA standards, and maps are available at the Touring Center. Snowmobiles are not allowed, except to groom trails. The Country Club system connects with trails from The Hermitage (see separate entry) and with numerous other trails and unplowed roads in the Green Mountain National Forest.

The Touring Center includes a rental shop, retail shop, luncheon area, and waxing room. Snacks are available. Rentals, instruction, moonlight tours, and golf on skis are offered. There is a $3.00 trail fee.

Broad Brook Trail

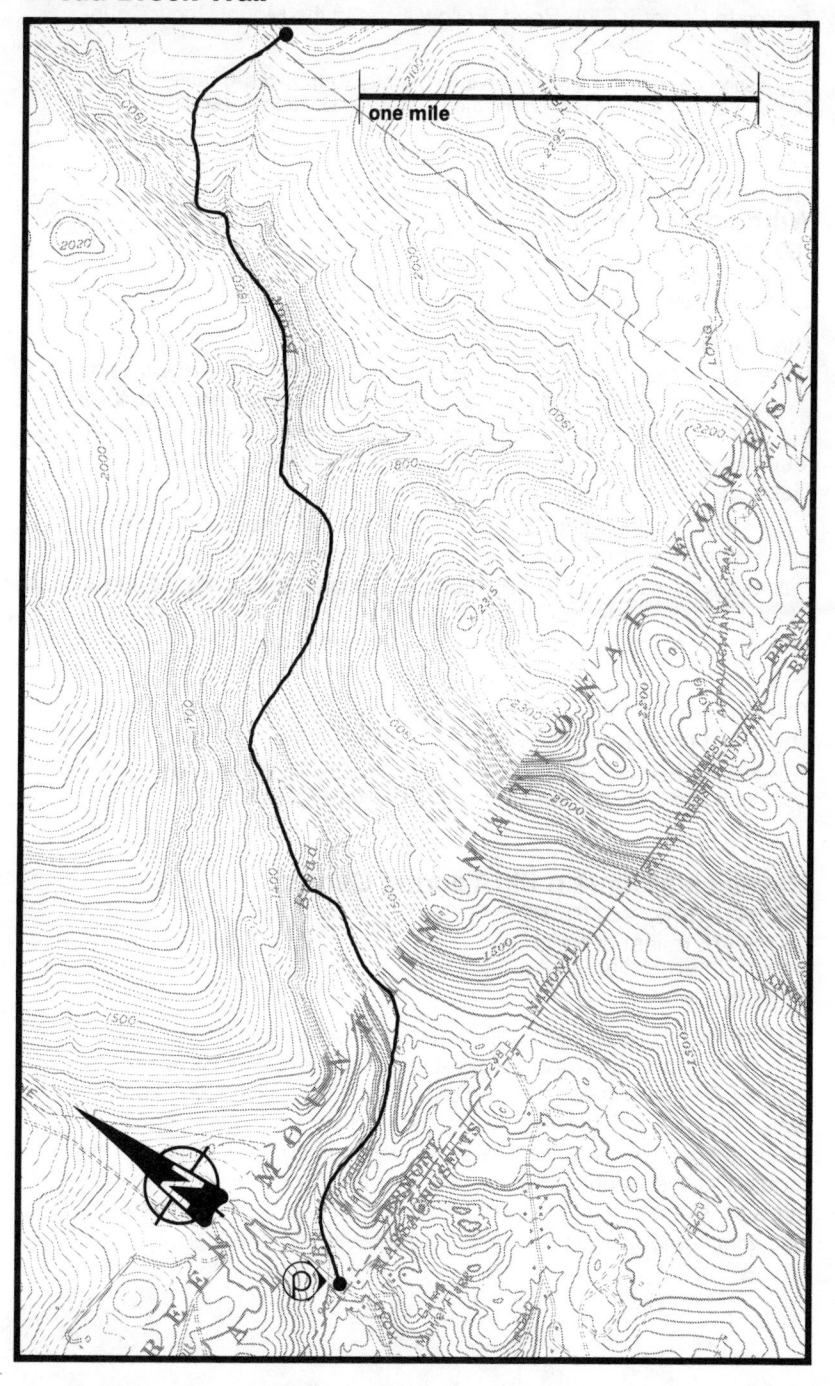

one mile

139   Southern Vermont

Driving directions: From Wilmington, drive north on Route 100 about 7 miles to Country Club Road. Follow signs to the Mount Snow Country Club.

Suggestion courtesy of Jim McGovern, Country Club Cross-Country Touring Center, Country Club Road, Wilmington, Vermont 05363 (802-464-5642).

Hermitage Ski Touring Center
Wilmington, Vermont
100 acres
novice–intermediate–advanced
USGS: Willmington

The Hermitage is a small country inn with its own ski touring center. Trails run through wooded, protected areas with some open fields between Mount Snow and Haystack Ski Areas. They connect with trails from the Country Club Touring Center (see separate entry) to make a much larger network. Snowmobiles are permitted only to groom trails. Maps are available at the Touring Center.

Meals and lodging are available at the Inn. The Touring Center offers rentals and certified instruction and sponsors an annual Saint Patrick's Day race. A 20-mile, guided overnight tour from the Inn to Stratton Pond, Stratton Mountain, and the north face of Mount Snow may be arranged. The Hermitage also offers sleigh rides. The trail fee is $3.00.

Driving directions: Follow Route 100 north from Wilmington; turn left onto Coldbrook Road, and continue 3½ miles to the Touring Center.

Suggestion courtesy of Jim McGovern, Hermitage Ski Touring Center, Box 291, Coldbrook Road, Wilmington, Vermont 05363 (802-464-3759).

Haystack Mountain Ski Touring Center
Wilmington, Vermont
26 km (16 miles) of trails
novice–intermediate–advanced
USGS: Willmington

Trails from Haystack Mountain go through primarily wooded areas in the Green Mountain National Forest and over the former Haystack Golf Course. Features include maple groves with a sugar house, old stone walls, and several brooks. At the far end of the trail system is the Chimney Hill warming hut. Trails are well marked, and maps are distributed at the Touring Center. Snowmobiles are not allowed. Haystack trails connect with those from The Hermitage (see separate entry) and with numerous logging roads in the National Forest.

The Ski Touring Center is adjacent to the base lodge of Haystack Ski Area. The lodge has a lounge, restaurant, and snack bar. Rentals and instruction are offered. Special events are scheduled every weekend, including citizens' races, family day races, Bill Koch League races, telemark turn contests, guided tours, moonlight tours, and ski orienteering events. The trail fee is $2.00 per day; $1.00 for skiers staying at satellite inns. Season passes and group rates are available.

Driving directions: From Route 100 north of Wilmington, turn west onto Coldbrook Road, then left onto the Haystack access road.

Suggestion courtesy of Donald C. Race, Jr., Haystack Mountain Ski Touring Center, Coldbrook Road, Wilmington, Vermont 05363 (802-464-8641).

The White House Touring Center
Wilmington, Vermont
15 miles of trails
novice–intermediate–advanced
USGS: Wilmington

The White House is an old, turn-of-the-century mansion, and many trails cross the old golf course and woodlands of the estate. Much of the area is hardwood forest, with an abandoned sugar bush and stands of pine. There are a number of attractive novice trails, several open "telemark" hills, and steep twisting trails for advanced skiers. One trail passes an active beaver pond; another recently-cut trail makes an approximately 10-km loop to a nearby lake. All trails are groomed and very well marked. Maps are distributed at the Touring Center.

The White House Touring Center includes a full rental shop and a waxing room with a bench, tools, and iron. Rooms and meals are available. Ski touring instructors are EPSTI certified. Other activities include guided tours (by appointment), moonlight tours, and the annual USSA spring triathalon.

Driving directions: The White House is on Route 9, ½ mile east of Wilmington.

Suggestion courtesy of Kel Kahler, Cross-Country Director, The White House Touring Center, Box 757C, Route 9, Wilmington, Vermont 05363 (802-464-2135).

Sitzmark Ski Touring Center
Wilmington, Vermont
20 miles of trails/2000 acres
novice-intermediate-advanced
USGS: Wilmington

Sitzmark Ski Touring Center maintains a network of trails that branch out in all directions from the Center. The golf course provides excellent novice skiing, with attractive brooks and bridges. Other trails follow logging roads and carriage trails in surrounding wooded areas. Some lead to old hunting cabins, apple orchards, and maple groves. One popular route is the Ellis Brook Trail, which links the Sitzmark with the town of West Dover. All trails are groomed and marked with red arrows and standard trail difficulty signs. Maps are distributed at the Touring Center. Snowmobiles are prohibited. On The Rocks Lodge, nearby, has a series of nature trails that connect with those from the Sitzmark and offers special nature tours.

The ski shop is located on the ground floor of an old barn adjoining Sitzmark Lodge. It has a waxing room heated by a wood stove. Overlooking the ski shop is a lounge, with hot spiced wine and cider. Lunch is served daily at the Sitzmark, and accommodations are available at several lodges in the area. Rentals, EPSTI certified instruction, and moonlight tours are available. Sitzmark is a host of the Fleischmann's Margarine Sprint Relays. There is a $2.50 trail fee.

Driving directions: From I-91 in Brattleboro, follow Route 9 west 21 miles to Wilmington. Turn right (north) onto Route 100, and continue 4 miles to East Dover Road. Turn right at the Sitzmark Ski Touring sign.

Suggestion courtesy of Eddie Flaim, Director, Sitzmark Ski Touring Center, Sitzmark Lodge, Wilmington, Vermont 05363 (802-464-3384).

Living Memorial Park Cross-Country Trail
Brattleboro, Vermont
1 mile
novice-intermediate
USGS: Brattleboro

This trail was constructed by the Brattleboro Outing Club and is lighted for night use. Though there is no map available, it is an easy trail to find and follow. Starting at the top of the T-bar, it loops through a wooded area, with some uphill and downhill stretches. Snowmobiles are not allowed on the trail.

The park has a heated shelter, snack bar, and toilets.

Driving directions: From Brattleboro, take Route 9 west 1 mile, crossing the covered bridge to Living Memorial Park.

Suggestion courtesy of Frank Dearborn, Brattleboro Recreation and Parks Department, Brattleboro, Vermont.

Brattleboro Country Club Ski Touring Center
Brattleboro, Vermont
100 acres
novice–intermediate–advanced
USGS: Brattleboro

Part of the Brattleboro trail system follows the perimeter of the golf course, with loops back to the Touring Center. Other trails go through adjacent wooded areas. The terrain varies from flat to hilly. Trails are shown on a map and marked with standard NSTOA signs. Snowmobiles are used only for grooming trails. Dogs are not allowed.

Rentals, instruction, and snacks are available at the Touring Center. There is a fireplace, a wood stove, and rest rooms. Moonlight tours are held each month, and the Washington's Birthday Race every February. There is a fee for trail use.

Driving directions: From Brattleboro, take Route 30 west to Upper Dummerston Road.

Suggestion courtesy of Joe and Bitsy Jacques, Brattleboro Country Club Ski Touring Center, Box 525, Brattleboro, Vermont 05301 (802-257-7380).

West Hill Ski Touring Center
Putney, Vermont
7 km (4 miles) of trails
novice–intermediate
USGS: Brattleboro/Saxton's River

Trails from the West Hill Shop are groomed and traverse predominantly flat, open land between I-91 and the Connecticut River. There are many other superb trails in the Putney area; check at the shop for current information and directions.

West Hill offers retail sales, rentals, and instruction. There is no trail fee.

Driving directions: The Touring Center is right off I-91, at Exit 4.

Suggestion courtesy of Neil Quinn, West Hill Ski Touring Center, RD #2, Box 14, Putney, Vermont 05346 (802-387-5718).

Ski Touring
Massachusetts and Rhode Island
CHAPTER 4

Massachusetts has many fine, skiable trails and open areas. These include state parks and forests, town lands, wildlife management areas, and some Metropolitan District Commission (MDC) lands. There are several excellent ski areas within the metropolitan Boston region, such as the Middlesex Fells and Blue Hills Reservations (see individual entries), which are easily accessible from the city. Cape Cod and other coastal sections of Massachusetts and Rhode Island offer some nice opportunities for skiing, though snow cover is usually sparse.

Many Massachusetts state parks and forests are suitable for ski touring, though some receive heavy snowmobile use. Many now have designated trails for skiing (foot use) and snowmobiling; check at individual parks or forests, or at regional headquarters for further information. Region 1 (southeastern Massachusetts) Headquarters is at Myles Standish State Forest, P.O. Box 66, South Carver 02566 (617-295-2135); Region 2 (northeastern Massachusetts) at Willard Brook State Forest, P.O. Box 111, West Townsend 01474 (617-597-8802); Region 3 (central Massachusetts) at Clinton Nursery, P.O. Box 155, Clinton 01510 (617-365-5908); Region 4 (Connecticut Valley area) at Amherst Nursery, P.O. Box 484, Amherst 01002 (413-549-1461); and Region 5 (Berkshires) at Pittsfield State Forest, Cascade Street, Pittsfield 01201 (413-442-8992).

The state issues a pamphlet, "Camping in Massachusetts," which lists state-run and private campgrounds and state day-use areas. Facilities and recreational activities, including ski touring, are listed for each area. Write to the Massachusetts Department of Commerce and Development, Division on Tourism, Box 1775, Boston, Massachusetts 02105.

25 Ski Tours in Western Massachusetts, by John Frado, Richard Lawson, and Robert Coy, includes maps, driving directions, and detailed trail descriptions for selected tours.

Berkshire Trails for Walking and Ski Touring, by Whit Griswold, describes hiking and ski trails for all levels of ability and includes maps, driving directions, and detailed trail descriptions.

The following guides to hiking trails in Massachusetts may be useful to the ski tourer. All include trail descriptions and maps. Unless trails are evaluated specifically for ski touring, it is best to consult topographic maps or have summer experience on a trail before attempting it on skis.

The AMC *Massachusetts and Rhode Island Trail Guide* is the most comprehensive guide to trails in Massachusetts. It also describes the Rhode Island Inter-Park Trails, many of which are good for ski touring with sufficient snow cover. This book describes trails in all parts of Massachusetts, including many state lands, wildlife sanctuaries, and other non-mountain areas where the terrain is fairly gentle. Many of the trails, therefore, are skiable. The following maps come with the book, or may be purchased separately: Mount Greylock, Pittsfield State Forest,

Mount Tom/Holyoke Range, Mount Toby, Rhode Island Inter-Park Trails (northwestern and southwestern), Dogtown (Cape Ann), Wachusett Mountain, and Blue Hills Reservation.

The *Guide to the Appalachian Trail in Massachusetts and Connecticut* covers the Appalachian Trail and some side trails (including a chapter on Mount Greylock trails) in Massachusetts. Most of this trail is too rugged to ski, but some sections are suitable. Snowmobiles are not permitted on the Appalachian Trail.

Fifty Hikes in Massachusetts, by Paul and Ruth Sadlier, describes many hikes that are also excellent on skis. Among the best possibilities are the Beech Forest Trail, Fort Hill Trail, Yarmouth Botanic Trails, Ashumet Holly Reservation, Braintree Town Forest, Ravenswood Park, Crane Reservation, Phillips Academy Bird Sanctuary, Cook's Canyon Sanctuary, Harvard Forest, Arcadia Wildlife Sanctuary, Stebbins Wildlife Refuge, Dorothy Frances Rice Sanctuary, Borden Mountain, Smith Mountain, Mount Prospect, Mount Wilcox, and Pleasant Valley Sanctuary. Refer to *Fifty Hikes* for driving directions, maps, and detailed trail information.

Short Walks on Cape Cod and the Vineyard, also by Paul and Ruth Sadlier, describes 25 short trips, most under 2 miles. Snow conditions on the Cape are not reliable, but with sufficient snow cover most of these trails can be skied.

Hiking Cape Cod, by J.H. Mitchell and Whit Griswold, includes excellent background information on Cape Cod history and environment, as well as detailed descriptions of ten hikes (including maps and parking directions).

Country Walks Near Boston, by Alan Fisher, is published by the Appalachian Mountain Club. All of these walks are accessible by public transportation. Some, including Fowl Meadow, Stony Brook Reservation, Belmont and South Concord, are recommended specifically for ski touring. Trail descriptions are supplemented by interesting historical and environmental information.

The *Guide to the Metacomet-Monadnock Trail in Massachusetts and New Hampshire* is described in the Metacomet-Monadnock Trail entry under Western Massachusetts.

25 Walks in Rhode Island, by Ken Weber, includes maps, driving directions and detailed trail descriptions. With sufficient snow cover, most of these trails should be skiable.

Northeastern Massachusetts Ski Touring Areas

1. Riverwood Ski Touring Center, Winchendon *150*
2. Mount Watatic Ski Touring Center, Ashby *150*
3. Townsend State Forest, Townsend *151*
4. Willard Brook State Forest, West Townsend/Ashby *151*
5. Wachusett Mountain Ski Area, Princeton *152*
6. Oak Hill, Littleton *152*
7. Hartwell Hill, Littleton *154*
8. North Country Ski Touring Center, Carlisle *156*
9. Manning State Forest, Billerica *154*
10. Lowell-Dracut State Forest, Lowell *156*
11. Weir Hill Reservation, North Andover *154*
12. Andover Village Improvement Society, Andover *158*
    Harold Parker State Forest, Andover/North Andover *158*
    Charles W. Ward Reservation, Andover *159*
    Bald Hill–Wood Hill Reservation, Andover *159*
13. Boxford State Forest, Boxford/North Andover *160*
    Boxford Wildlife Sanctuary, Boxford *160*
14. Walnut Lane Cross-Country Skiing, Middleton *162*
15. Crane Pond Wildlife Management Area, Newbury/Georgetown/Groveland *163*
16. Old Town Hill Reservation, Newbury *162*
    Kents Island, Newbury *163*
17. Parker River National Wildlife Refuge, Newburyport *166*
18. Willowdale State Forest, Ipswich *166*
    Bradley Palmer State Park, Topsfield/Hamilton *167*

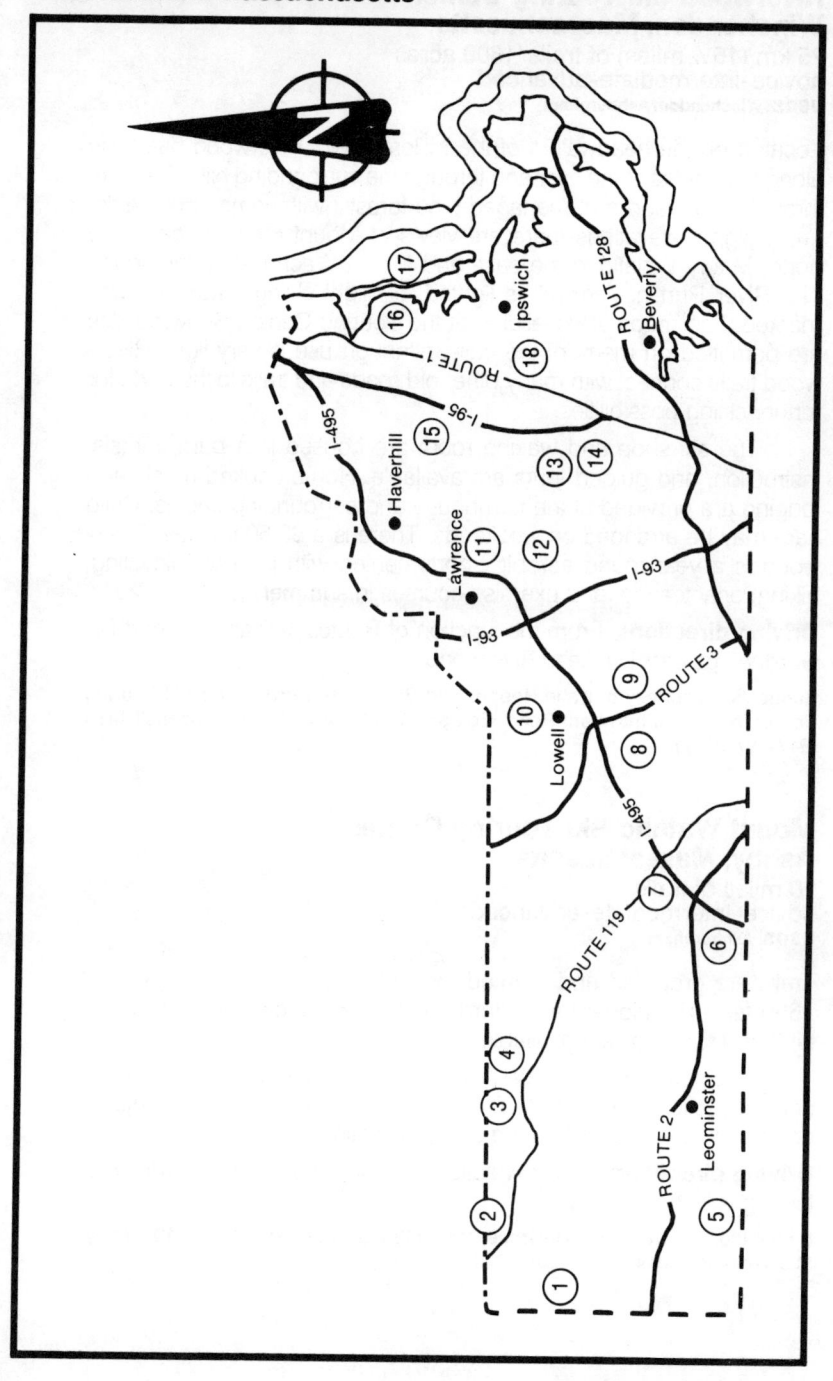

Northeastern Massachusetts

149   Northeastern Massachusetts

Riverwood Ski Touring Center
Winchendon, Massachusetts
25 km (15½ miles) of trails/1600 acres
novice-intermediate-advanced
USGS: Winchendon/Ashburnham

Located on the headwaters of the Millers River, Riverwood has trails along both sides of the river and through the surrounding hills. Trails go through hardwood and managed pine forests, with some open fields. From higher elevations there are views of Mount Monadnock to the north, Mount Watatic to the east, and Mount Wachusett to the south. The River Run novice trail is lighted for night skiing. Trails are well marked, and maps are available at the Touring Center. Snowmobiles are permitted on many of the trails, although use is very light. Riverwood trails connect with many other old roads and trails to the north for further skiing possibilities.

The ski shop and waxing room are housed in a barn; rentals, instruction, and guided tours are available. Home cooked meals and lodging are provided at the farmhouse and surrounding cabins. Child care may be arranged on weekends. There is a $2.50 trail fee. Riverwood is a year-round aerobic sports center, with jogging, bicycling, hiking, orienteering, and exercise courses in summer.

Driving directions: From the junction of Routes 140 and 12, north of Gardner, go east ½ mile to Riverwood.

Suggestion courtesy of Katie Hooper and Burt Porter, Riverwood Ski Touring Center, North Ashburnham Road, Box 54, Winchendon, Massachusetts 01475 (617-297-2257).

Mount Watatic Ski Touring Center
Ashby, Massachusetts
20 miles of trails
novice-intermediate-advanced
USGS: Ashburnham

Trails are groomed and marked, with elevations between 1250 and 1650 feet. The higher trails afford great views. Snowmobiles are prohibited. Trail maps are available.

The new Touring Center has a retail shop and snack bar. Rentals and instruction are offered. There is a $2.00 trail fee. The center is open on weekends and during school vacation weeks.

Driving directions: Mount Watatic is just off Route 119 in Ashby. Follow signs to the ski area.

Suggestion courtesy of Al DeGrace, Mount Watatic Ski Area, Route 119, Ashby, Massachusetts 01431 (617-386-7921).

Townsend State Forest
Townsend, Massachusetts
7 miles of trails
novice-intermediate
USGS: Townsend

Townsend State Forest offers ski touring on wood roads running through hardwood and pine forests. The trails are fairly hilly. Separate trails are designated for ski touring and snowmobiling. Trails east of Fessenden Road (unplowed), and a loop off Old Turnpike Road are for skiing; trails between Fessenden Road and Barker Hill Road are open for snowmobiling. Trail maps are available through the Massachusetts Department of Natural Resources, or at Willard Brook State Forest in West Townsend (see separate entry).

Driving directions: From I-495, take Route 119 west to Townsend. To ski the eastern section of the Forest, turn right at the light on Route 13 and continue to the state line, where there is a snowplow turnaround. It is possible to park here when it is not snowing. If snowplows are working, park alongside the road. To ski the western portion of the Forest, continue on Route 119 through Townsend and bear right on Old Turnpike Road. Continue on this road until it is no longer plowed (usually at the railroad track); park here.

Suggestion courtesy of Robert O. Goguen, Supervisor, Willard Brook State Forest, West Townsend, Massachusetts.

Willard Brook State Forest
West Townsend/Ashby, Massachusetts
6 miles of trails/2000+ acres
novice-intermediate
USGS: Ashby

This is a hilly state forest with open hardwoods and hemlock. Trails are designated specifically for ski touring (foot use) or for snowmobiling. Maps are available at the Forest headquarters. One good loop for ski touring starts across the road from the headquarters. If skiing clockwise, turn right before the trail joins the snowmobile trail. Ski northwest across the field; upon reaching the trail along the brook, turn right. This trail leads back to the headquarters.

Driving directions: From I-495, take Route 119 west. Continue on Route 119 through Townsend, entering the Forest 1.4 miles west of West Townsend. The headquarters, with a plowed parking area, is on the right. There is also a plowed parking lot at the Pearl Hill area, south of Route 119 on the New Fitchburg Road.

Suggestion courtesy of Robert O. Goguen, Supervisor, Willard Brook State Forest, West Townsend, Massachusetts.

Wachusett Mountain Ski Area
Princeton, Massachusetts
18 km (11 miles) of trails
novice-intermediate-advanced
USGS: Wachusett Mtn./Gardner

Wachusett Mountain is the highest point in eastern Massachusetts. Tracks are set on unplowed roads and ski trails through Wachusett Mountain State Reservation. There are also some skiable hiking trails in the area. Trails are marked according to NSTOA standards, and maps are free at the ski area. Snowmobiles are not permitted in the Reservation.

Rentals, instruction, and a snack bar are available, and there is a Nordic Patrol on weekends. The trail fee is $2.00.

Driving directions: From Route 2 west of Fitchburg, go south on Route 140 for 3 miles. Turn right on Mile Hill Road, which leads to the ski area.

Suggestion courtesy of Tom Smith, Nordic Director, Wachusett Mountain Ski Area, Mountain Road, Princeton, Massachusetts 01541 (617-464-2355).

Oak Hill
Littleton, Massachusetts
2 miles of trails/200 acres
novice-intermediate
USGS: Ayer

This hilly area is covered with stands of oak, maple, and evergreens, and offers views of Boston. Trails are marked by paint blazes on trees. Blue trails are for skiing and snowshoeing, red marks all-purpose trails, and yellow is used for difficult trails. Snowmobiling is not allowed.

Driving directions: From Littleton, go south on Oak Hill Road. A small, cleared parking area is located about ¼ mile from town, at the northeast corner of the reservation. Extra cars may park along the road.

Suggestion courtesy of Littleton Conservation Commission, Littleton, Massachusetts.

Oak Hill

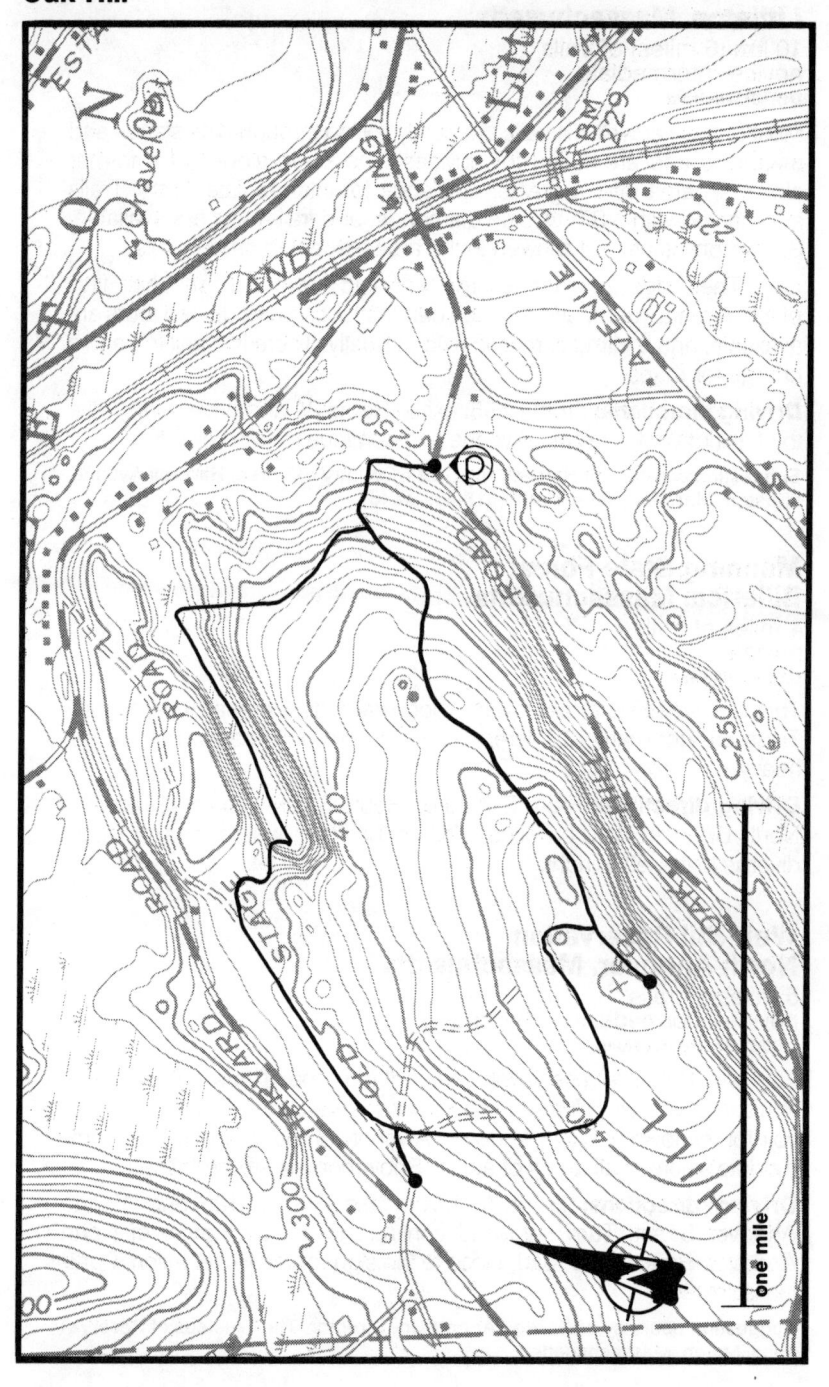

Northeastern Massachusetts

Hartwell Hill
Littleton, Massachusetts
10 km (6 miles) of trails
novice-intermediate
USGS: Westford

Most of the Hartwell Hill trails are gently rolling through pine stands and meadows and are suited for novices. The steep slopes of a former alpine ski area offer a greater challenge for intermediate skiers. Trails are marked with NSTOA blue diamonds, and trail maps are available. Snowmobiles are not allowed in the area, except to groom trails.

The lodge includes a large warming room with an open fireplace, a rental room, and a snack bar. Instruction and guided tours are available, and a citizens' race is held annually. There is a trail fee and a charge for maps.

Driving directions: From I-495, exit at Route 2A and drive north. Take the first right onto Hartwell Avenue and continue to Hartwell Hill.

Suggestion courtesy of Hartwell Hill Cross-Country Ski Area, Hartwell Avenue, Littleton, Massachusetts 01360 (617-486-4546).

Manning State Forest
Billerica, Massachusetts
4 miles of trails
novice
USGS: Billerica

This is a small state forest with wood roads over primarily flat terrain. Trails are not marked. There is some snowmobile traffic, but it is not heavy.

Driving directions: From Exit 28 off Route 3, take Route 129 toward North Billerica. Park on either side of the road, where logging roads diverge to the left or right.

Weir Hill Reservation
North Andover, Massachusetts
5 miles of trails
novice-intermediate-advanced
USGS: South Groveland

This is a 177-acre reservation of woodland, open fields, and wetlands surrounding Weir Hill and bordering on Lake Cochichewick, a reservoir for the town of North Andover. A variety of roads and trails accommodate skiers at all levels of ability. Snowmobiles are prohibited.

Driving directions: From Andover, take Routes 125 and 133 to Andover Street. Turn right and continue to the old center of North Andover. Park on the road, close to the sign for the Reservation. Parking is limited.

Suggestion courtesy of Gordon Abbott, Jr., Director, The Trustees of Reservations, Milton, Massachusetts.

Manning State Forest

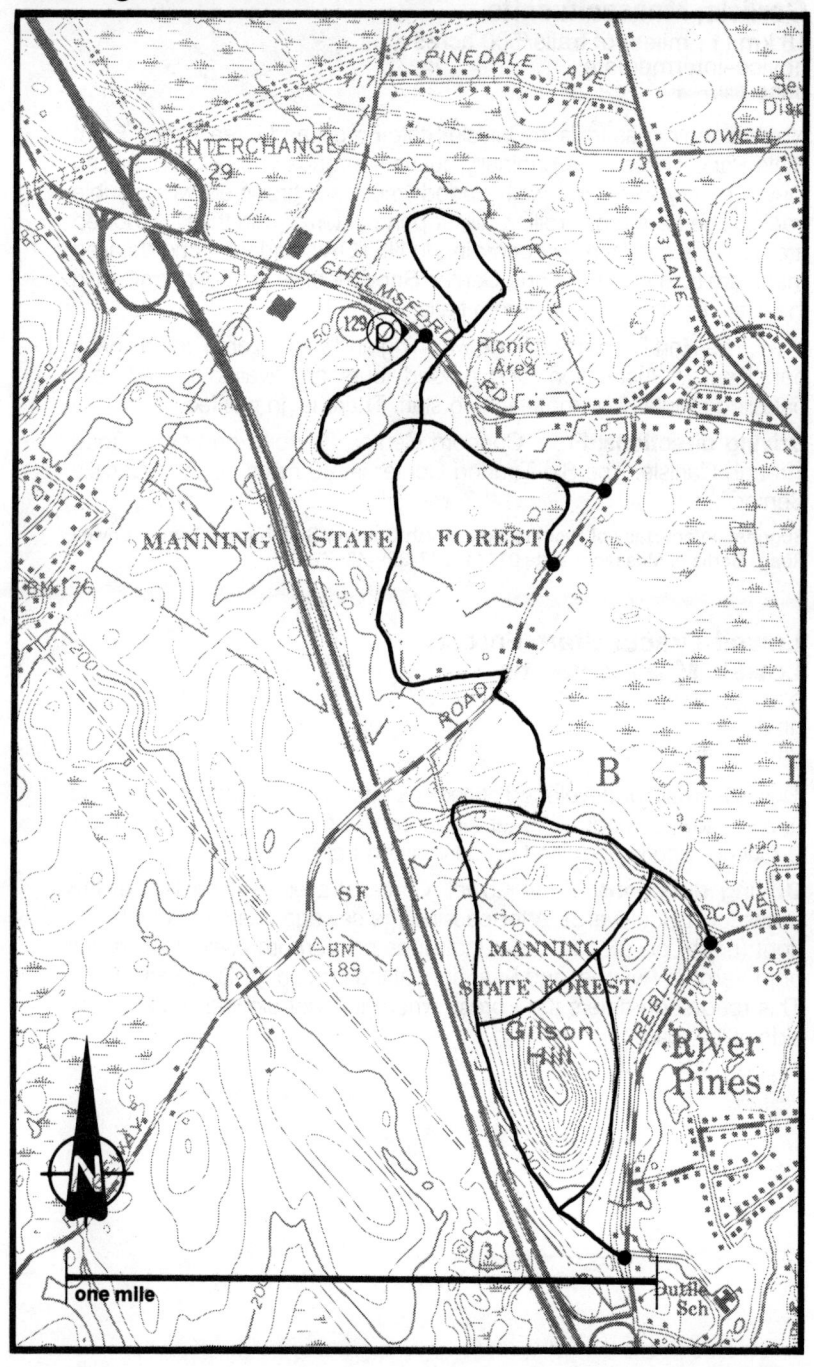

Northeastern Massachusetts

North Country Ski Touring Center
Carlisle, Massachusetts
18 km (11 miles) of trails/500 acres
novice-intermediate
USGS: Billerica

North Country has trails in Carlisle State Forest and Great Brook Farm State Park. These were originally cut as fire roads and bridle paths, so they are very wide and well graded; most are groomed with double tracks. The trails cross rolling hills, open pastures, and thickly wooded areas. Trails are marked according to NSTOA standards, and detailed maps are sold at the Touring Center. Snowmobiles are not permitted in the State Park, except to groom trails.

The Hart Barn has a large warming and waxing area and a snack bar. Rentals, instruction, and guided tours are available. Trails are patrolled regularly by the teaching staff. There is no trail fee.

Driving directions: From Concord Center, go north on Lowell Road through Carlisle. The Ski Touring Center is 1.9 miles north of Carlisle Center.

Suggestion courtesy of Richard Fox, North Country Ski Touring Center, Lowell Road, Carlisle, Massachusetts 01741 (617-369-4327).

Lowell-Dracut State Forest
Lowell, Massachusetts
9 miles of trails
novice
USGS: Lowell

This is a small, undeveloped state park offering pleasant skiing on trails and unplowed roads. The terrain is gentle; much of it is swampland. Snowmobiling is permitted on designated trails.

Driving directions: From Lowell Center, travel west on Route 113 (Pawtucket Boulevard). After passing the sewage treatment plant, turn right (north) on a short street that ends on Varnum Avenue. Turn left onto Varnum Avenue, and bear right at the fork on Trotting Park Road. This road soon enters the Forest, where it is not plowed. Park on the side of the road.

Lowell-Dracut State Forest

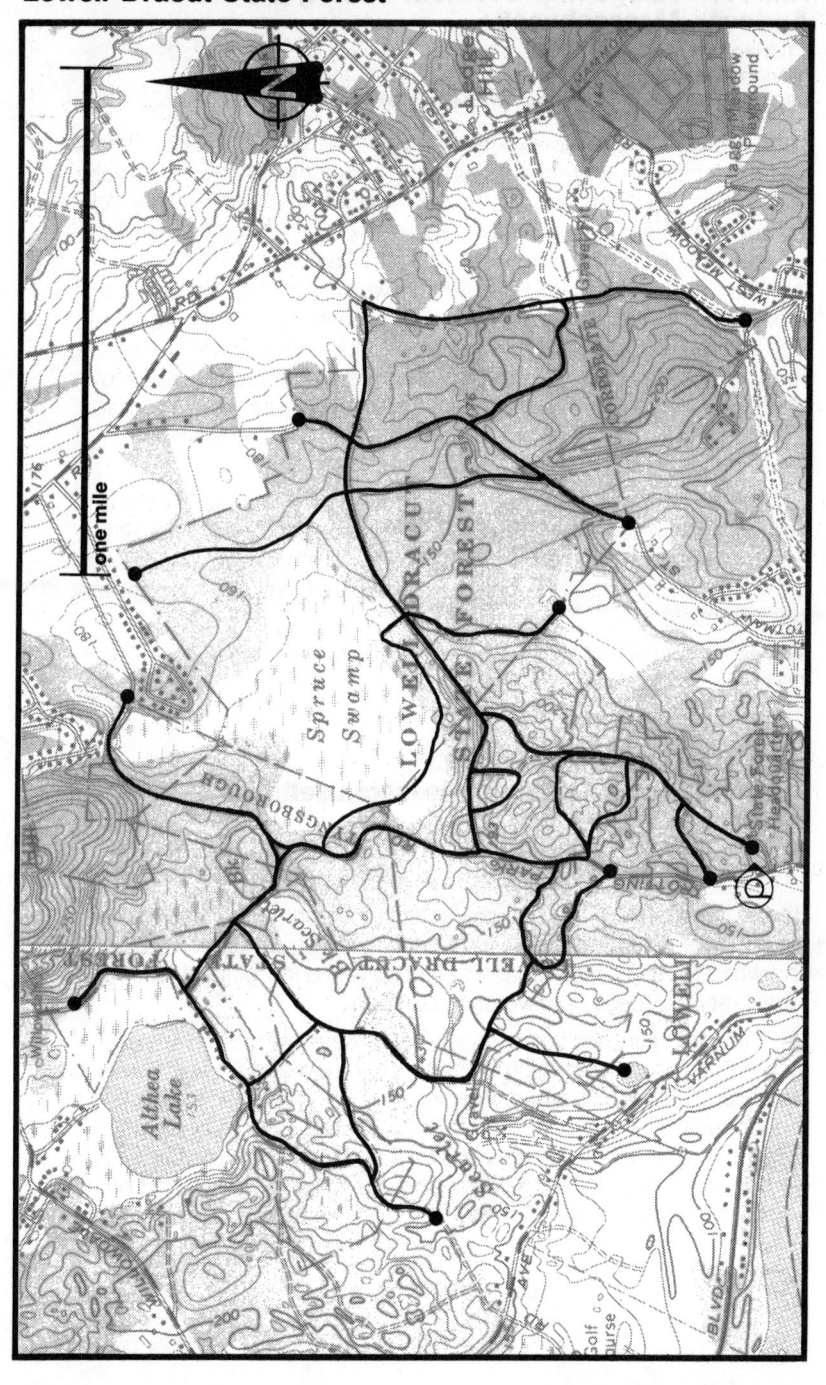

Northeastern Massachusetts

Andover Village Improvement Society
Andover, Massachusetts
11 miles of trails
novice-intermediate
USGS: Lawrence/South Groveland/Wilmington/Reading

The Andover Village Improvement Society maintains a number of trails suitable for ski touring. Flat areas along the banks of the Shawsheen and Meririmack Rivers are particularly recommended. The Harold R. Rafton Reservation has steeper grades. Baber's Meadow and the Indian Ridge Reservation have good trails. The Doyle Link Trail, forming a loop between Plain Road and Lowell Street, offers 1.6 miles of intermediate skiing. Some trails are over private property; skiers should stay on the trails. Snowmobiling is prohibited. The Andover Conservation Commission has recently published an Open Space Map showing both town and AVIS lands open to the public. The map is available at the Town Clerk's Office or the Conservation Office on the first floor of the Andover Town Hall.

Driving directions: From I-93, exit at Lowell Street and follow signs to Andover. Drive for about 1 mile to the intersection of Lowell Street, Beacon Street, Shawsheen Road, and Reservation Road. Most areas are within a short distance of this intersection. Consult a map for further information.

Suggestion courtesy of Virginia H. Hammond, Andover Conservation Commission, Andover, Massachusetts.

Harold Parker State Forest
Andover/North Andover, Massachusetts
9 miles of trails/3000 acres
novice-intermediate
USGS: Reading/South Groveland

Harold Parker State Forest is characterized by primarily flat terrain with a number of natural and man-made ponds. Trails are unplowed gravel and wood roads through hardwood forest with a few pines. Most of the Forest receives heavy snowmobile use.

In the main section of the Forest, there are about 4 miles of recommended trails. The circuit around Brackett and Collins Ponds is particularly attractive, though designated for snowmobile use. The Woodchuck Hill section of the Forest is separated from the main area; skiing is on 5 miles of abandoned town and logging roads. There is a clearing at the top of the hill that is a good picnic spot. This part of the Forest is adjacent to the Charles W. Ward Reservation (see separate entry).

Driving directions: From Route 28 (Main Street) in Andover, go south to Gould Road. Turn left and cross Route 125 near the State Police headquarters. After passing between the large gateposts, bear left and follow Harold Parker Road (Mill Street), which goes through the Forest. Park along the road or in a plowed area. To reach the Woodchuck Hill area, see directions to the Charles W. Ward Reservation.

Suggestion courtesy of Virginia H. Hammond, Andover Conservation Commission, Andover, Massachusetts.

Charles W. Ward Reservation
Andover, Massachusetts
5 miles of trails
novice-intermediate-advanced
USGS: South Groveland

This is a Trustees of Reservations tract of some 595 acres of wooded highlands and lowlands. Two high hills—Holt Hill and Boston Hill—offer views of Boston, Mount Monadnock, Temple Mountain, and Mount Kearsarge. Due to the variety of terrain, the area accommodates skiers of all abilities. Some trails are narrow in spots, which makes them more difficult. There is a fire tower on the top of Holt Hill, the highest hill in Essex County. The trail over Holt and Boston Hills is 5 miles, round trip. Holt Hill Circle is 2.5 miles, and Elephant Rock Trail is 0.8 miles. A trail map is available. Snowmobiling is prohibited.

Driving directions: East of the center of Andover, Routes 114 and 125 divide. From this intersection, follow Route 125 south for about 1¾ miles, and turn left onto Prospect Road. There is a parking area off Prospect Road, close to the Reservation entrance sign.

Suggestion courtesy of Gordon Abbott, Jr., Director, The Trustees of Reservations, Milton, Massachusetts; and Virginia H. Hammond, Andover Conservation Commission, Andover, Massachusetts.

Bald Hill-Wood Hill Reservation
Andover, Massachusetts
200+ acres
novice-intermediate-advanced
USGS: Lawrence

This is a splendid area for skiing, offering vistas of the Boston skyline and the church steeples of Andover. The Reservation includes Bald Hill Drumlin and the eastern flank of Wood Hill Drumlin, with some steep slopes. A 1978 CETA project created a large parking area and a large number of trails, including a racing trail. Not all are adequately marked at this time. Trail maps are available for a portion of the Reservation; the remainder is being mapped. Trails in the eastern section join those of the adjacent Harold R. Rafton Reservation of the Andover Village Improvement Society.

Driving directions: From I-93, exit at Lowell Street (Route 133) and go east toward Andover Center. After about ¼ mile, go left at the traffic light onto Greenwood Road, and continue for 1 mile to High Plain Road. Turn left, crossing Routes 93 and 495, and park in the lot at the top of the hill.

Suggestion courtesy of Virginia H. Hammond, Andover Conservation Commission, Andover, Massachusetts.

Boxford State Forest
Boxford/North Andover, Massachusetts
7 miles of trails/500 acres
novice-intermediate
USGS: South Groveland

This undeveloped state forest has trails over rolling terrain through stands of hardwood and pine. Most trails are suitable for novices. Trails are unmarked but are not difficult to follow. Bald Hill is open to the southeast and offers views of Boston and the surrounding countryside. This area connects with trails in Boxford Wildlife Sanctuary (see separate entry). Snowmobile use is light.

Driving directions: From Route 1 in Danvers, take Route 114 northwest toward Lawrence. Turn right near the Middleton/North Andover town line onto a paved road (see accompanying map). Park at the end of the road. The Forest is not marked by signs.

Suggestion courtesy of Parker E. Gifford, Supervisor, Boxford State Forest, c/o Willowdale State Forest, Ipswich, Massachusetts.

Boxford Wildlife Sanctuary
Boxford, Massachusetts
3 miles of trails/321 acres
novice-intermediate
USGS: South Groveland/Georgetown

Managed by the Massachusetts Division of Fisheries and Wildlife, Boxford Wildlife Sanctuary is an area of gently rolling, wooded terrain. Trails connect to those in Boxford State Forest (see separate entry). Snowmobiles are prohibited.

Driving directions: From I-95, take the Middleton Road exit in Boxford. Follow Middleton Road northwest to the Sanctuary on the left. Park at the beginning of Bald Hill Road, which leads to Crooked Pond in the Sanctuary. Parking is limited.

Suggestion courtesy of Tom Sheehan, Massachusetts Division of Fisheries and Wildlife, Acton, Massachusetts.

Boxford State Forest and Boxford Wildlife Sanctuary

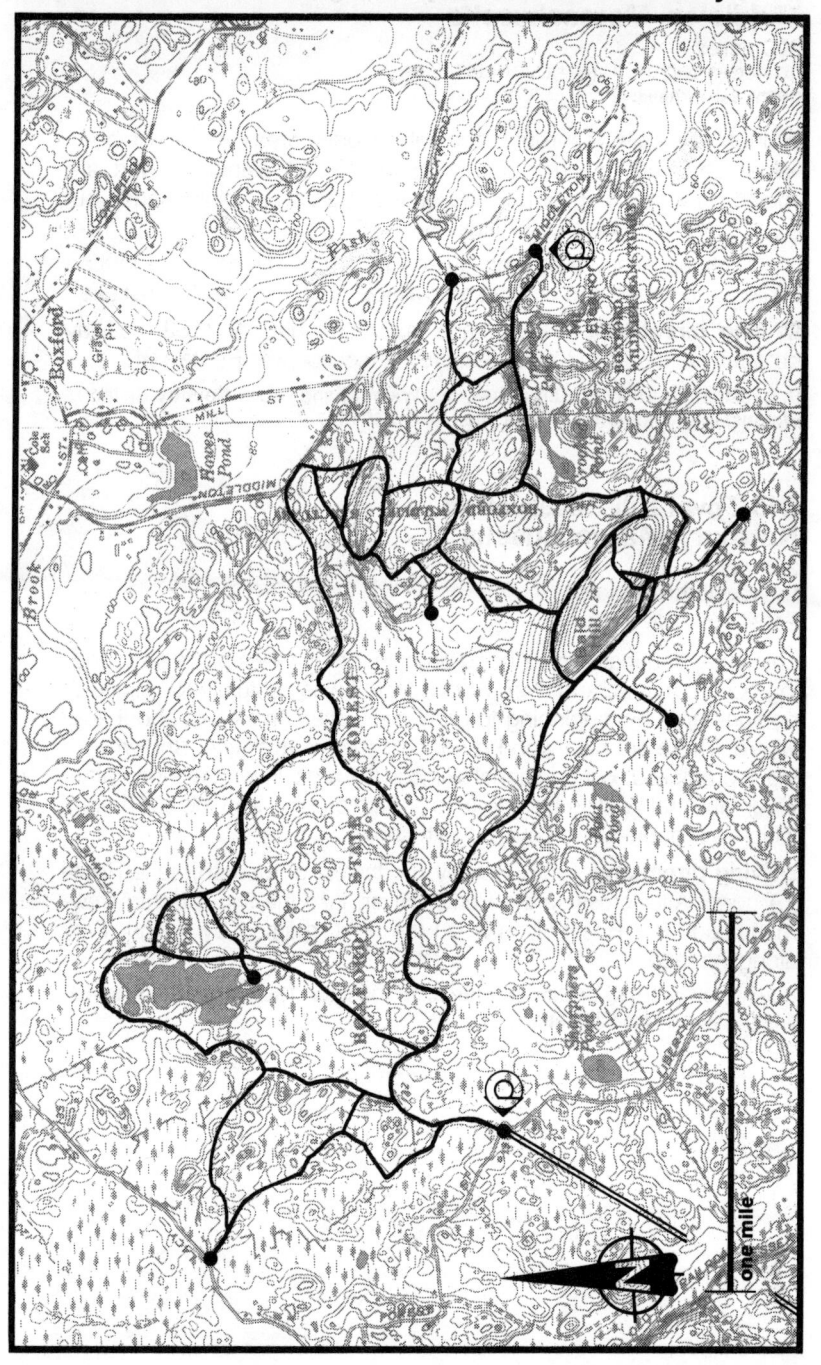

Northeastern Massachusetts

Walnut Lane Cross-Country Skiing
Middleton, Massachusetts
600 acres
novice–intermediate–advanced
USGS: Salem/Reading

Walnut Lane trails go through primarily wooded areas, with some open fields. They are marked according to NSTOA standards and are shown on a trail map. Snowmobiles are used on adjoining lands but are not permitted on the ski trails.

Rentals, instruction, and guided tours are offered at the touring center, and coffee and cocoa are available. There is a fee for trail use.

Driving directions: Walnut Lane is located on Route 62, halfway between Route 1 and I-495, near the intersection with Route 114.

Suggestion courtesy of Earl Jones, Jr., Walnut Lane Cross-Country Skiing, 7 Walnut Lane, Middleton, Massachusetts 01949 (617-774-8511).

Old Town Hill Reservation
Newbury, Massachusetts
261 acres
novice–intermediate
USGS: Newburyport East

This area, dominated by a huge drumlin, offers views of the surrounding ocean, marsh, and river. At one time it was pastureland. Although portions are now beginning to grow over, one can ski just about anywhere. There are also wood roads. No map is available. Snowmobiling is prohibited. For additional skiing in the area, investigate the Parker River National Wildlife Refuge (see separate entry) and the salt marsh, which is suitable when covered with snow.

Driving directions: From Rowley (northwest of Ipswich), take Route 1A north. After crossing the Parker River, take the first left onto Newman road. The Reservation is on the right, marked by a sign. Park along the road.

Suggestion courtesy of Gordon Abbott, Jr., Director, The Trustees of Reservations, Milton, Massachusetts.

Kents Island
Newbury, Massachusetts
1500 acres
novice-intermediate
USGS: Newburyport East/Newburyport West

This is an area of relatively easy skiing over gentle hills. Some of the area is wooded, but much is open, overlooking the Parker River and salt marsh meadows. At present there is only one trail, but with sufficient snow cover, some fields are also skiable. Snowmobiles are prohibited.

Driving directions: From Route 1 heading north, turn right on Boston Street. From Boston Street, take the first right onto Kents Island Road. The parking lot is not plowed in winter.

Suggestion courtesy of Tom Sheehan, Massachusetts Division of Fisheries and Wildlife, Acton, Massachusetts.

Crane Pond Wildlife Management Area
Newbury/Georgetown/Groveland, Massachusetts
2500 acres
novice-intermediate-advanced
USGS: Newburyport West/South Groveland/Georgetown

This is a large area managed by the Massachusetts Division of Fisheries and Wildlife. It consists of slightly rolling lowland and some swampland, with a few areas offering fine views. The trail system is composed partially of wood roads. All trails are unmarked. Snowmobile use is moderate.

Driving directions: From I-95, take Route 97 to Georgetown Square, then follow Pond Street to the area. There are no plowed parking areas. Use caution when parking along the road.

Suggestion courtesy of Tom Sheehan, Massachusetts Division of Fisheries and Wildlife, Acton, Massachusetts.

Trail map appears on following page.

Crane Pond Wildlife Management Area

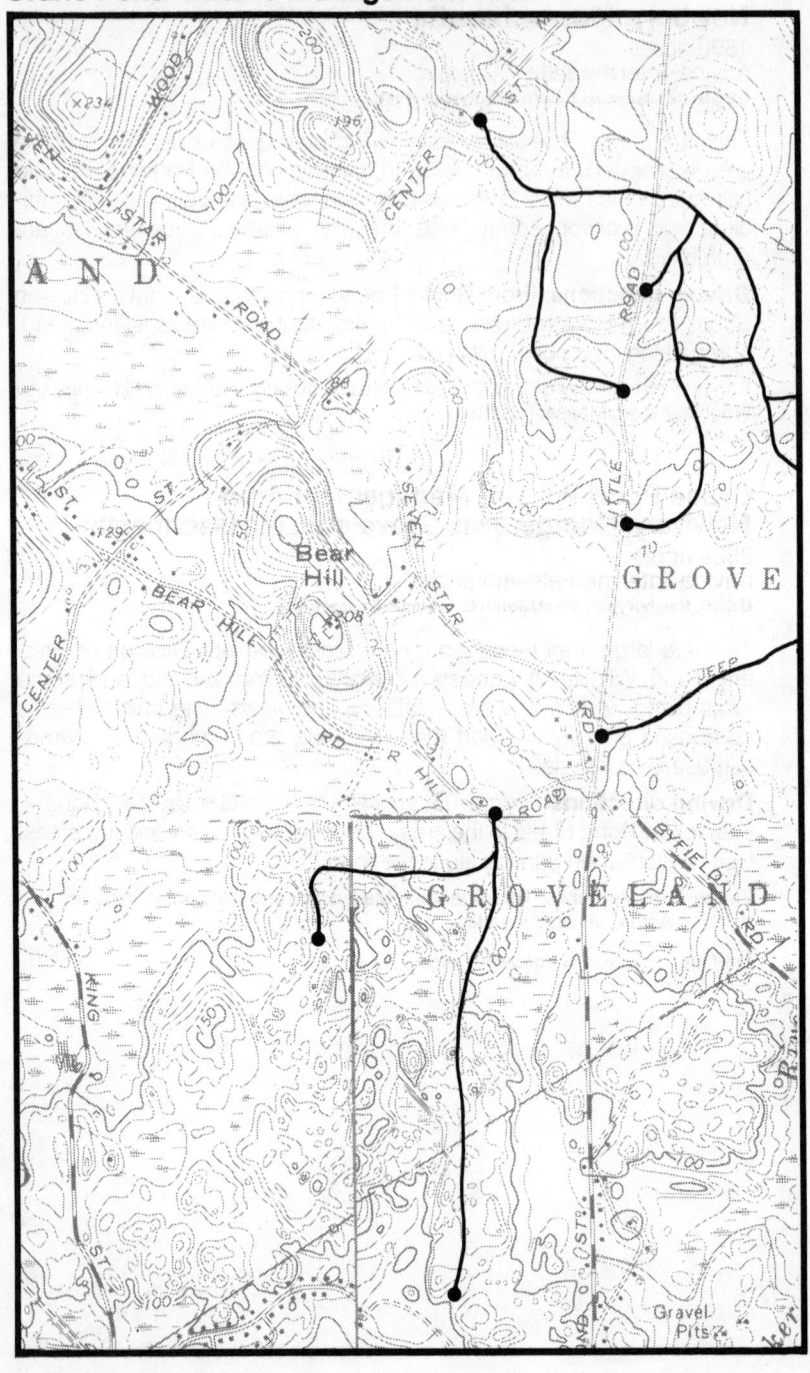

Northeastern Massachusetts

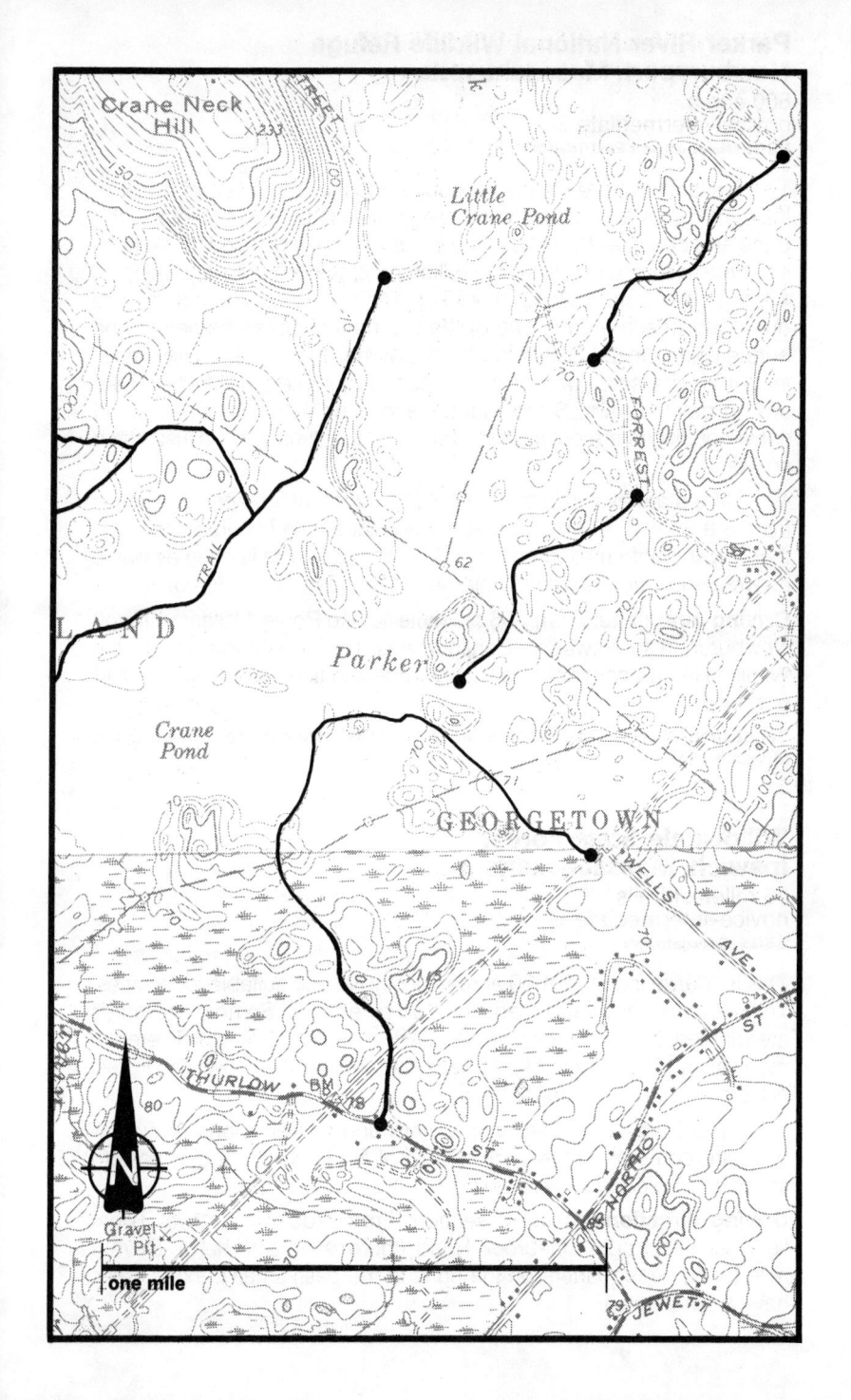

165   Northeastern Massachusetts

Parker River National Wildlife Refuge
Newburyport, Massachusetts
600 acres
novice-intermediate
USGS: Newburyport East/Ipswich

This National Wildlife Refuge occupies most of Plum Island. Most of the 4650 acres are salt- or freshwater marshes, but two sections of the dune and beach area east of the access road may be used for ski touring. One section extends from the Refuge entrance south to parking lot #3, the other from parking lot #5 south to the Refuge boundary. The dune and beach area is one of the last natural ocean barriers in the northeastern United States, and most of the dunes are heavily vegetated with grasses, low growing shrubs, and some small trees. There are no defined trails. Since Plum Island is right on the ocean, good snow conditions are often short-lived. The best time to ski is just after a snowfall.

Maps are available at the Refuge headquarters, open weekdays from 8 a.m. to 4:30 pm., and at the entrance gate (when someone is there). Other information on natural history or wildlife is often available as well. Snowmobiles are not allowed in any part of the Refuge.

Driving directions: From I-95 or Route 1, take Route 113 east through Newburyport to Newbury. Continue east to Plum Island and to the Wildlife Refuge entrance. Park only in designated lots (#1-#7, or #11 or beyond).

Suggestion courtesy of Parker River National Wildlife Refuge, Newburyport, Massachusetts.

Willowdale State Forest
Ipswich, Massachusetts
25 miles of trails
novice-intermediate
USGS: Georgetown

This is a large forest of 1600 acres, mostly flat and suitable for novices. Trails are over old wood roads through pine forest. Some of the roads are marked, but these receive the heaviest snowmobile use. There are many suitable, unmarked loop roads that are easy to follow. The Forest headquarters has trail maps.

The Forest is divided into eastern and western parts: snowmobiles are common in the section west of Route 1; the larger, eastern section is closed to snowmobiling.

Driving directions, eastern section: From Route 1 north of Topsfield, turn east onto Linebrook Road (there is no sign here). Drive 1 mile to the headquarters on the right. In the past, small parking areas have been plowed.

Driving directions, western section: From Route 1, turn west onto Linebrook Road. Follow it past the intersection of Newbury Road, shortly beyond the intersection with Rowley Road. A parking area for the Forest is on the right.

Suggestion courtesy of Parker E. Gifford, Supervisor, Willowdale State Forest, Ipswich, Massachusetts.

Bradley Palmer State Park
Topsfield/Hamilton, Massachusetts
6+ miles of trails/720 acres
novice-intermediate
USGS: Georgetown

Bradley Palmer State Park offers excellent opportunities for ski touring with its open fields and hilly terrain and developed system of wide bridle paths. Wildlife is abundant because hunting is prohibited. Separate trails are designated for snowmobiling and ski touring. Maps specifying these trails are available in limited supply at the Park headquarters. Ski touring trails are indicated by blue markers.

Driving directions: From Route 1, take Ipswich Road east for about 2½ miles to Ashbury Street. Turn right, then take the first left on the access road leading to the headquarters. Do not park on the roadways.

Suggestion courtesy of George Houghton, Supervisor, Bradley Palmer State Park, Topsfield, Massachusetts.

Southeastern Massachusetts and Rhode Island Ski Touring Areas

1. Stow Town Forest, Stow   170
2. Great Meadows National Wildlife Refuge, Concord   170
3. Walden Pond State Reservation, Concord   170
4. Lincoln Conservation Commission and Lincoln Land Trust, Lincoln   171
   Lincoln Guide Service, Lincoln   171
5. R.J. Callahan State Park, Framingham   172
6. Nobscot Scout Reservation, Framingham/Sudbury   172
7. Breakheart Reservation, Saugus/Wakefield   173
8. Middlesex Fells Reservation, Stoneham/Medford/Winchester/Melrose/Malden   173
9. Lynn Woods, Lynn   174
   Lynn Woods Ski Touring Center, Lynn   174
10. Charles River, Boston/Cambridge   175
11. Weston Ski Track, Weston   175
12. Newton Recreation Areas, Newton   176
13. Brookline Reservoir, Brookline   176
    Larz Anderson Park, Brookline   177
    Putterham Meadows Golf Course, Brookline   177
14. Rocky Woods Reservation, Medfield   178
15. Hale Reservation, Westwood   178
16. Blue Hills Reservation, Milton/Quincy/Canton/Randolph   179
17. Ponkapoag Pond, Canton/Randolph   179
    Ponkapoag Outdoor Center, Canton   180
18. Borderland State Park, Easton/Sharon   180
19. World's End, Hingham   180
20. Whitney and Thayer Woods Reservation, Cohasset/Hingham   181
21. Pulaski State Park, Burrillville, Rhode Island   181
22. Beach Pond Parks, Exeter/West Greenwich, Rhode Island   182
23. Caratunk Wildlife Refuge, Seekonk   182
24. Freetown–Fall River State Forest, Assonet   183
25. Myles Standish State Forest, Plymouth/Carver   183
26. Sandy Neck, Barnstable   184
27. Nickerson State Park, Brewster   184
28. Great Island, Wellfleet   185

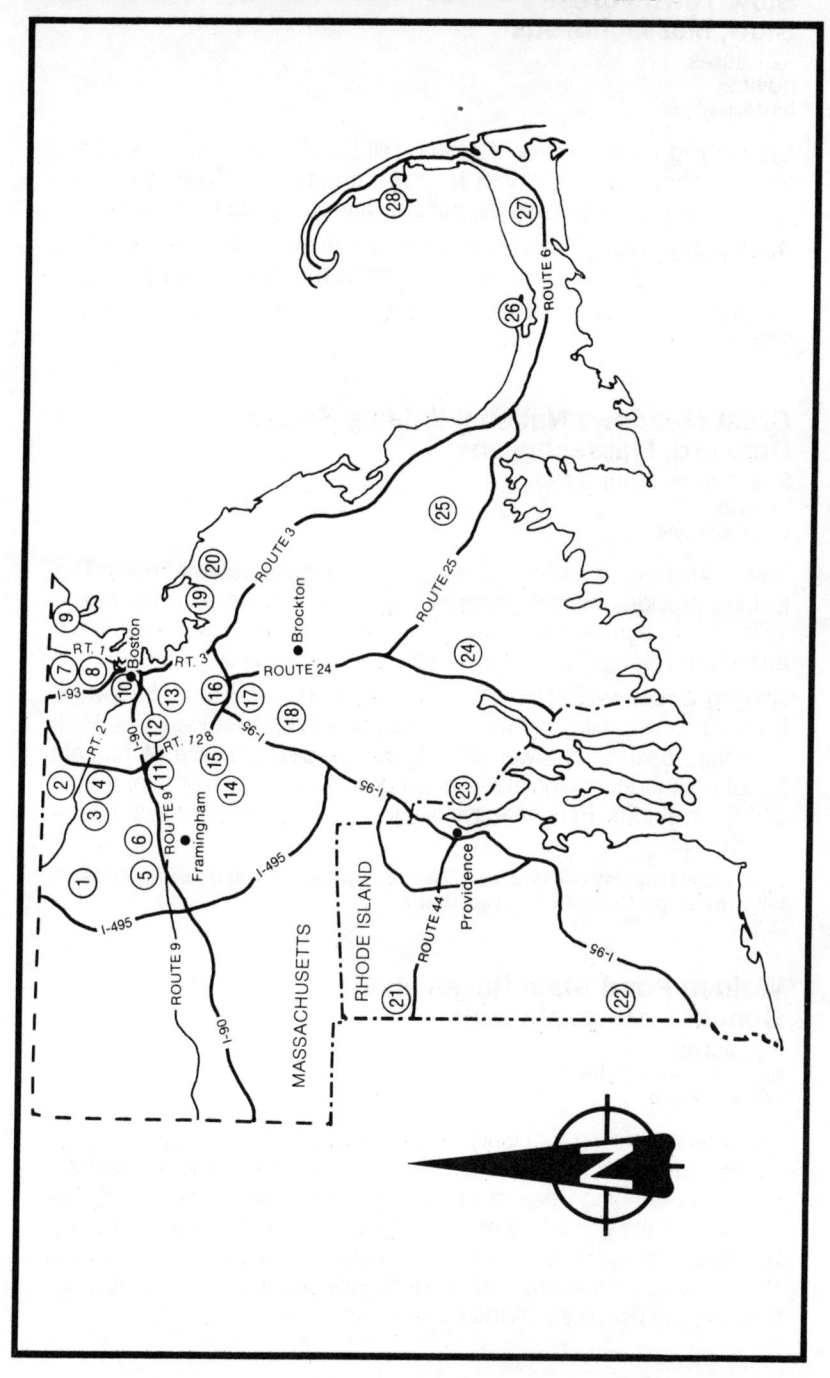

Southeastern Massachusetts and Rhode Island

Stow Town Forest
Stow, Massachusetts
324 acres
novice
USGS: Maynard

Old logging roads in Stow Gardner Hill Land have colored markers and are shown on the USGS Maynard quadrangle. Trails are occasionally used by snowmobiles, but they are prohibited on Sundays.

Driving directions: From Stow, drive east on Great Road (Route 117), and turn right onto Bradley Lane. Park at the end of the plowed road.

Suggestion courtesy of Stow Conservation Commission, Stow, Massachusetts.

Great Meadows National Wildlife Refuge
Concord, Massachusetts
2 or 4 miles, round trip
novice
USGS: Concord

This is a flat marsh and river bottom land along the Concord River. The Refuge provides habitat for many species of wildlife and has nature trails and an observation tower. Ski on dikes, nature trails, or along the abandoned railroad bed. Snowmobiles are prohibited.

Driving directions: From Concord Common, take Route 62 toward Bedford for 1.2 miles to Monsen Road and follow Refuge signs. Park near the observation tower and ski on the dike. Or take Monument Street next to the Colonial Inn and continue to the parking lot for the Old North Bridge. Park here and ski down the road bordering the lot on the east side.

Suggestion courtesy of David Beall, Refuge Manager, Great Meadows National Wildlife Refuge, Concord, Massachusetts.

Walden Pond State Reservation
Concord, Massachusetts
300 acres
novice–intermediate
USGS: Concord

This was the setting for Henry David Thoreau's *Walden*. When frozen, the 65-acre pond may be used for skiing, and there are several trails on the surrounding Reservation land. Terrain is hilly and wooded. The trail around the pond (1.9 miles) is shared with snowshoers and may be heavily traveled. A longer tour is possible by skiing from Walden Pond to Lincoln on conservation lands (see separate entry). Snowmobiles are not permitted on the Reservation.

Driving directions: From Route 2, go south on Route 126. Park in the lot on the right, about 0.4 miles from Route 2.

Suggestion courtesy of Walden Pond State Reservation, Concord, Massachusetts.

Lincoln Conservation Commission and Lincoln Land Trust
Lincoln, Massachusetts
about 12 miles of trails
novice-intermediate
USGS: Concord

The town of Lincoln has an extensive network of trails on public and private lands, some of which are good for ski touring. The Conservation Commission offers an excellent ski touring map showing designated trails around Mount Misery, Sandy Pond, and Walden Pond State Reservation (see separate entry). These trails are on predominantly public lands and are marked with signs and yellow plastic discs. It is possible to ski short loops, or to make longer tours by skiing from one area to another. Maps are distributed in parking areas where there is an attendant, such as the one near the Lincoln railroad station.

Driving directions: There are four designated parking areas. One is at Walden Pond State Reservation in Concord; see separate entry for driving directions. Another is off Lincoln Road by the railroad tracks, just north of Route 117. To get to Mount Misery, go west on Route 117 for 0.7 miles past Route 126. The parking area is on the right. To ski near Sandy Pond, park next to Smith School, off Lincoln Road between Route 117 and Lincoln Center.

Suggestion courtesy of William Preston, Lincoln Conservation Commission and Lincoln Land Trust, Lincoln, Massachusetts.

Lincoln Guide Service
Lincoln, Massachusetts
20 acres
novice-intermediate
USGS: Concord

The Lincoln Guide Service shop offers a number of services and programs, using primarily Lincoln town conservation land (see preceding entry). The shop has waxing rooms and a snack bar and offers rentals, instruction, and guided tours.

Driving directions: Lincoln Guide Service is on Lincoln Road at the railroad tracks just north of Route 117.

Suggestion courtesy of Mike Farny, Lincoln Guide Service, Lincoln, Massachusetts 01773 (617-259-9204).

R. J. Callahan State Park
Framingham, Massachusetts
about 7 miles of trails/425 acres
novice–intermediate
USGS: Framingham

This State Park is mostly wooded, gently rolling land, with many open fields. Trails consist of wood roads, hiking trails, and bridle paths. They are well marked and easy to follow; trail maps are available at Cochituate State Park. Snowmobiles are prohibited. There are additional trails on the adjacent Sudbury Valley Trustee Land.

Driving directions: From Exit 12 off the Massachusetts Turnpike (I-90), drive east on Route 9 to Framingham Center. Turn north on Edgell Road, and continue for about 0.3 mile to Belknap Road. Turn left and drive for ½ mile to Millwood Street; turn right and continue for about 0.3 mile to the Park entrance, opposite the Millwood Farm Golf Course. Parking may be a problem since there is no plowed area.

Suggestion courtesy of Jonathan M. Geer, Forest and Park Supervisor, Cochituate State Park, Cochituate, Massachusetts 01778.

Nobscot Scout Reservation
Framingham/Sudbury, Massachusetts
600+ acres
novice–intermediate
USGS: Framingham

Nobscot Scout Reservation, a training camp for the Norumbega Council, Boy Scouts of America, includes approximately 15 miles of old roads and trails. Terrain is mostly rolling upland, with one large, nearly flat section especially suited to novice use. An area cleared years ago for a proposed rope tow can be used as a practice slope. Use is very light on weekdays; moderate to heavy on weekends. Maps are available from the ranger. Motorized vehicles, other than camp service vehicles, are not permitted on the Reservation.

Visitors are required to register with the ranger before entering the property. On several weekends during the ski season the Reservation is closed to visitors; check in advance (617-443-5161). Fires are not permitted. Water is available near the ranger's cabin. All users are asked to stay out of cabins and other structures reserved for Scout use. Trails are not maintained or patrolled. For overnight use (fee and advance reservations required), organized groups may apply to Norumbega Council, B.S.A., 2044 Beacon Street, Waban, Massachusetts 02168 (617-332-2220).

Driving directions: From Route 128, go west on Route 20 to South Sudbury. After passing the Sudbury Plaza shopping center on the left, take a sharp left onto Nobscot Road (just past the railroad tracks). Continue for 1 mile to the entrance to Nobscot Reservation on the right. Park in the outer lot and register at the ranger's cabin.

Suggestion courtesy of the Camping Committee (Fred Berman, Chairman), Norumbega Council, B.S.A., Waban, Massachusetts.

Breakheart Reservation
Saugus/Wakefield, Massachusetts
6 miles of trails
intermediate
USGS: Boston North

This is a fairly rough area of rock outcroppings and woodland maintained by the Metropolitan District Commission. Skiing is on unplowed paved roads. The foot trails have not been cleared recently and are difficult to follow. Maps are available at the Reservation for $.25. Snowmobiling is prohibited.

Driving directions: From Route 1 in Saugus, take Main Street west. Turn right onto the Lynn Fells Parkway, then left on Forest Street, which is the main entrance to the Reservation. Park behind the maintenance building.

Suggestion courtesy of MDC Parks, Middlesex Fells Division, Stoneham, Massachusetts.

Middlesex Fells Reservation
Stoneham/Medford/Winchester/
Melrose/Malden, Massachusetts
400 acres
novice-intermediate
USGS: Boston North/Lexington

This Reservation is maintained by the Metropolitan District Commission. There are several miles of skiing on wood roads, bridle paths, and hiking trails. Numerous brooks and ponds make this a pleasant area to explore. Although near the city, the area resembles New Hampshire woodlands. Terrain is variable but seldom steep. Trails are not marked, but trail maps are available at the office during working hours, Monday through Friday. Snowmobiles are prohibited.

Driving directions, eastern section: From Fellsway West in Medford, go east on Elm Street to the rotary. Continue north on Woodland Road. Park along the road or in the parking lot near the skating rink, just south of the New England Sanitarium.

Driving directions, western section: To reach the southern end of this section, go west on South Border Road from the Fellsway West, and park along the road. To reach the northern side, follow Fellsway West to North Border Road. Turn left and park along the road.

Suggestion courtesy of MDC Parks, Middlesex Fells Division, Stoneham, Massachusetts.

Lynn Woods
Lynn, Massachusetts
12+ miles of trails
novice-intermediate
USGS: Lynn

This is a primarily wooded area, including a pond and a chain of granite hills. There are views of the ocean from a number of locations and views of the New Hampshire mountains from the stone tower on Burrill Hill. Skiing is on unplowed roads. A large map of the area may be obtained from the Lynn Parks Department for $.50. Both the northern and southern sections are heavily used on weekends.

Driving directions, southern section: Take the Walnut Street (Lynn) exit off Route 1 in Saugus. Go past the reservoir on the right, and turn left at the lights onto Pennybrook Road. The entrance to Lynn Woods is at the end of the road.

Driving directions, northern section: Take the Lynnfield Street exit off Route 1 in Lynnfield. Continue for several miles to Great Woods Road by Sluice Pond. The western gate parking area is at the end of the road.

Lynn Woods Ski Touring Center
Lynn, Massachusetts
2200 acres
novice-intermediate
USGS: Lynn

Trails wind over a golf course and follow fire roads in Lynn Woods (see separate entry). They are being marked, and maps are available. The Touring Center offers rentals, instruction, and guided tours, with special group rates. There is a large area for relaxing, and refreshments are available.

Driving directions: From Boston, go north on Route 1 for about 15 miles, then east 2 miles on Route 129.

Suggestion courtesy of Bob Williamson, Lynn Woods Ski Touring Center, Great Woods Terrace, Lynn, Massachusetts 01904 (617-598-4212).

Charles River
Boston/Cambridge, Massachusetts
novice
USGS: Boston South/Newton

With good snow, there is fine skiing along the banks of the Charles River. Icy footprints can be annoying, so it is best to ski on new snow. The section closest to downtown Boston is good for night skiing. A good starting point is behind the Boston University Chapel off Commonwealth Avenue, east of the B.U. Bridge. There is a walkway over Storrow Drive. The area close to Harvard Stadium, along Soldiers Field Road, is also nice and a little quieter. There are parking areas off Soldiers Field Road. The Cambridge side of the river is also good for skiing. The section opposite Soldiers Field Road can be reached via Greenough Street.

Suggestion courtesy of the Metropolitan District Commission, Boston, Massachusetts.

Weston Ski Track
Weston, Massachusetts
300 acres
novice–intermediate
USGS: Natick

The landscaped, open areas and gently rolling terrain of the Leo J. Martin Golf Course are especially suited to novice skiers. There is skiing on both sides of a very attractive stretch of the Charles River. Trails are well marked, and a map is available. Trails are lighted for evening use and have snowmaking to provide good conditions when snowfall has been inadequate. Snowmobiles are not permitted.

The touring center is at the golf course club house and has been developed especially as a beginners' instruction center. Facilities include a waxing room, locker and shower rooms, snack bar, and retail shop. Rentals, instruction (including evening instruction), and guided tours are available. There is a trail fee.

Driving directions: From Route 30 heading west, take the first left after Route 128, following signs for the Massachusetts Turnpike. Go straight, past the entrance to the Turnpike. The touring center is on the left about 0.3 mile after the railroad underpass. From Route 16 heading west, go right at the traffic light in Newton Lower Falls (before Route 16 crosses the river). Continue on that road until it crosses the river into Weston. There is ample parking at the touring center.

Suggestion courtesy of the Metropolitan District Commission, Boston, Massachusetts.

Newton Recreation Areas
Newton, Massachusetts
novice
USGS: Newton/Natick

Edmands Park, Blake Street, Newtonville; 32 acres. This park has lots of woods, trails, a pond, and some open land on rolling terrain.

Driving directions: From Commonwealth Avenue in Newton, go north on Centre Street, then turn left onto Mill Street. The park is on the right. Park along the street.

Auburndale Park, West Pine Street, Auburndale, 30 acres. This recreation area provides open space along the Charles River.

Driving directions: From Commonwealth Avenue in Auburndale, drive north on Melrose Street, then turn left onto West Pine Street. There is a plowed parking area.

Webster Conservation Land, Warren Street, Newton Centre. This is a sizeable parcel of wooded land. The area is flat; trails are unmarked but easily followed.

Driving directions: Access is from the west side of Hammond Pond. Parking is off the Hammond Pond Parkway, north of Route 9.

Cold Springs Recreation Park, Newton Highlands, 65 acres. This is a fairly large park traversed by an aqueduct that is suitable for skiing. There are also several open areas.

Driving directions: From the intersection of Beacon and Walnut Streets in Newton Highlands, go south on Walnut Street. Turn right onto Duncklee Road and continue to the parking area.

Infirmary Land, Oak Hill, 25 acres. This is a fairly flat, open area along the Charles River, away from residential areas.

Driving directions: From Route 9 in Newton Highlands, go south on Needham Street. Bear left on Winchester Street at Countryside Pharmacy and continue to the Charles River Country Club. The infirmary land is across the street from the Club.

Suggestion courtesy of Marge Lesbirel, Newton Recreation Department, Newton, Massachusetts.

Brookline Reservoir
Brookline, Massachusetts
32 acres
novice
USGS: Newton

This is a small but pretty spot with flat terrain. It is possible to ski a one-mile loop around the Reservoir. Since the area is used for jogging, icy footprints may be a problem. The best place to ski is south of the Reservoir; there is more land and enough light for night skiing. Snowmobiles are prohibited.

Driving directions: The Reservoir is bordered by Route 9 to the north and Lee Street to the west. From Brookline Village, drive west for about 1 mile on Route 9, then turn left on Warren Street. Take the first right onto Dudley Street. Park along the east side of the Reservoir.

Suggestion courtesy of Brookline Parks and Recreation Commission, Brookline, Massachusetts.

Larz Anderson Park
Brookline, Massachusetts
80 acres
novice
USGS: Newton

This is a hilly, open area close to downtown Boston. People walk here, but footprints are generally not a problem. Snowmobiles are prohibited.

Driving directions: From Brookline Village, drive west on Route 9 for about 1.4 miles. Turn left onto Lee Street, just past Brookline Reservoir. Continue to Clyde Street, and turn left onto Newton Street. The main entrance is to the left, ¼ mile from Clyde Street. Parking is also available in a small lot off Goddard Street. To reach Goddard Street, take the first left fork off Newton Street; the lot is on the right.

Suggestion courtesy of Brookline Parks and Recreation Commission, Brookline, Massachusetts.

Putterham Meadows Golf Course
Brookline, Massachusetts
5 miles around course
novice
USGS: Newton

This open area is excellent for ski touring, especially for beginners. Skiing is along fairways over low, gentle hills. Snowmobiles are not allowed.

Driving directions: From Brookline Village, take Route 9 west to Lee Street. Turn left and continue south to Clyde Street. Turn right onto Newton Street and, after ¾ mile, bear right following Newton Street. The golf course entrance is about ½ mile ahead on the right.

Suggestion courtesy of Brookline Parks and Recreation Commission, Brookline, Massachusetts.

Rocky Woods Reservation
Medfield, Massachusetts
12 miles of trails
novice-intermediate
USGS: Medfield

This is a pleasant area of 441 acres with open woods and extensive trails. A few sections have fairly steep climbs, but they are rewarding. Cedar Hill, with a lookout tower, offers good views. Chickering Pond, about 5 acres in size, offers a unique ice skating program. The Reservation is open from 10:30 AM to sunset and is closed on Mondays. Equipment rentals and trail maps are available. Snowmobiling is prohibited.

Driving directions: From the center of Medfield, take Route 109 northeast for approximately 1½ miles to Hartford Street. Bear left. Proceed on Hartford Street for about 0.6 mile to the Reservation entrance on the left. There is a $1.00 admission fee.

Suggestion courtesy of Gordon Abbott, Jr., Director, The Trustees of Reservations, Milton, Massachusetts.

Hale Reservation
Westwood, Massachusetts
16 miles of trails
novice-intermediate
USGS: Norwood/Medfield

The 1200-acre Hale Reservation has a system of trails, mostly over old cart roads, that wind through hilly forest terrain, along the edges of ponds, across brooks, and through meadows. All trails are groomed with set tracks and are well marked. Maps are available. Snowmobiles are not permitted in the area. Hale Reservation trails connect with those of the Powissett Farm, which has 1000 acres open to skiing.

There is a warming hut with rest rooms at the Reservation. Rentals, instruction, a ski safety patrol, and guided natural history tours are available. The trail fee is $2.00 for adults, $1.00 for children.

Driving directions: From Route 128, take Route 109 west to Dover Road, then turn onto Carby Street and continue to the Reservation.

Suggestion courtesy of Leonard Myers, Hale Reservation, 80 Carby Street, Westwood, Massachusetts 02090.

Blue Hills Reservation
Milton/Quincy/Canton/Randolph, Massachusetts
novice-intermediate
USGS: Blue Hills

This is a large area with an extensive trail system close to downtown Boston and maintained by the Metropolitan District Commission. Skiing is possible on numerous hiking trails, bridle paths, and unplowed roads. Trails are shown on the AMC Blue Hills Reservation map, and some are described in the AMC *Massachusetts and Rhode Island Trail Guide*. Maps are also available at the MDC Police Station on Hillside Street.

Driving directions: To park near the MDC Police station, take the Blue Hills Parkway south from Mattapan, which turns into Unquity Road. Just after Unquity Road joins Hillside Street, the police station appears on the right. To park near Great Blue Hill, go south from Mattapan on Route 138 (Blue Hill Avenue), which becomes Washington Street. The parking area is on the left shortly beyond the Trailside Museum.

Suggestion courtesy of the Metropolitan District Commission, Boston, Massachusetts.

Ponkapoag Pond
Canton/Randolph, Massachusetts
novice
USGS: Blue Hills

There is a network of trails around Ponkapoag Pond and a golf course on the western shore. It is possible to ski a 3½-mile circuit around the pond on old, unplowed roads. Trails are shown on the AMC Blue Hills Reservation map, and on a map available from the MDC Police headquarters on Hillside Street. Some of the trails are described in the AMC *Massachusetts and Rhode Island Trail Guide*. Snowmobiling is restricted.

Driving directions: From Route 128, take Route 138 south through Ponkapoag. Turn left onto Randolph Street. After 1.2 miles there is a riding stable on the right and a crosswalk opposite the driveway to the stables. Park here and ski in on the unplowed road that leads into the woods on the left.

Suggestion courtesy of the Metropolitan District Commission, Boston, Massachusetts.

Ponkapoag Outdoor Center
Canton, Massachusetts
1200 acres
novice–intermediate
USGS: Blue Hills

The YMCA Ponkapoag Outdoor Center uses Reservation trails in the vicinity of Ponkapoag Pond (see separate entry). Main cross-country ski trails are marked, and MDC trail maps are available. Interesting natural features in the area include the pond, the quaking bog, and marsh areas. Snowmobiles are not permitted. Snowshoe and ski rentals and instruction are available.

Driving directions: From Route 128, take Exit 65 and head south on the dirt road. The Outdoor Center and parking area are indicated by signs, about ¾ mile from Route 128. Parking is limited to people who are renting equipment.

Suggestion courtesy of Laura Burke, Ponkapoag Outdoor Center, Greater Boston YMCA, Canton, Massachusetts 02021 (617-696-4520).

Borderland State Park
Easton/Sharon, Massachusetts
5 miles of trails
novice
USGS: Mansfield

Ski touring trails are over old roads through the woods and over farmland. This park offers a nice 3-mile loop around Leach Pond. The loop can be shortened by taking the road between the pond and the overflow area. Trails are not marked. Maps are available at the Park headquarters. The park is closed to snowmobiling.

Driving directions: From Sharon, take Pond Street south to Massapoag Avenue. Continue past Massapoag Lake to the Park headquarters on the left.

Suggestion courtesy of the Massachusetts Department of Natural Resources, Division of Forests and Parks, Boston, Massachusetts.

World's End
Hingham, Massachusetts
250 acres
novice–intermediate–advanced
USGS: Hull/Nantasket Beach

The reservation consists of two drumlins—one jutting into Boston Harbor, the other on the mainland, joined by a narrow beach. There are rolling, open pastures and unplowed roads lined with hardwoods. The area closes at sundown. There is a charge of $1.00 per person 15 years of age or older. Snowmobiles are prohibited.

Driving directions: From Route 3A north of Hingham, take Summer Street northeast at the Hingham traffic circle, and turn north onto Martin's Lane. There is a parking area for the reservation at the end of the lane.

Suggestion courtesy of Gordon Abbott, Jr., Director, The Trustees of Reservations, Milton, Massachusetts.

Whitney and Thayer Woods Reservation
Cohasset/Hingham, Massachusetts
12 miles of trails
novice–intermediate
USGS: Cohasset

This is a wooded, hilly area of 783 acres with a view of Cohasset Harbor from Turkey Hill. Major trails are the Howe's Lane Trail (1 mile), Boulder Lane Trail (¾ mile), Whitney Road Trail (1¾ miles), Turkey Hill Loop (1½ miles), and the Swamp Border Trail (⅞ mile). These and other trails are described in the AMC *Massachusetts and Rhode Island Trail Guide.* Snowmobiling is prohibited.

Wompatuck State Park, which adjoins the Reservation on the west, is also an excellent area for ski touring.

Driving directions: The entrance to the Reservation is on the south side of Route 3A, opposite Sohier Street, east of Hingham Center. Parking is limited.

Suggestion courtesy of Gordon Abbott, Jr., Director, The Trustees of Reservations, Milton, Massachusetts.

Pulaski State Park
Burrillville, Rhode Island
13 miles of trails
novice–intermediate–advanced
USGS: Thompson

The state of Rhode Island grooms and tracks several trails in Pulaski State Park. They form loops that begin and end at the warm-up hut and are designed to be skied one way. All are well marked, and trail maps are available.

The State Park has a warm-up hut with a wood stove and tables and a heated sanitary facility. There are a number of ski touring programs, including indoor workshops, guided tours, winter natural history tours, and free instruction.

Driving directions: From I-295, take Route 44 west to Glocester. Turn right at the entrance sign and continue for 1 mile to the parking area.

Suggestion courtesy of Kenneth Rogers, Pulaski State Park, Glocester, Rhode Island.

Beach Pond Parks
Exeter/West Greenwich, Rhode Island
15-20,000 acres
novice-intermediate-advanced
USGS: Hope Valley

There are numerous hiking trails and unplowed roads in Dawley, Arcadia, and Beach Pond State Parks that are good for ski touring. They are shown on a map that is available from the Beach Pond Park Caretaker, Escoheag Hill, Escoheag, Rhode Island 02821; they are also shown on the AMC Interpark Trails map. Snowmobiles use the trails, mostly on weekends.

Driving directions: From I-95, go west on Route 165 and turn right at the Escoheag Post Office. There are several free parking areas.

Suggestion courtesy of Kenneth G. Melbourne, Park Caretaker Foreman, Escoheag, Rhode Island.

Caratunk Wildlife Refuge
Seekonk, Massachusetts
about 5 miles of trails
novice
USGS: East Providence

The Refuge has 159 acres of abandoned farmland, with fields and woodlands, ponds and a stream. Trails were cut for hiking, so there are a few rough spots, but most sections are suitable for novice skiers. Maps are available at the Refuge. Snowmobiles are prohibited.

Various ski touring programs are held at the Refuge, snow conditions permitting. These include instruction, natural history tours, and moonlight skiing. Contact the Refuge for further information.

Driving directions: Caratunk Wildlife Refuge is located on Brown Avenue, off Route 152 in Seekonk, Massachusetts, 7 miles east of Providence, Rhode Island. There is a $1.00 parking fee; members of the Audubon Society of Rhode Island may park for free.

Suggestion courtesy of Carolyn Stefanik, Audubon Society of Rhode Island, Caratunk Wildlife Refuge, Brown Avenue, Seekonk, Massachusetts 02771 (617-761-8230).

Freetown-Fall River State Forest
Assonet, Massachusetts
5500 acres
novice
USGS: Assonet/Fall River East

This is a gently rolling, wooded area with old logging roads for trails. Snow cover here is more reliable than at Myles Standish State Forest, but there is quite a bit of snowmobile activity.

Driving directions: From Route 128, take Route 24 south. Take the Assonet exit. Drive through town, and take Route 79 north. Cross the river and take Slab Bridge Road straight, where Route 79 veers sharply left. Park at the State Forest headquarters.

Suggestion courtesy of the Massachusetts Department of Natural Resources, Division of Forests and Parks, Boston, Massachusetts.

Myles Standish State Forest
Plymouth/Carver, Massachusetts
14,000 acres
novice
USGS: Wareham

This is a large area of gently rolling terrain with skiable roads, trails, and firebreaks. It is wooded except for some small open fields that serve as bird feeding stations. There are numerous ponds. Snow cover is inadequate at times. It would be best to ski immediately after a storm; even then the snow tends to be wet. Snowmobile use can be heavy here.

Driving directions: From Route 128, take Route 24, then Route 25 south. Get off at the Route 58 interchange, 10 miles south of Middleboro. Go north on Route 58, and when it turns sharply to the left, go straight ahead, continuing past the South Carver Post Office. Take the next right onto Cranberry Road. Drive 2 miles on Cranberry Road; the State Forest headquarters and parking area are on the left. From Route 3 heading south, take Exit 5, and turn right onto Long Pond Road. Continue to the State Forest sign, and follow signs to the headquarters.

Suggestion courtesy of Philip Whitten, Senior Forest and Park Superintendent, Myles Standish State Forest, South Carver, Massachusetts.

Sandy Neck
Barnstable, Massachusetts
12 miles, round trip
novice
USGS: Hyannis

From the parking area, ski along the beach, and return by way of a jeep trail between the dunes and the salt marsh. There are several short trails between the two, so it is possible to ski loops of varying lengths. Views are of Cape Cod Bay to the north and of Barnstable Harbor to the south. As with other beach areas, Sandy Neck is best skied right after a storm.

Driving directions: From Sandwich, go west on Route 6A, and turn left (south) onto Sandy Neck Road. From Barnstable, go east on Route 6A and turn right. Park at the end of the road.

Suggestion courtesy of Brad Amer, Hyannis, Massachusetts.

Nickerson State Park
Brewster, Massachusetts
1778 acres
novice
USGS: Harwich

Nickerson State Park has a network of bicycle trails that are excellent for skiing when there is sufficient snow cover. This is a lovely area, with pine forests and several ponds. Maps may be obtained at the shop office, near the main entrance, until 4:30 PM.

Driving directions: Nickerson State Park is south of Route 6A, about 3 miles west of Route 6.

Suggestion courtesy of Brad Amer, Hyannis, Massachusetts.

Great Island
Wellfleet, Massachusetts
6 miles, round trip
novice
USGS: Wellfleet

This is a lovely area of pine forests, salt marshes, and beaches, with nice views of Cape Cod Bay and Wellfleet Harbor. The trail follows an old road the length of the peninsula, with a short side loop to the site of an old tavern. Good snow conditions are short-lived, and winds can occasionally mix sand with the snow to render it unskiable, so Great Island is best skied immediately after a storm.

Driving directions: From Route 6 in Wellfleet, take the Wellfleet Center exit. Turn left at the Town Pier sign onto Chequesset Neck Road, and continue to the end of the road. The trail begins at the parking area.

Suggestion courtesy of Brad Amer, Hyannis, Massachusetts.

Western Massachusetts Ski Touring Areas

1. Taconic Crest Trail, Petersburg, New York *188*
2. R.R.R. Brooks Trail, Williamstown *188*
3. Notch Road, Mount Greylock State Reservation, North Adams *190*
   Bellows Pipe Trail, North Adams *190*
   Hopper Trail, South Williamstown *191*
   Appalachian Trail on Saddle Ball Mountain, Adams *194*
4. Spruce Hill, Florida/Savoy *194*
5. Stump Sprouts Ski Touring, Charlemont *195*
6. Notchview Reservation, Windsor *196*
7. Cummington Farm Ski Touring Center, Cummington *196*
8. D.A.R. State Forest, Goshen *197*
9. Conway State Forest, Conway *200*
10. Bucksteep Manor Ski Touring Center, Washington *200*
11. Hickory Hill Touring Center, Worthington *202*
12. The Center at Foxhollow, Lenox *202*
13. Oak n' Spruce Resort, South Lee *203*
14. Tyringham Cobble Reservation, Tyringham *203*
15. Riverrun North, Sheffield *204*
16. Butternut Ski Touring, Great Barrington *204*
17. Red Fox Ski Touring Center, New Marlborough *205*
18. Otis Ridge Ski Center, Otis *205*
19. Northfield Mountain Ski Touring Center, Northfield *206*
20. Stratton Mountain Tour, Northfield/Warwick *206*
21. Bearsden Conservation Area, Athol *208*
22. Birch Hill Wildlife Management Area, Winchendon/Royalston/Templeton *209*
23. Mount Orient and Poverty Mountain, Pelham *210*
    Metacomet-Monadnock Trail, Southwick Massachusetts to Jaffrey, New Hampshire *209*
24. Ware River Watershed, Hubbardston/Barre/Rutland/Oakham *212*
25. Peaceful Acres Touring Center, Hubbardston *212*
    Hubbardston Wildlife Management Area, Hubbardston *213*
26. Wilder Ski Track, Springfield *213*
27. Quaboag Wildlife Management Area, Brookfield/West Brookfield *214*

Western Massachusetts

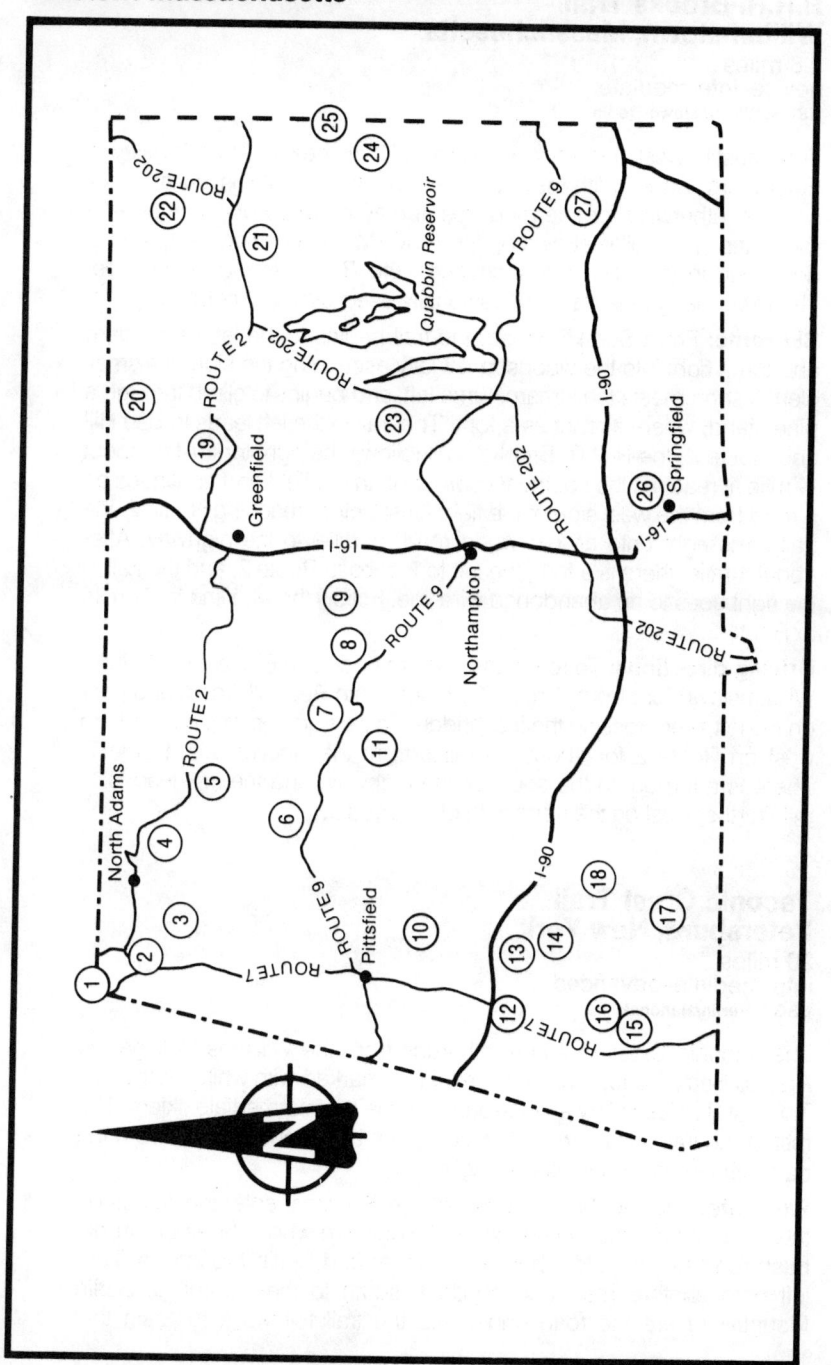

R.R.R. Brooks Trail
Williamstown, Massachusetts
2.8 miles
novice–intermediate
USGS: Williamstown/Berlin

From east to west, this trail ascends a strikingly beautiful brook valley to Petersburg Pass. With new powder snow, the trail is suitable for novices, otherwise for intermediates. It may be skied one way or as a round trip. The trail is shown on the AMC, Mount Greylock map and is described in the AMC *Massachusetts and Rhode Island Trail Guide*. The lower half of the trail is occasionally used by snowmobiles.

Ski route: From Bee Hill Road, the trail begins to the left of the dam and turns right into the woods, gradually ascending the side of a small glen. It soon meets the stream, turns left, and begins to climb through a pine stand, where it reaches a fork. The trail to the left leads to Bee Hill and Route 2; the R.R.R. Brooks Trail follows the right fork. After about ¾ mile, it reaches the southeast corner of an old field and continues on a road from the west side of the field. Just before reaching Route 2, the trail turns right onto an old wood road, parallel to the highway. After about 1 mile, there is a fork; the left fork goes to Route 2, and the trail to the right goes to an abandoned wire line. Follow the wire line for ¼ mile to Route 2.

Driving directions: To reach the eastern end, take Route 7 south from Williamstown for about ¼ mile. Turn right onto Bee Hill Road, and park on the left after crossing the first bridge. To ski from the western end, go west on Route 2 for about 3.3 miles from the junction with Route 7. There is a turnout to the south of the highway, and the trailhead is ¼ mile further west on the north side of the road.

Taconic Crest Trail
Petersburg, New York
20 miles
intermediate–advanced
USGS: Berlin/Hancock

The Taconic Crest Trail currently runs from the Williams College Ski Area to Berry Pond, Massachusetts. It is marked with white diamonds. The first 3 miles follow an old road suitable for intermediate skiers. The rest of the trail is narrow and steep. There are beautiful views from the ridge. Snowmobile use is fairly light.

Ski route: Leaving the Williams College Ski Area, enter the woods on the north side of the parking lot and follow the white blazes up an old bush road to the saddle between Raimer and Berlin Mountains. Turn left onto another road and continue south to the summit of Berlin Mountain. Here the road ends, and the trail follows a footpath that

R.R.R. Brooks Trail

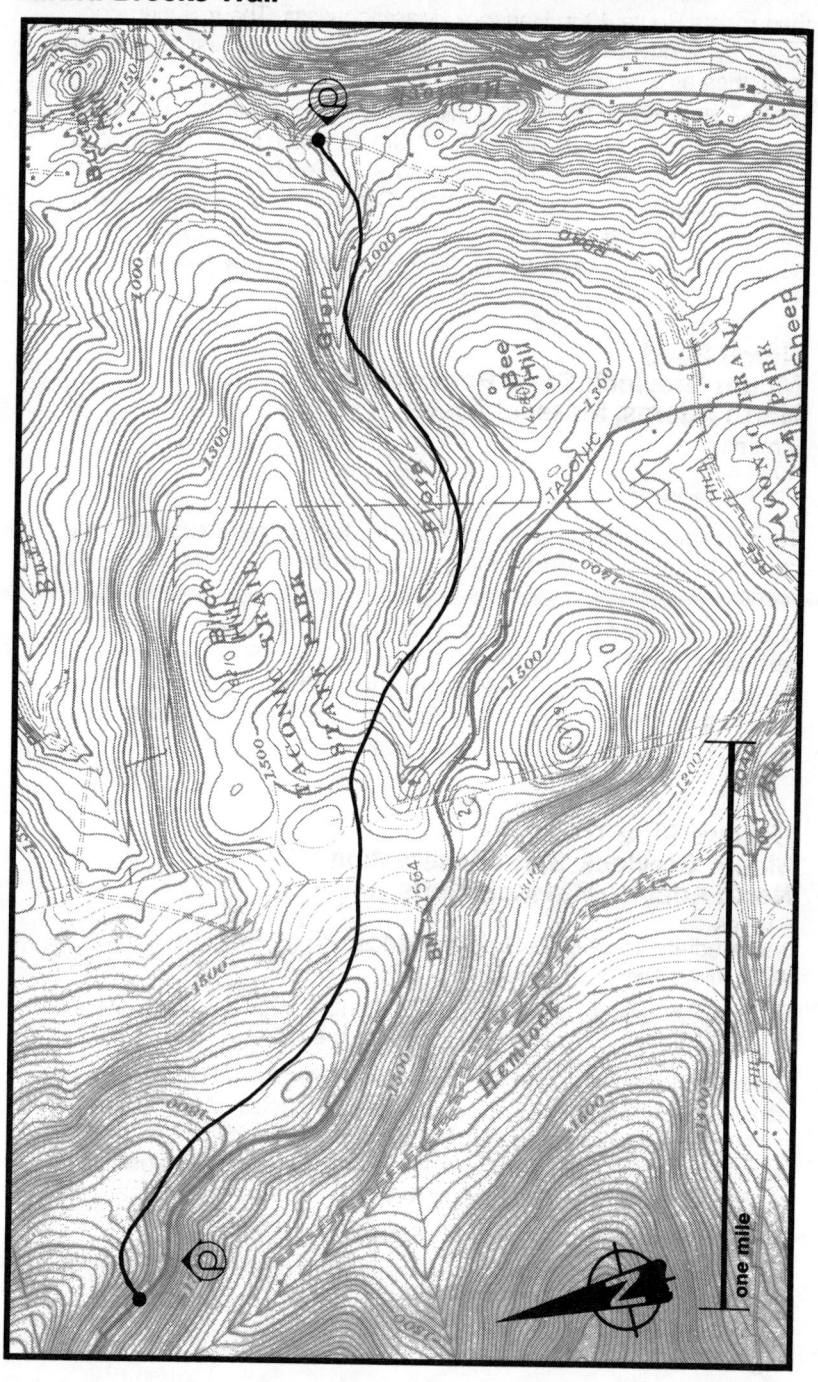

Western Massachusetts

crosses access trails at Southeast, Bentley, and Rathburn Hollows, then meets Route 43 in Hancock, Massachusetts. The trail then continues up a paved road where it reenters the woods, first as a bush road, then as a footpath, ending at Berry Pond.

Driving directions: From Williamstown, Massachusetts, take Route 2 west. At the crest of Petersburg Pass, turn right onto the access road to the Williams College Ski Area. The road is marked by white blazes, and there is a sign to the Carmelite Fathers. Continue for about 3 miles, and park at the Ski Area.

Suggestion courtesy of Betty Regan, Taconic Hiking Club, Troy, New York.

Notch Road
Mount Greylock State Reservation
North Adams, Massachusetts
6 miles
novice
USGS: Williamstown

This unplowed, paved road provides ski tourers easy access to the summit of Mount Greylock. The grade is gentle, and snowmobiles are prohibited.

Driving directions: Take Route 2 to North Adams, and turn southwest onto Notch Road. Just before Mount Williams Reservoir, the road intersects Pattison Road; take a very sharp left turn. Continue on this road to the Notch Reservoir. The Bellows Pipe Trail heads south from here, and the Notch Road goes to the west.

Bellows Pipe Trail
Mount Greylock State Reservation
North Adams, Massachusetts
4 miles
intermediate (to Bellows Pipe)–advanced (to summit)
USGS: Williamstown

This is an excellent summit tour up Mount Greylock. Snowmobiles are prohibited on the section of trail within the State Reservation.

Ski route: From the Notch Reservoir, ski 2 miles to the Bellows Pipe, a pass between Mount Greylock and Ragged Mountain. At the top of the pass, turn right onto an overgrown trail. Within 100 yards, the trail becomes distinct; follow the switchbacks to the summit. It is possible to cross over to the Thunderbolt Trail if conditions are better there.

Driving directions: See directions to the Notch Road.

Suggestion courtesy of the Massachusetts Department of Natural Resources, Division of Forests and Parks, Boston, Massachusetts.

Hopper Trail
Mount Greylock State Reservation
South Williamstown, Massachusetts
4 miles
intermediate-advanced
USGS: Williamstown

The Hopper Trail up Mount Greylock is suitable for intermediates when there is substantial fresh snow, making the descent skiable in a straight run. Otherwise, the run involves much snowplowing and sideslipping. Avoid this trail when it is icy or crusty. This trail is shown on the USGS Williamstown quadrangle and the AMC Mount Greylock map. The AMC *Massachusetts and Rhode Island Trail Guide* includes a trail description. Snowmobiles are prohibited in the area north of the summit.

Ski route: Pass through the gate at Haley's Farm and continue straight on a wood road to a second gate. The Hopper Trail begins after a slight descent of 100 yards. It leads off to the right for about 100 yards, then turns right and ascends to a field. The Money Brook Trail branches left from the Hopper Trail 0.2 miles from the road. The Hopper Trail enters the woods at the southeast corner of the field by a large elm tree. It then ascends the north slope of Stony Ledge and at 2 miles reaches Sperry Road west of the campground. Turn left onto Sperry Road and continue to a rise in the road; here Sperry Road turns right and the Hopper Trail goes left. Ski past the Overlook Trail on the left and the hairpin turn on Rockwell Road to the right. From here, turn right onto Rockwell Road for a more gradual ascent, or continue on the Hopper Trail by turning left just beyond a piped spring. The trail ascends steeply for 0.2 miles before rejoining Rockwell Road opposite the Cheshire Harbor Trail. Turn left and follow the road, which is part of the Appalachian Trail. At the fork, leave the road and continue straight on the Appalachian Trail to the summit.

Driving directions: From Williamstown, drive east on Route 2 to Route 43. Turn right, drive 2½ miles, and turn left onto Hopper Road at the entrance to Mount Hope Farm. Continue for about 1 mile, turn left at a fork, then drive another ½ mile to Haley's Farm. Park well off the road.

Trail map for Notch Road, Bellows Pipe Trail *and* Hopper Trail *appears on following page.*

Notch Road, Bellows Pipe Trail, and Hopper Trail

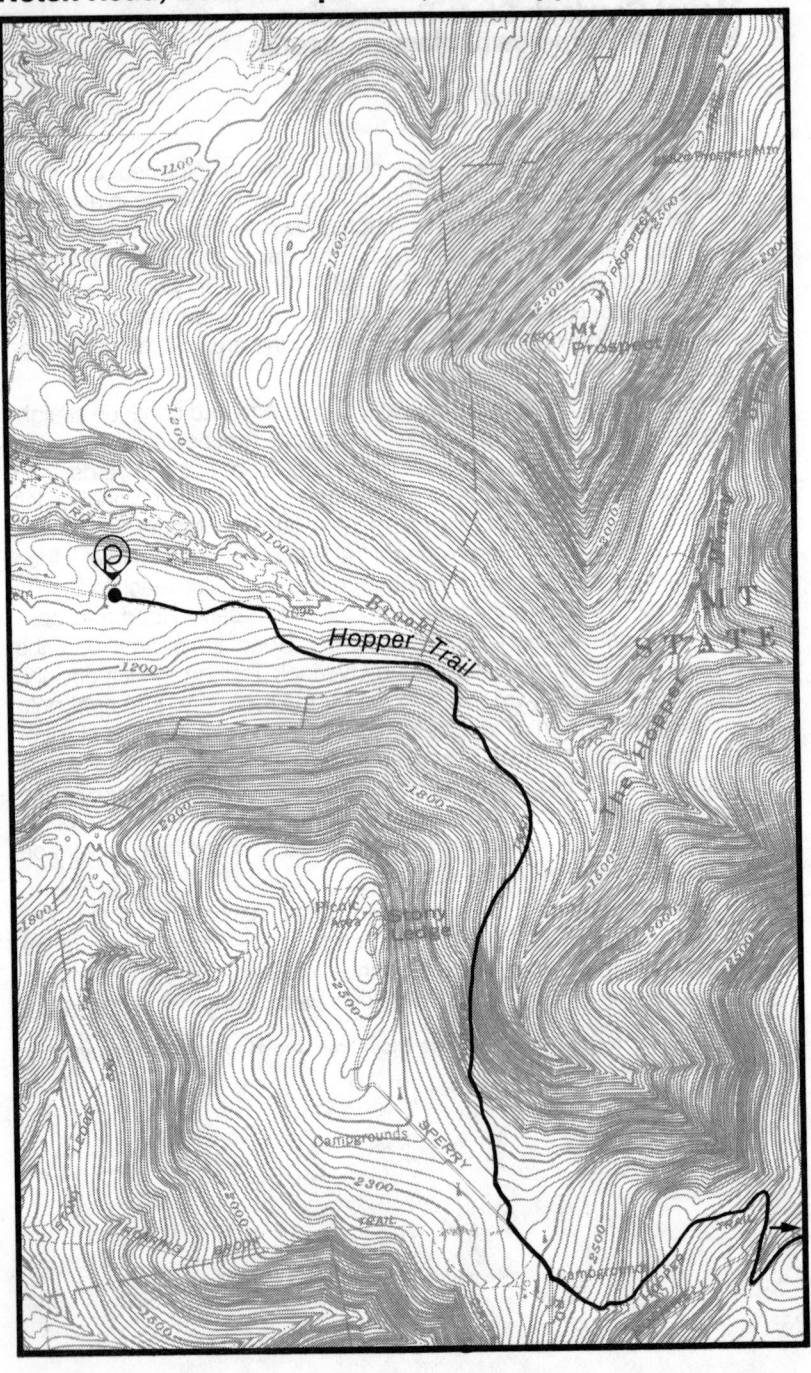

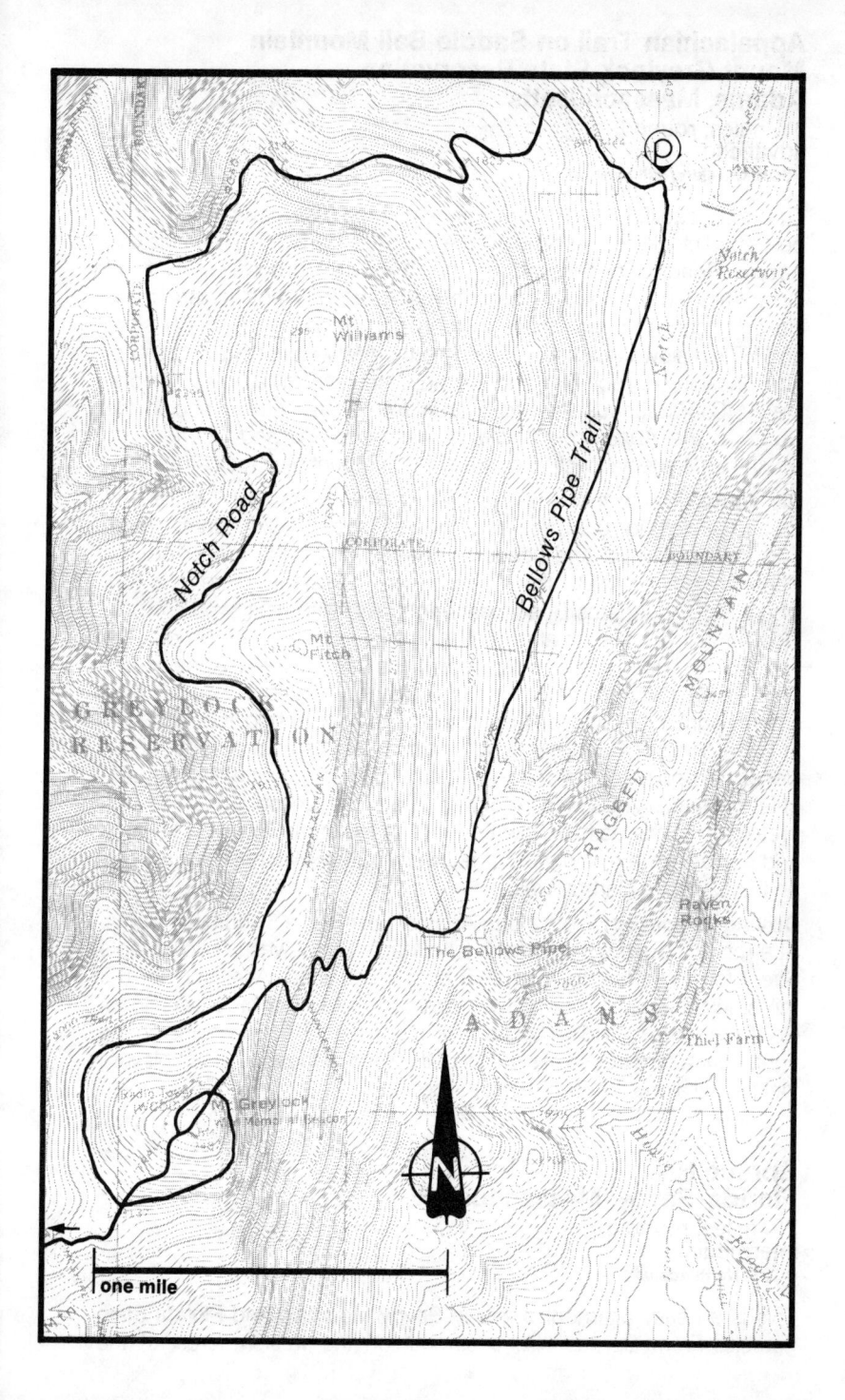

Western Massachusetts

Appalachian Trail on Saddle Ball Mountain
Mount Greylock State Reservation
Adams, Massachusetts
9½ miles, round trip
advanced
USGS: Cheshire/Williamstown

This is a beautiful ridgetop tour offering some nice views. The loop is best skied clockwise. Ascend via the Cheshire Harbor Trail and the Old Adams Road, and descend on the Cheshire Harbor Trail. Both of these trails receive heavy snowmobile use, but the Appalachian Trail is closed to snowmobiles. These trails are shown on the USGS Cheshire and Williamstown quadrangles and on the AMC Mount Greylock map. The Cheshire Harbor Trail and the Appalachian Trail are described in the AMC *Massachusetts and Rhode Island Trail Guide* and in the *Guide to the Appalachian Trail in Massachusetts and Connecticut*, which has a special section on trails in the Mount Greylock area.

Ski route: Follow the Cheshire Harbor Trail (marked by white and orange circles) for 0.9 miles, and turn left onto the Old Adams Road. This trail stays level and heads southwest. About 1½ miles from the Cheshire Harbor Trail, after three stream crossings, there is a fork where the Old Adams Road bears right. After the next stream crossing, the trail bears right and continues straight to Kitchen Brook. The Old Adams Road ends here; continue straight on the Appalachian Trail. The Appalachian Trail climbs steeply, turning right, then left, then sharply right. From Jones Nose, it dips into a dense bog, then ascends to the summit of Saddle Ball Mountain. It follows a long ridge, occasionally dropping down on the western side. Shortly after the Appalachian Trail intersects with Rockwell Road, the Cheshire Harbor Trail breaks off to the east. Follow the road to the summit of Mt. Greylock and back (1-mile round trip), or return directly to West Mountain Road on the Cheshire Harbor Trail.

Driving directions: From North Adams, take Route 8 south to Adams. At a rotary around a monument, take Maple Street west. Follow Maple Street for 0.4 miles, then turn left onto West Road. After another 0.3 miles, just after a brook crossing, turn right onto West Mountain Road. Continue on this road for as far as it is plowed. The trail begins on the right, near a farmhouse at the end of the road. If the road is not plowed that far, ski along the road to the trailhead.

Spruce Hill
Florida/Savoy, Massachusetts
2¼ miles, round trip
intermediate
USGS: North Adams

This is an easy afternoon's tour in Savoy Mountain and Florida State Forests. From Spruce Hill, a summit on the western crest of the

Hoosac Range, there are excellent views of the Eastern Plateau, the Hoosac Valley, and Mount Greylock. The trail is shown on the USGS North Adams quadrangle. Snowmobile use is fairly light.

Ski route: The trail begins at the sharp turn on Shaft Road and is marked by a sign. It heads due north and crosses two power lines before starting a gradual ascent. After about 1 mile, the trail passes an abandoned cellar hole and turns sharply up and to the left. Following the trail is difficult in the open hardwood forest; if it is lost, ski uphill and slightly to the left to the final steep slope. It is best to leave skis at the base of the summit and to walk the final 100 yards. On the descent, make traverses across the hardwood slope.

It is also possible to head west from the same starting point on the Old Florida Road for 1.3 miles. This route is suitable for novices, but it is also a popular snowmobile trail.

Driving directions: From North Adams, take Route 2 east for 4.4 miles to Shaft Road. Turn right and continue to the service building for the state forests, 200 yards before the sharp turn in the road. Park in the lot, and ski to the turn where the trail begins.

Stump Sprouts Ski Touring
Charlemont, Massachusetts
20 km (12½ miles) of trails
novice-intermediate-advanced
USGS: Plainfield

The Touring Center at Stump Sprouts is based in a farmhouse on a hill that offers fine views. The trails, at elevations ranging from 1500 to 1870 feet, boast good, natural snow cover. Terrain is mostly wooded with some open areas. Trails vary from broad, gentle logging roads to steep, narrow runs. They are marked according to difficulty, and maps are available at the farmhouse. About 3 km of unplowed roads are shared with snowmobiles. Trails from Stump Sprouts connect with those in the Mohawk Trail State Forest for further skiing opportunities.

The farmhouse includes a warming room and rental shop, with snacks and hot beverages. There is also a waxing hut. Meals and lodging will be available in the near future. Rentals, instruction, moonlight tours, and nature tours are offered. The trail fee is $1.50.

Driving directions: From Charlemont, drive south for 7 miles on Route 8A, then turn right onto West Hill Road. Continue for 1 mile to Stump Sprouts.

Suggestion courtesy of Lloyd Crawford, Stump Sprouts Ski Touring, West Hill Road, Charlemont, Massachusetts 01339 (413-339-4265).

Notchview Reservation
Windsor, Massachusetts
3000 acres
novice-intermediate
USGS: Windsor/Peru

Notchview Reservation is located in the Hoosac Range. Most of the land is at elevations over 1900 feet and offers good views. Two brooks cross the Reservation, and the hillsides are covered with spruce and hardwood. To the south there are open fields, houses, and barns. There is a network of wood roads and hiking trails, a segment of which goes over Judges Hill. A trail map is available. Snowmobiles are prohibited. There is a charge of $1.00 per person 15 years of age or older. For more skiing in the area, investigate Windsor Jambs State Park and Windsor State Forest.

The Arthur D. Budd Visitor Center, open Friday through Sunday, provides a handy facility for trail information, picnic tables, and ski waxing.

Driving directions: From I-91, take Route 9 west through Cummington. Shortly after entering Windsor, look for a Notchview Reservation sign on the right. Turn right at the sign; the first left is a plowed parking area. If the parking area is full, cars may park along the road.

Suggestion courtesy of Gordon Abbott, Jr., Director, The Trustees of Reservations, Milton, Massachusetts.

Cummington Farm Ski Touring Center
Cummington, Massachusetts
40 km (25 miles) of trails
novice-intermediate-advanced
USGS: Cummington/Ashfield

Cummington Farm is a 700-acre gentleman's farm in the Berkshires. The area is mainly forested, with 50 acres of open fields, and has two major streams, a pond, and two working beaver bogs. Elevations from 1200 to 1450 feet provide nice views of the surrounding countryside. The 40 km of maintained and groomed trails include a 2½-km lighted trail for night skiing. All trails are well marked, and maps are free at the Touring Center. Trails are patrolled by the Nordic Ski Patrol. Snowmobiles are prohibited.

The Ski Touring Center has a full retail shop, rental shop, restaurant and lounge, canteen, dormitory, and overnight cabins heated by wood stoves. Winter camping is permitted. EPSTI certified instruction, full moon night tours, waxing clinics, and special instructor's clinics are offered. Cummington Farm sponsors two major races annually, including the Cummington Farm Bread Race (PEP series), and has a Bill Koch League program. There is a fee for trail use, with season memberships available.

Driving directions: From Northampton, go west on Route 9 to Cummington Center and bear right into town, then follow signs to Cummington Farm.

Suggestion courtesy of David Alvord, Cummington Farm Ski Touring Center, South Road, Cummington, Massachusetts 01026 (413-634-2111).

D.A.R. State Forest
Goshen, Massachusetts
40+ miles of trails
novice–intermediate–advanced
USGS: Goshen

In 1975, the State Forest Ranger, in coordination with the Goshen Conservation and Recreation Commissions and a local Boy Scout troop, opened the existing road system of the D.A.R. State Forest into a year-round recreational use area. A number of new trails have been cut, and additional trails in the Goshen area connect with them to form a large network that extends into Chesterfield and Cummington. There are over 20 miles of nature trails in the vicinity of the DAR campground, Upper Highland Lake, and Moore Hill. Many other trails follow wide, partially-graded routes that are used as bridle paths in the summer. The fire tower on Moore Hill (elevation 1800 feet) offers extensive views of the Connecticut River Valley and the Berkshires.

Trails in the D.A.R. State Forest are well marked: ski trails in blue, snowmobile/ski trails in orange, and horseback routes in red. Maps of trails in the vicinity of Highland Lake are available at the State Forest Headquarters, East Street, Goshen and Highlander Farm Lodge. Snowmobile trails to the south and west of the State Forest are not marked. Highlander Farm Lodge, a partially furnished home adjacent to trails in Goshen center, is available to skiers nightly or weekly, on a caretaker basis. For guide service and further information contact Jerry Weene, Box 47, Goshen, Massachusetts 01032 (617-864-0567 or 413-268-7543).

There is an open shelter, tables, and a fireplace near the D.A.R. State Forest day-use entrance (Moore Hill Road). Picnics are permitted; fire permits may be obtained at Forest Headquarters. This is also a good place to obtain information about trails and current conditions.

Driving directions: From I-91 in Northampton, take Route 9 west for about 13 miles to Goshen Center. From Route 2 take 112 south to the intersection with Route 9 in Goshen. Park at the Goshen General Store, the State Forest Headquarters on East Street, Center School (when not in session), or at Dresser's Mobile Station. Moore Hill Road goes into the D.A.R. State Forest from Route 112. Park along the highway as there is no plowed area.

Suggestion courtesy of Jerry Weene, Goshen, Massachusetts.

Trail map appears on following page.

D.A.R. State Forest

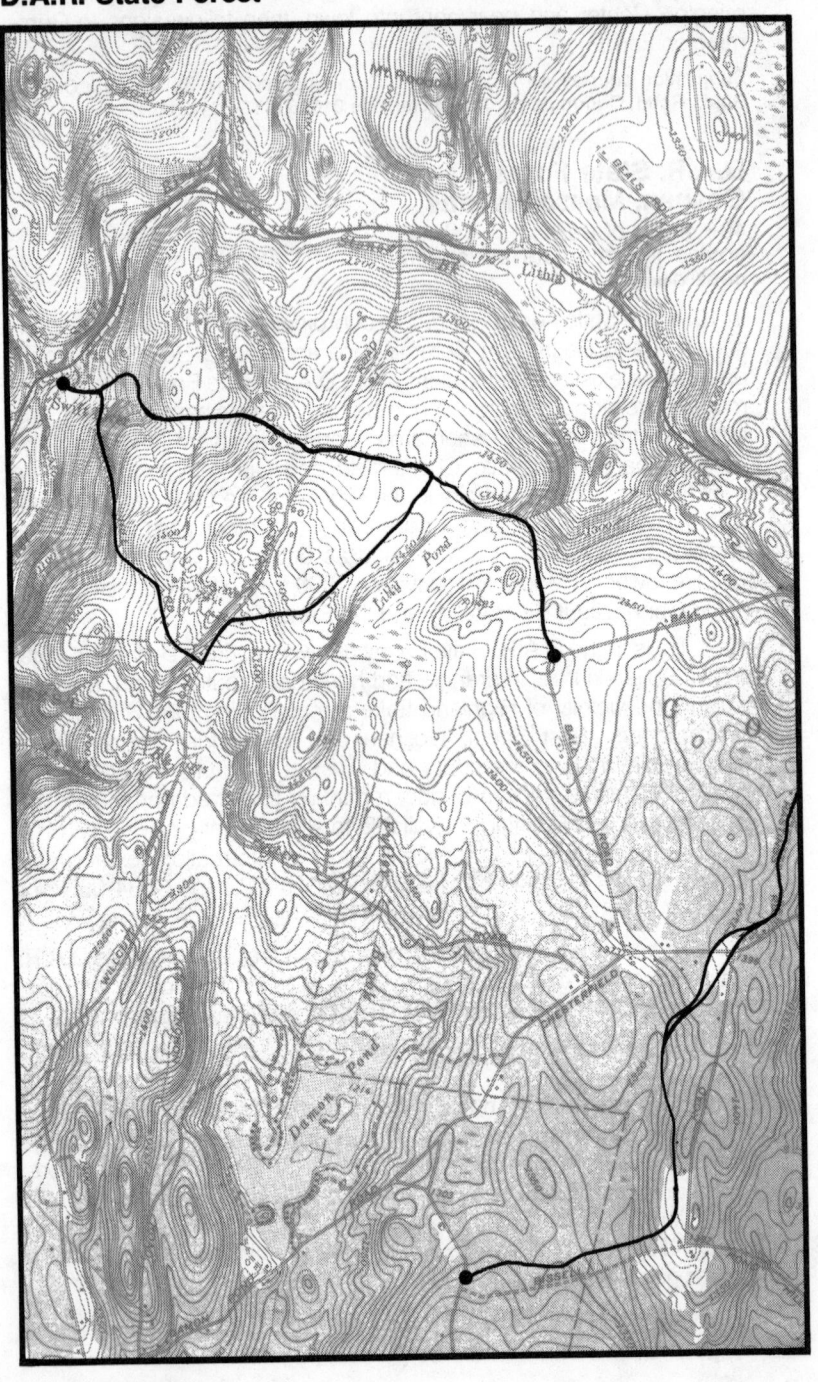

Western Massachusetts

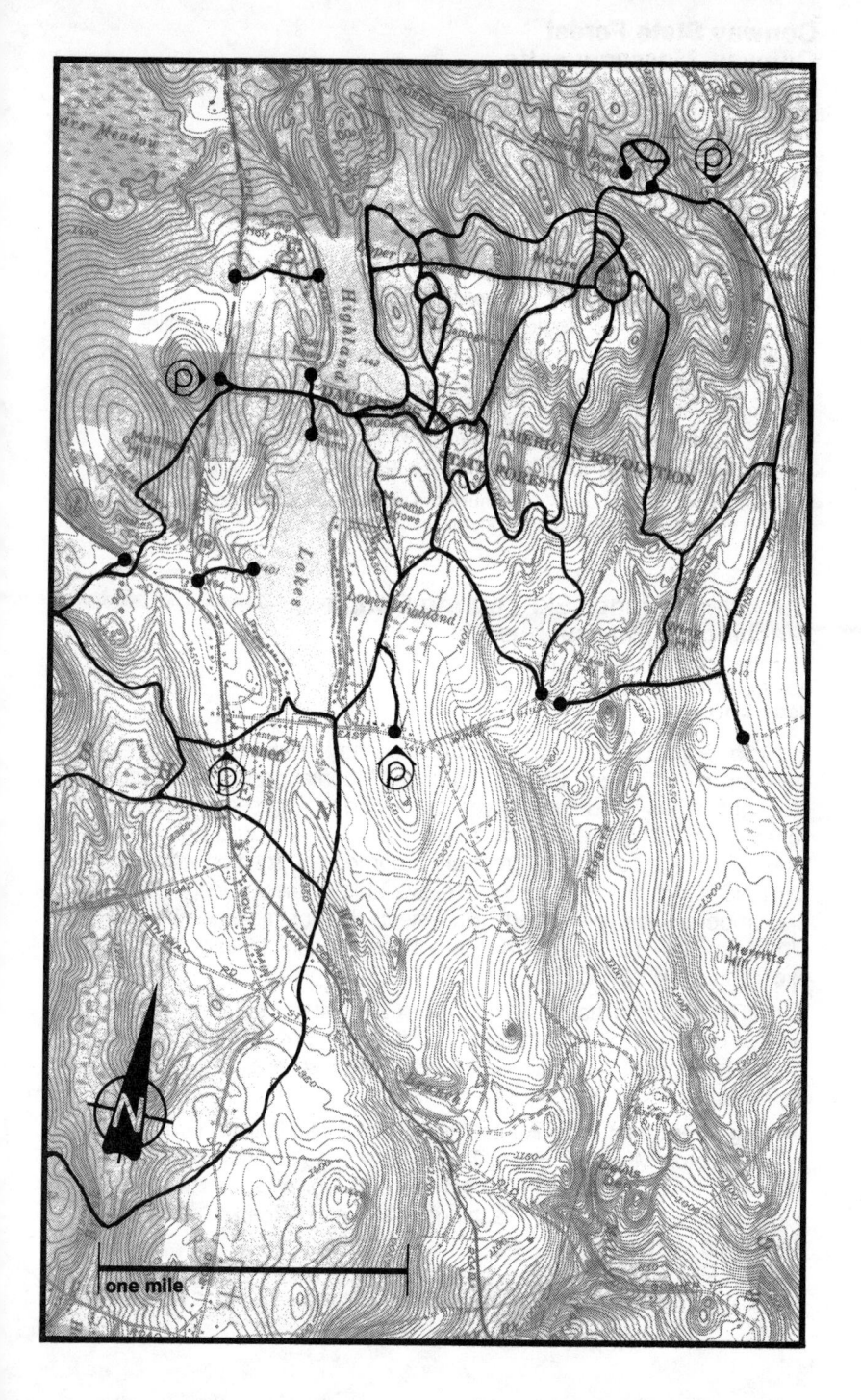

Western Massachusetts

Conway State Forest
Conway, Massachusetts
8 miles of trails
novice-intermediate
USGS: Williamsburg

This is a hilly, wooded state forest traversed by a number of unplowed roads. There are some nice flat stretches and some excellent downhill runs. Snowmobiles use the area, but are less likely to be encountered in the mornings or on weekdays.

Driving directions: From Greenfield, go south on I-91 for about 7 miles. Turn west onto Route 116 in South Deerfield. Drive 6 miles to Conway, and turn left on the Conway-West Whately Road. After 1.8 miles, turn right onto a side road; park after 0.8 miles where a side road enters from the left. To park at the southern end of the Forest, continue on the Conway-West Whately Road to West Whately. Turn right onto Williamsburg Road and go 1½ miles to a trailhead on the right.

Suggestion courtesy of the Massachusetts Department of Natural Resources, Division of Forests and Parks, Boston, Massachusetts.

Bucksteep Manor Ski Touring Center
Washington, Massachusetts
15 miles of trails/300 acres
novice-intermediate-advanced
USGS: East Lee

Bucksteep Manor is an old, turn-of-the-century estate. Located at an elevation of 1900 feet, between October Mountain and Washington Mountain, it has good snow cover and a long touring season. Terrain varies from flat, open land for novices to hilly pine and hardwood forests for advanced skiers. Trails are groomed and marked with standard NSTOA signs, and maps are available at the Touring Center. Snowmobiles are prohibited. Bucksteep Manor adjoins October Mountain State Forest, which has a large network of trails that are excellent for ski touring.

The ski shop has a waxing room and offers rentals and retail sales. Instruction, citizens' races, ski orienteering events, and guided tours into October Mountain State Forest are also available. The trail fee is $2.50 on weekends, $2.00 weekdays.

Driving directions: From Route 7 in Pittsfield, take William Street east to Washington Mountain Road. Turn right and go south to Bucksteep Manor on the left. From the Massachusetts Turnpike (I-91), take Route 8 north, and turn left onto Washington Mountain Road. Continue to Bucksteep Manor.

Suggestion courtesy of Domenick Sacco, Bucksteep Manor Ski Touring Center, Washington Mountain Road, Washington, Massachusetts 01223 (413-623-5535).

Conway State Forest

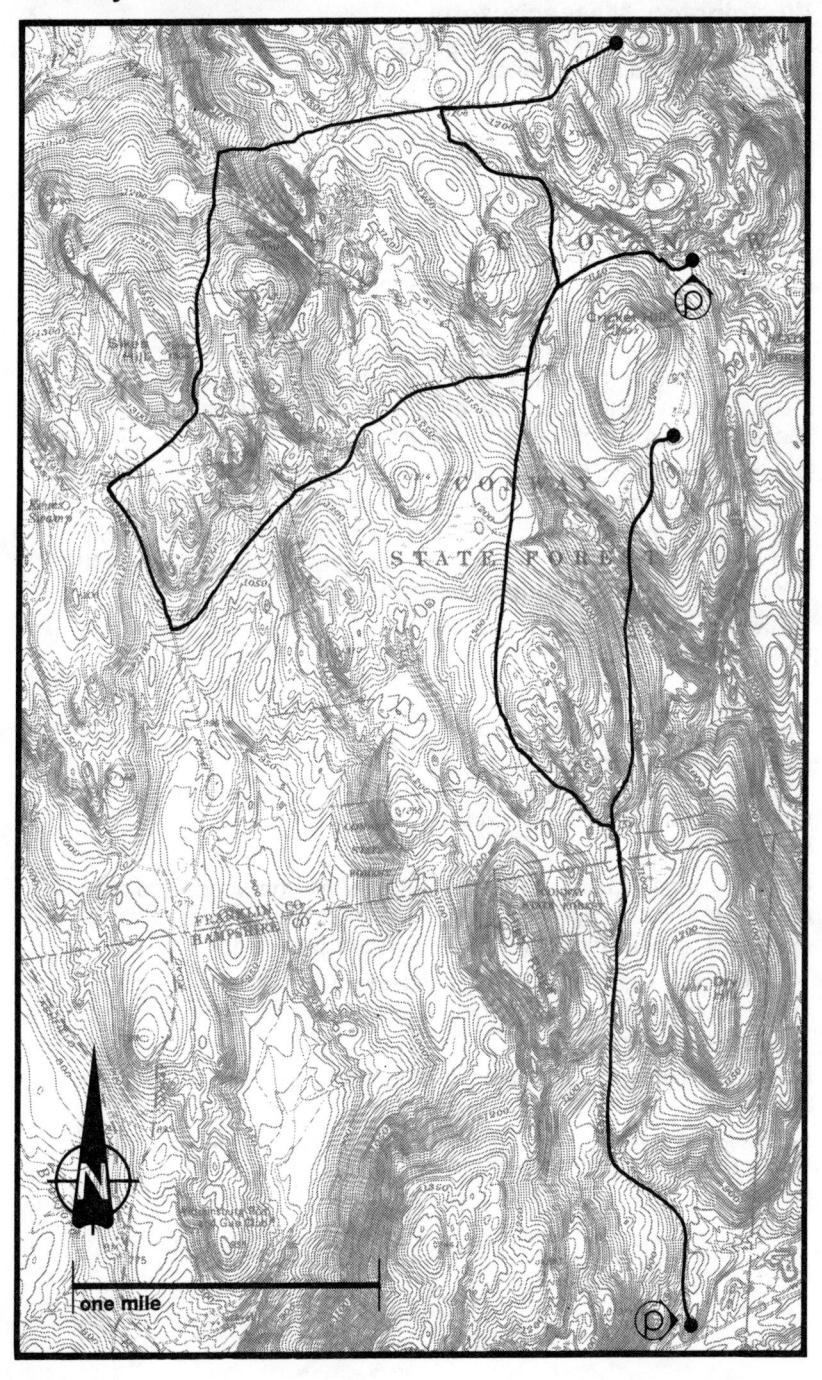

201   Western Massachusetts

Hickory Hill Touring Center
Worthington, Massachusetts
30 km (18½ miles) of trails/650 acres
novice-intermediate-advanced
USGS: Worthington

Hickory Hill has an extensive trail system in the central Berkshires, with elevations from 1600 to 1800 feet. The area is primarily forested with hardwoods and pine groves. There are two large fields for novices; more difficult trails wind through the hills, over brooks, and past beaver ponds. There are some nice views to the south and west. Trails are well marked and maps are available. Snowmobiles are prohibited, except for trail maintenance and first aid.

The Touring Center is housed in a barn with a large fireplace, a kitchen offering homemade soups and baked goods, rest rooms, and a bar. Rentals, instruction, maple sugar tours, a pig roast, and other special activities are offered. There is a trail fee.

Driving directions: From Connecticut and Springfield, take I-91 to Route 20, and go west to Huntington. Turn right (north) onto Route 112, and continue to Worthington. Go left at the traffic light onto Buffington Hill Road. From Northhampton, drive west on Routes 9 and 143 to Worthington, and go straight at the traffic light.

Suggestion courtesy of Paul and Tim Sena, Hickory Hill Touring Center, Buffington Hill Road, Worthington, Massachusetts 01098 (413-238-5813).

The Center at Foxhollow
Lenox, Massachusetts
10 miles of trails/285 acres
novice-intermediate-advanced
USGS: Stockbridge

Foxhollow offers a network of groomed trails through woods and open meadows. They are marked with standard Nordic signs, and trail maps are available. Snowmobiles are not permitted in the area.

Rentals, instruction, and guided tours are offered. Lodging is available at the inn; the dining room and lounge are open to day skiers. There is a $2.00 trail fee.

Driving directions: Fox hollow is on Route 7 between Stockbridge and Lenox.

Suggestion courtesy of John Baker, The Center at Foxhollow, Route 7, Lenox, Massachusetts 01240 (413-637-2000).

Oak n' Spruce Resort
South Lee, Massachusetts
25+ miles/12,000 acres
novice-intermediate
USGS: Stockbridge

This Berkshire resort has a large network of trails through woods and open meadows, across frozen wetlands and a golf course, and includes seven miles of unplowed country roads. Trails connect to those in nearby Beartown State Forest. Maps of the area are posted. Snowmobiling is allowed, but use is limited.

The Resort offers meals and lodging and has a ski rental shop. Winter activities include alpine skiing, skating, tobogganing and snowmobiling, as well as ski touring. The main lodge includes a gift shop, indoor pool, and a night club. Use of ski trails is free to guests at the Resort.

Driving directions: From the Massachusetts Turnpike (I-90), take Exit 2. Drive south on Route 102 for about 2 miles to the Resort. There is ample parking.

Suggestion courtesy of F. J. Prinz, Oak n' Spruce Resort, South Lee, Massachusetts 01260 (413-243-3500).

Tyringham Cobble Reservation
Tyringham, Massachusetts
206 acres
novice-intermediate-advanced
USGS: Monterey

Tyringham Cobble Reservation is composed mostly of steep upland pasture and woodland. From Cobble Hill there are views of the Berkshires to the southwest and the Tyringham Valley to the East. No map is available. Beartown and Otis State Forests are within a 5-mile radius. Snowmobiling is prohibited.

Driving directions: From the Massachusetts Turnpike, take Exit 2 and Route 102 south. Almost immediately, turn south on Tyringham Road. In Tyringham, turn right onto Jerusalem Road. After about ½ mile, look for the Reservation sign on the right. Park close to the sign.

Suggestion courtesy of Gordon Abbott, Jr., Director, The Trustees of Reservations, Milton, Massachusetts.

Riverrun North
Sheffield, Massachusetts
7 km (4 miles) of trails
novice-intermediate
USGS: Great Barrington

Set along the Housatonic River, Riverrun North has gentle and largely open terrain, with some wooded sections. Trails are marked according to NSTOA standards, and maps are available at the touring center. Snowmobiles are permitted only for trail maintenance and rescue. Beartown State Forest is nearby, with further ski touring possibilities.

Facilities include a rental and repair shop, warming area, waxing area, and beverage bar. Instruction, moonlight tours, and babysitting are available, and there is a ski club. Trail fees are voluntary.

Driving directions: Riverrun North is midway between Great Barrington and Sheffield on Route 7, near Exit 2 off the Massachusetts Turnpike (I-90).

Suggestion courtesy of of John Pogue, Riverrun North, Route 7, Sheffield, Massachusetts 01257 (413-528-1100).

Butternut Ski Touring
Great Barrington, Massachusetts
12 miles of trails
novice-intermediate-advanced
USGS: Great Barrington

Novice and intermediate trails wind through the woods at Butternut Basin Ski Area; the expert trail crosses alpine ski trails and continues into East Mountain State Forest. Trails are marked according to NSTOA standards. Snowmobiles are permitted only for trail grooming and rescue. Maps of Butternut trails, Beartown State Forest, and Mount Washington are available at the ski touring center.

Butternut offers rentals and EPSTI certified instruction. Ski tourers may use the ski area facilities, which include a cafeteria and a nursery. There is a $2.00 trail fee.

Driving directions: From Great Barrington, go east on Route 23 to Butternut Basin.

Suggestion courtesy of Bill Lorch and Polly Pulver, Butternut Ski Touring, Route 23, Great Barrington, Massachusetts 01230 (413-528-0610).

Red Fox Ski Touring Center
New Marlborough, Massachusetts
1800 acres
novice-intermediate-advanced
USGS: South Sandisfield

With trails in the vicinity of the Red Fox Music Barn and Sandisfield State Forest, Red Fox Ski Touring Center has developed a rather large network of trails for all levels of skiing ability. These connect with wood roads in York State Forest. Trails are marked according to the standard NSTOA system, and maps are available. Snowmobiles are permitted in York State Forest, though use is fairly light.

The Touring Center has a waxing room, rental shop, retail shop, and snack bar. Rentals and instruction are offered. There is a fee for trail use.

Driving directions: From Winsted, Connecticut, take Route 183 north for 17 miles. From New Marlborough, Massachusetts, take Route 183 south to the Red Fox Music Barn.

Suggestion courtesy of Rick Mansfield, Red Fox Ski Touring Center, P.O. Box 45, Southfield, Massachusetts 01259 (413-229-7790).

Otis Ridge Ski Center
Otis, Massachusetts
14+ miles of trails
novice-intermediate-advanced
USGS: Otis

There are two trails within the 200-acre forest at Otis Ridge Ski Center: a 1-mile novice trail that is flat and groomed for instruction, and a 3-mile intermediate trail. The expert trail crosses a bridge into Otis State Forest, where it connects with the Knox Bicycle Trail and miles of unplowed roads with ski touring possibilities. Several spots along the trails offer spectacular views. Trails are well marked, and maps are free at the Ski Center. Snowmobiles are used in the State Forest, but not on the other trails. There is an hourly shuttle bus to the upper touring trails and Otis State Forest.

The base lodge includes a cafeteria, bar, restaurant, and an inn and lodge. Rentals and instruction are available, and special events are scheduled each winter. There is a $2.00 trail fee.

Driving directions: From Springfield, Massachusetts, take Route 20 west, then Route 23 south to Otis Ridge Ski Center.

Suggestion courtesy of Richard Wiseman, Otis Ridge Ski Center, Route 23, Otis, Massachusetts 01253 (413-269-4444).

Northfield Mountain Ski Touring Center
Northfield, Massachusetts
25+ miles of trails/4000 acres
novice-intermediate-advanced
USGS: Millers Falls

Northfield Mountain trails are situated on the eastern slopes of the Connecticut River Valley, overlooking the French King Gorge. Trails are wide carriage roads that meander over rolling and hilly terrain. The area is heavily forested and rich in wildlife, and affords excellent views. All trails are marked, and intersections are numbered to correspond with the trail map. Snowmobiles are prohibited. Trails are groomed daily, conditions permitting. In addition to ski trails, there are 6 miles of scenic snowshoe trails.

Facilities at Northfield Mountain include a rental shop, lounge, lunch room, classroom, and outdoor food service (weekends and holidays). The "Chocolate Pot," halfway up the mountain, is run by the ski patrol and sells hot beverages and snacks. Rental equipment and EPSTI certified instruction are available. Northfield's Nordic Ski Patrol and ranger staff offer free films and educational programs to the public. Topics include orienteering, survival, first aid, and waxing. There is a fee for trail use.

Driving directions: Northfield Mountain is on Route 63, between Millers Falls (Route 2) and Northfield.

Suggestion courtesy of John Frado, Northfield Mountain Ski Touring Center, RR #1, P.O. Box 377, Northfield, Massachusetts 01360 (413-659-3713).

Stratton Mountain Tour
Northfield/Warwick, Massachusetts
2.7 mile trail
novice
USGS: Northfield/Mt. Grace

This tour over Stratton Mountain offers excellent views from the field at the summit. There is also a very interesting colonial house at the top.

Ski route: Ski up the unplowed, heavily snowmobiled section of the road to the top of Stratton Mountain. The field on the right offers fine views of the Connecticut Valley. After 2 miles, snowmobile traffic turns left. Continue straight (east) to a house and clearing where the road is plowed near the top of the rise.

Driving directions: From Northfield, go east on Maple Street, following signs to Erving. About 1.2 miles from Northfield, bear left onto a plowed dirt road where Gulf Road forks right. Continue 1.2 miles up a gradually steepening grade to the house on the left bearing the sign "Sportsmen Welcome." Park here. To spot a car at the other end of the trail, take Warwick Road from Northfield for about 7 miles, following signs for Warwick. Warwick Road becomes Northfield Road after crossing the town line. At the second intersection with White Road, take a sharp right and park where the road is no longer plowed.

Stratton Mountain Tour

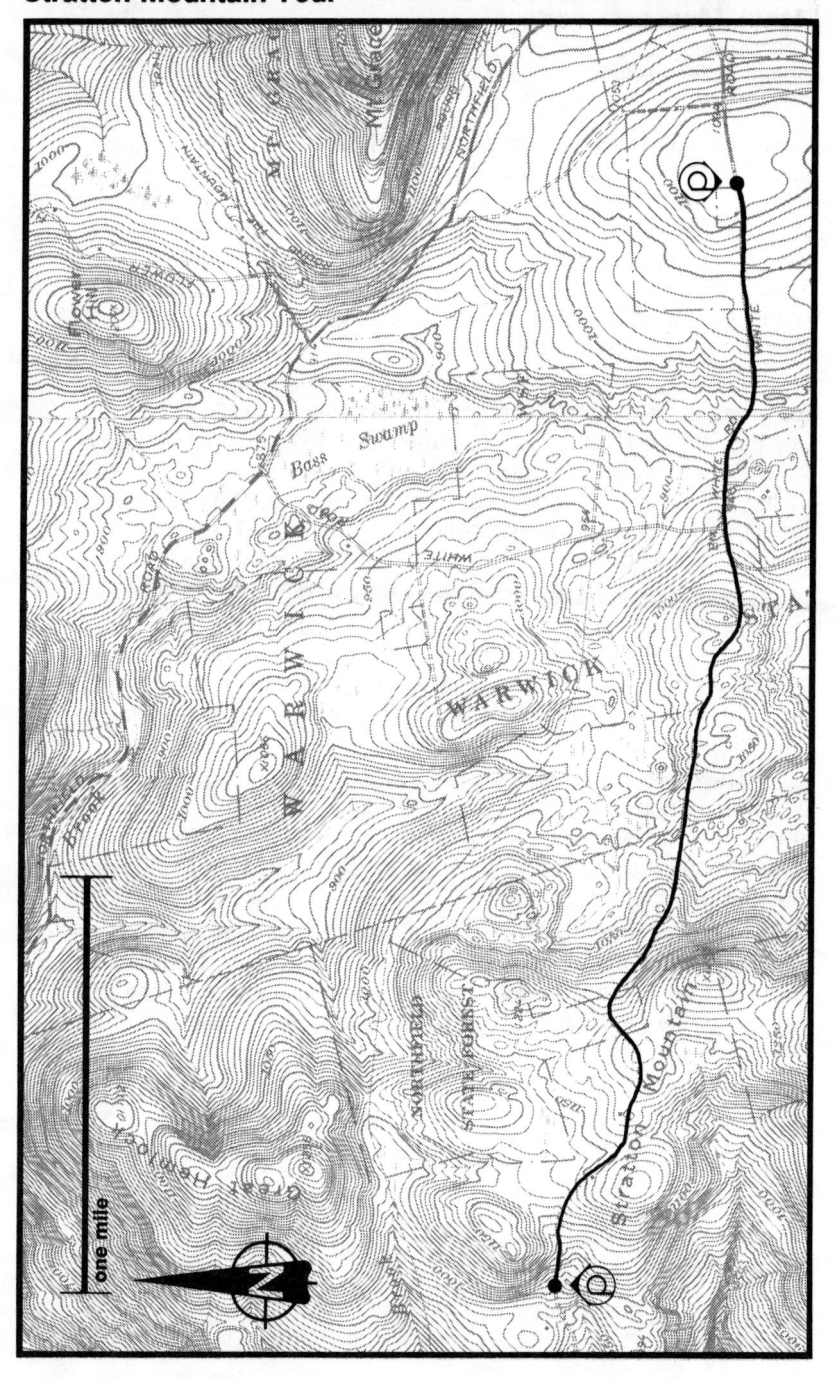

Bearsden Conservation Area
Athol, Massachusetts
1000 acres
novice-intermediate
USGS: Athol

This area was so named because bears used to frequent the rocky forest ledges. It is bounded on the north and west by the Millers River and includes two small reservoirs and a duck pond. The terrain is hilly; vegetation is mostly second-growth forest. Sheep Rock, in the northwest corner of the forest, offers nice views of the river valley. Round Top, in the southwest corner, has a vista of three states and the surrounding towns. The area is quite remote; it is possible to ski 4 or 5 miles through an uninhabited region.

The hills are crossed by many fire roads and trails. Most of the roads are gently sloping. The only trail too steep for skiing runs north and east of Little Round Top. Most trails are marked by dots on trees or by wooden markers with painted shapes. Snowmobiles are permitted in the forest. Use is moderate to heavy on weekends, mostly on Bearsden Road and over adjacent roads and trails. The local snowmobile club has built bridges over some of the brooks.

A trail map is posted at the parking area. The Athol Conservation Commission publishes a booklet, "Athol Conservation Commission Lands and Waters," and a pamphlet, "Athol Conservation Areas," that include an excellent map of the forest. They are free on request from the Athol Conservation Commission, Memorial Building, Athol, Massachusetts 01331.

There are picnic tables in several spots throughout the forest; fires are not permitted. Paige Cabin, ½ mile south of the parking area, is available for overnight use by adults (call 617-249-3460 to make arrangements). There is also an Appalachian shelter west of the parking area.

Driving directions: From Route 2A, turn onto Bearsden Road opposite the hospital about 1½ miles east of Athol Center. Continue for about 2 miles to the Conservation Area. Parking is about ½ mile after the end of the paved part of the road. Do not park at the end of the paved road.

Suggestion courtesy of J. R. Greene, Athol Conservation Commission, Athol, Massachusetts

Birch Hill Wildlife Management Area
Winchendon/Royalston/Templeton, Massachusetts
30 miles of roads plus 400 acres
novice
USGS: Winchendon

This area offers skiing on 400 acres of fields where snowmobiling is prohibited. In addition, there are 30 miles of unplowed roads through mixed hardwood and coniferous forest; these receive heavy snowmobile use. Terrain varies from flat to rolling. Ski touring is not advised until the close of deer hunting season in mid-December. Maps are available from the Massachusetts Division of Fisheries and Game, Temple Street, West Boylston, Massachusetts. Note: the map indicates a bridge on Alger Street; it has washed out and will not be replaced.

Driving directions: From Route 2, go north on Route 202 toward Winchendon. Parking is on Denison Street, south of Lake Denison, and west of Route 202.

Suggestion courtesy of Carl Prescott, District Manager, Massachusetts Division of Fisheries and Game, West Boylston, Massachusetts.

Metacomet-Monadnock Trail
Southwick, Massachusetts to Jaffrey, New Hampshire
intermediate-advanced
**USGS: West Springfield/Mt. Tom/Easthampton/Mt. Holyoke/Belchertown
Shutesbury/Millers Falls/Northfield/Mt. Grace/Monadnock**

This trail begins in the Hanging Hills of Meriden, Connecticut, and follows mountain ridges along the Connecticut Valley north into New Hampshire, where it ends on Mount Monadnock. The Connecticut part of the trail, known as the Metacomet Trail, is part of the Connecticut Blue Trail system. In Massachusetts and New Hampshire, it is maintained by the AMC, Green Mountain Club, and other organizations. The *Guide to the Metacomet–Monadnock Trail in Massachusetts and New Hampshire,* published by the Berkshire Chapter of the AMC, includes excellent maps. The trail is marked by white rectangular blazes. Some sections are heavily snowmobiled. Most of the trail crosses private property; skiers should stay on the trail and should not build fires.

The trail was designed for hiking, so some sections are too steep for ski touring. Most of the trail has not been field checked on skis. Consult topographic maps, or those in the trail guide, to find potentially suitable areas.

The Metacomet-Monadnock Trail along the Holyoke Range between the Connecticut River and Route 116 is quite steep. There are numerous trails south of the range, and a few to the north, however, that are excellent for skiing. Sections of the trail around Mount Orient and Orient Springs are also quite rugged, but there is good skiing east of this area on trails in the Romer Estate. From Mount Orient north through Leverett, the trail is very good for skiing. The brookside section north of Ruggles Pond in Wendell is skiable but fairly rough. There is excellent skiing nearby in Wendell State Forest.

Driving directions: Refer to the trail guide or topographic maps. Parking may be a problem on some roads during winter.

Suggestion courtesy of Walter Banfield (AMC Berkshire Chapter), Amherst, Massachusetts.

Mount Orient and Poverty Mountain
Pelham, Massachusetts

4¼ miles, one way; 4½ miles, round trip
novice (Poverty section)—intermediate (Orient section)
USGS: Shutesbury

These trails can be skied either one way or as a loop. Skied as a loop, there is a beautiful ridge section with views, and a section over an old wood road through a ravine. As a one-way tour, either the ridge route or the ravine may be taken, and then the trail skirts the south side of Poverty Mountain. Snowmobiles may be encountered on these trails.

Ski route: From the southern end, the trail starts as a dirt road and goes off to the left just below a farmhouse. Ski about ⅛ mile and turn right at the fork. There is another fork about ½ mile from the start. To do the Mount Orient loop, take a right at the fork, following the white dot marks for the Metacomet-Monadnock Trail. This section is steep and difficult and may require side stepping. Once on the ridge, the view is wonderful and the descent gradual. After descending the second hump of the ridge, the trail joins a logging road leading from the ravine; take a left and return via the ravine.

To make a one-way trip, take either the right fork to Mt. Orient or the left fork through the ravine. After the ridge trail rejoins the logging road, continue north for another ½ mile and turn left where the road divides. The trail goes southwest around the south shoulder of Poverty Mountain, then curves northwest and ends at another trail. Turn right and ski ⅛ mile to Pratts Corner Road.

Driving directions: For a one-way tour, spot a car first. From the center of Amherst, take Pelham Road east. At East Village, take a left onto Northeast Street and a right onto Shutesbury Road at the four-way intersection. Park at Pratts Corner, just beyond Adams Brook. To find the start of the trail, go back to Pelham Road and follow it east. At West Pelham, turn left onto Pelham Valley Road. Follow it for ½ mile and park as far off the road as possible. The trail begins on the left.

Mount Orient and Poverty Mountain

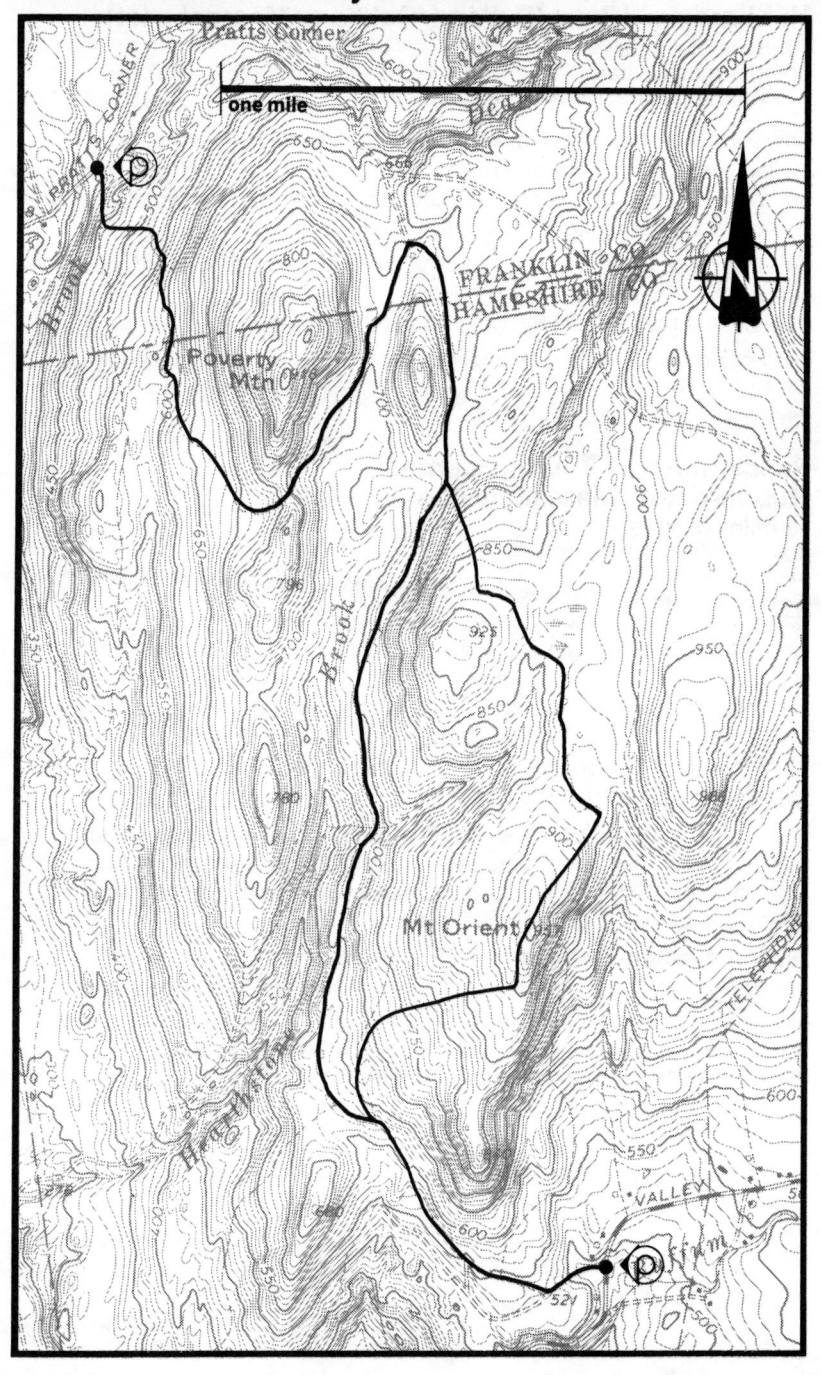

Western Massachusetts

Ware River Watershed
Hubbardston/Barre/Rutland/Oakham, Massachusetts
70 miles of roads
novice-intermediate
USGS: Barre/Wachusett Mtn./North Brookfield/Paxton

This 25,000-acre watershed is managed by the Massachusetts Metropolitan District Commission. Terrain is rolling, and wooded with pine and oak. All trails are over gravel roads and are heavily snowmobiled. A snowmobile trail map is available.

Driving directions: From Worcester, take Route 122 to the Watershed. From Route 2, go south on Route 140 and bear right onto Route 31. Turn right onto Route 62, which leads to the Watershed.

Suggestion courtesy of the Metropolitan District Commission, Belchertown, Massachusetts.

Peaceful Acres Touring Center
Hubbardston, Massachusetts
15 miles of trails/400 acres
novice-intermediate-advanced
USGS: Barre

Peaceful Acres trails wind over predominantly hilly terrain, with some flat sections. Some run along a river, passing ponds, dams and small falls. There are also good views of Wachusett Mountain. Trails are marked with colored markers on trees, and shown on a trail map. They connect with other trails in a nearby state forest, and with unplowed roads that lead to a power line. Snowmobiles are permitted in the state forest; however, use is fairly light.

Facilities include a heated lodge, a snack bar with homemade food, a retail shop, and rest rooms. Rentals and instruction are available. Special activities include moonlight skiing and citizens' races. There is a trail fee and a charge for maps.

Driving directions: From Route 68 in Hubbardston Center, take Williamsville Road for 1 mile. Turn right onto Mount Jefferson Road, then left onto Flagg Road. Peaceful Acres is at the end of the road.

Suggestion courtesy of Carol Curtis, Peaceful Acres Touring Center, Flagg Road, Hubbardston, Massachusetts 01452 (617-928-4413).

Hubbardston Wildlife Management Area
Hubbardston, Massachusetts
2200 acres
novice
USGS: Barre/Wachusett Mtn./Gardner

Much of this area is flat and open, with stands of hardwoods and conifers and some marshy areas. In the eastern section there are several unmarked roads and trails. Snowmobile use is moderate. Maps are available from the Massachusetts Division of Fish and Wildlife, Temple Street, West Boylston, Massachusetts 01583.

Driving directions: From Route 68 in Hubbardston, take Depot Road northeast for about 2 miles to the Management Area. Park alongside the road.

Suggestion courtesy of Carl Prescott, Massachusetts Division of Fish and Wildlife, West Boylston, Massachusetts.

Wilder Ski Track
Springfield, Massachusetts
6 miles of trails
novice-intermediate
USGS: Springfield South/Hampden

Wilder Ski Track is set in the middle of a metropolitan area, 5 miles from downtown Springfield. Trails wind over the open, rolling terrain of Veterans Golf Course and adjoining park land with woods, a stream, and a waterfall. All trails are groomed and marked according to the standard NSTOA system. Maps are available at the touring center.

Facilities include a waxing area and a retail shop with beverages and snacks, repair service, and rentals (including take-away rentals). Instruction for beginners, races, Bill Koch Ski League events, guided tours, and other special activities are held throughout the season. There is a trail fee.

Driving directions: From the Massachusetts Turnpike (I-90), take Exit 7 and drive south for 4 miles on Route 21. From I-91, take the Main Street exit in Springfield and drive north for 4 miles on Route 21. Wilder Ski Track is located on the South Branch Parkway just west of Route 21.

Suggestion courtesy of Carol Anderson, Wilder Ski Track, 1480 Parker Street, Springfield, Massachusetts 01129 (413-783-4411).

Quaboag Wildlife Management Area
Brookfield/West Brookfield, Massachusetts
3 miles of trails
intermediate
USGS: Warren/East Brookfield

This is an area of forestland, interspersed with open fields, marshes, and fire lanes. Trails are not marked. Snowmobiles are permitted on the trails, but not in surrounding open areas, and use is fairly light. Maps are available from the Massachusetts Division of Fish and Wildlife, Temple Street, West Boylston, Massachusetts 01583.

Driving directions: From West Brookfield, go south on Davis Road. Turn left onto Long Hill Road. Quaboag Wildlife Management Area is along the east side of the road. Parking areas are not plowed.

Suggestion courtesy of Carl Prescott, District Manager, Massachusetts Division of Fish and Wildlife, West Boylston, Massachusetts.

Ski Touring Connecticut

CHAPTER 5

Connecticut has many areas suitable for touring, including a number of ski touring centers and a well-developed state-wide trail system.

The Connecticut Department of Environmental Protection encourages cross-country skiing as an environmentally sound form of recreation. All state parks and forests are open to ski touring. In addition to several areas described in this Guide, the following are recommended to novice skiers: Sunnybrook State Park, Torrington (rolling meadows); Meshomasic State Forest, Portland (includes a portion of the Shenipsit Blue Trail); and Nathan Hale State Forest, Coventry (marked bridle trails).

Eleven state forests are open to snowmobiling: People's, Shenipsit, Nipmuck, Natchaug, Pachaug, Cockaponset (Turkey Hill and Cedar Swamp Blocks), Naugatuck, Pootatuck, Mohawk, and Housatonic. All other state forests and parks prohibit snowmobiling. Most state forests are open to hunting in season: skiers should avoid these areas in early winter.

The Connecticut Department of Environmental Protection Parks and Recreation Unit (State Office Building, Hartford 06115) issues an information sheet pertaining to ski touring in state parks and forests. They also have a pamphlet, *Connecticut: Recreation in State Parks and Forests.*

25 Ski Tours in Connecticut, by Stan Wass and David Alvord, includes maps, driving directions, and detailed trail descriptions for selected tours.

The Connecticut Outdoor Recreation Guide is published by the Connecticut Forest and Park Association as a reference to recreational facilities in the state. It contains descriptions of state forests and parks, sanctuaries, and other recreation areas.

There are several guides to hiking trails in Connecticut that can be very useful to the ski tourer. All have detailed trail descriptions and maps, though none evaluates the trails specifically for ski touring. It is best to consult topographic maps or to have summer experience on a trail before attempting it on skis. Keep in mind that, although negotiating stream crossings and finding parking areas may not pose a problem for summer hikers, they can be very difficult in winter.

The *Connecticut Walk Book* is a guide to the Connecticut Blue Trail system, a state-wide network maintained by the Connecticut Forest and Park Association. Most trails described are long through-trails, and many are on private land where motorized vehicles are prohibited. Substantial portions of the Blue Trails are used for skiing.

Short Walks in Connecticut, Volumes 1, 2, and 3, all by Eugene Keyarts, describe selected walks along the Blue Trail system, many of which have scenic, environmental, or historic interest.

The *Guide to the Appalachian Trail in Massachusetts and Connecticut* describes the Appalachian Trail and a few short side trails. Though in general the Appalachian Trail follows rough, high ground, some sections many be suitable for skiing. Motorized vehicles are prohibited.

Fifty Hikes in Connecticut, by Gerry and Sue Hardy, includes a number of trips with ski touring potential.

Connecticut Ski Touring Areas

1. Riverrunning and Ski Touring, Falls Village *220*
2. Blackberry River Ski Touring Center, Norfolk *220*
3. John Minetto State Park, Torrington *221*
4. Main Stream Touring Center, Pleasant Valley *221*
5. Tunxis State Forest, Hartland *221*
   Pine Mountain Cross-Country Ski Touring Center, East Hartland *222*
6. Great World Ski Touring Center, West Simsbury *223*
7. McLean Game Refuge, Granby *223*
8. Cedar Brook Farms Ski Touring Center, West Suffield *224*
9. Northwest Park, Windsor *224*
10. West Hartford Reservoir Reservation, West Hartford *225*
11. Winding Trails Recreation Area, Farmington *226*
12. Topsmead State Forest, Litchfield *226*
    White Memorial Foundation, Litchfield *227*
13. Woodbury Ski and Racquet, Woodbury *227*
14. Southford Falls State Park, Southbury *228*
    Larkin State Bridle Trail, Southbury to Waterbury *230*
15. Seth Low Pierrepont State Park, Ridgefield *228*
16. Collis P. Huntington State Park, Redding *230*
17. Osbornedale State Park, Derby *232*
18. Powder Ridge Ski Area, Middlefield *232*
19. Wadsworth Falls State Park, Middletown/Middlefield *234*
20. Gay City State Park, Hebron *234*
21. Nipmuck State Forest, Union *236*
22. Mansfield Hollow State Park, Mansfield *236*
23. James L. Goodwin State Forest, Hampton *238*
24. Natchaug State Forest, Eastford *238*
25. Mashamoquet Brook State Park, Pomfret *239*
26. Pachaug State Forest, Voluntown *239*

Connecticut

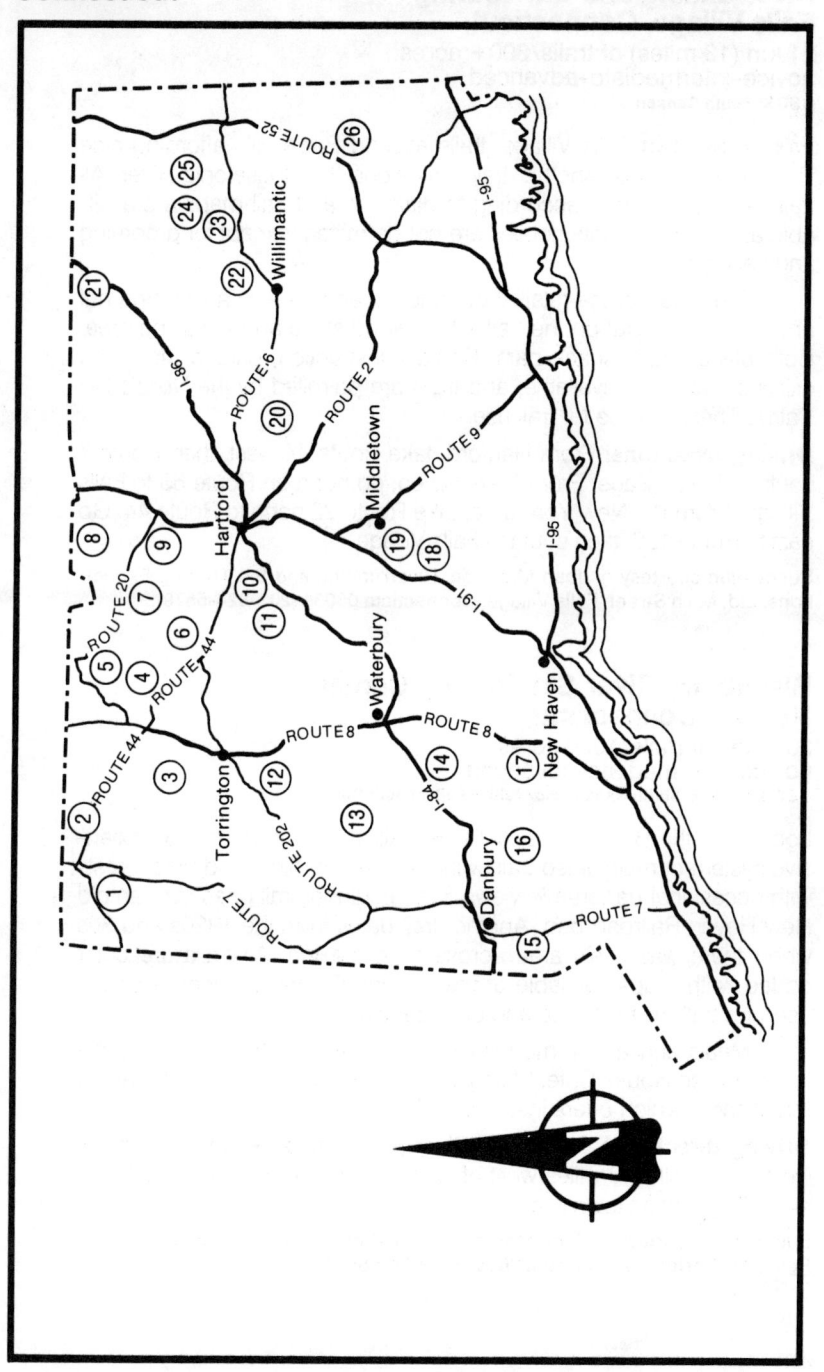

Riverrunning and Ski Touring
Falls Village, Connecticut
21 km (13 miles) of trails/300+ acres
novice-intermediate-advanced
USGS: South Canaan

From downtown Falls Village, trails ascend Battle Hill, affording nice views from the top. Another trail runs along the Housatonic River. All trails are color coded according to difficulty, and trail maps are available at the shop. Snowmobiles are not permitted, except for grooming and setting tracks.

Trails start at the retail shop in town, and there is a warming hut about 1¼ miles out on the trail with a wood stove and a waxing area. Both places have snack bars. Rentals, instruction, guided trips, and citizens' races are available, and trails are patrolled by the Nordic Ski Patrol. There is a fee for trail use.

Driving directions: From Hartford, take Route 44 west, then Route 7 south to Falls Village. From New Haven, go north on Route 63 to Falls Village. From the New York area, take Route 22 north to Route 44. Go east to Route 126, then south to Falls Village.

Suggestion courtesy of Joan Manasse, Riverrunning and Ski Touring Expeditions, Ltd. Main Street, Falls Village, Connecticut 06031 (203-824-5579).

Blackberry River Ski Touring Center
Norfolk, Connecticut
20 miles of trails/1000 acres
novice-intermediate-advanced
USGS: Norfolk/South Sandisfield/Ashley Falls/South Canaan

Located in the Berkshire foothills, Blackberry River Inn has an extensive system of maintained trails winding through birch and pine forests with occasional panoramic views. One beginner trail goes over an old New Haven Railroad bed. Another trail dates from the 1920s and 30s when there was a ski area across from the Inn. All trails are color coded, with maps available at the Touring Center. Snowmobiles are used for trail maintenance and emergencies.

Meals and accommodations are available at the Inn and at the two-story Ice House Cafe. Skiing facilities include a waxing room and a rental shop, which offers instruction. Trail donation is $2.50.

Driving directions: Blackberry River Ski Touring Center is 2½ miles west of Norfolk (40 miles west of Hartford) on the north side of Route 44, at the Canaan town line.

Suggestion courtesy of Rick Mansfield, Blackberry River Ski Touring Center, Route 44, Norfolk, Connecticut 06058 (203-542-5614).

John Minetto State Park
Torrington, Connecticut
150 acres
novice
USGS: West Torrington/Norfolk

John Minetto State Park offers skiing through open meadows and some lightly wooded areas. Forest roads are sometimes unplowed, but there are no marked trails. Snowmobiles are prohibited.

Driving directions: From Torrington, go north on Route 272 for about 8 miles to the state park entrance. Park in the plowed area.

Suggestion courtesy of Anthony Cantele, Connecticut Department of Environmental Protection, Pleasant Valley, Connecticut.

Main Stream Touring Center
Pleasant Valley, Connecticut
11 miles of trails
novice
USGS: New Hartford/Winsted

Main Stream trails traverse fairly gentle terrain, including streams and beaver ponds. Trails are marked, and maps are available at the shop. Snowmobiles are prohibited. The nearby People's State Forest has other trails that are good for skiing.

Rentals, EPSTI certified instruction, and moonlight tours are available at the Touring Center. There is no trail fee.

Driving directions: The Touring Center is in Pleasant Valley, where Routes 44 and 181 intersect.

Suggestion courtesy of John H. Casey, Main Stream Touring Center, Route 44, Pleasant Valley, Connecticut 06063 (203-379-1448).

Tunxis State Forest
Hartland, Connecticut
11 miles of trails
novice-intermediate
USGS: West Granville/New Hartford

Ski routes are on unplowed forest roads. The terrain is rolling and covered with mixed northern hardwoods, pine, and hemlock. Snowmobiling is not allowed. Trails are scattered throughout the Forest and are shown on USGS topographic maps. Caution: the Metropolitan District Commission lands surrounding the reservoir and within the boundaries of Routes 20, 181, and 179, are posted against all foot and motor travel.

Driving directions: Take Exit 2 from the Massachusetts Turnpike (I-90) and follow Route 8 south to Route 20. Go east on Route 20 through Hartland. There are several places to park along Routes 20 and 179; refer to USGS maps.

Suggestion courtesy of Anthony Cantele, Connecticut Department of Environmental Protection, Pleasant Valley, Connecticut.

Pine Mountain Cross-Country Ski Touring Center
East Hartland, Connecticut
15 miles of trails
novice-intermediate-advanced
USGS: New Hartford

Situated at the second highest point in Connecticut (1300 feet), Pine Mountain has snow conditions like those in the Berkshires further north. Terrain is varied, including hills and valleys, meadows and wooded areas. Trails are groomed, and tracks set. They are marked according to NSTOA standards and rated for degree of difficulty. A trail map is given to each skier, and there is a large map posted at the Touring Center. Snowmobiles are prohibited from Pine Mountain trails and from Tunxis State Forest (see separate entry) with which two trails connect.

The Touring Center is housed in a newly remodeled gambrel-roofed barn, with a large wood stove for warming, and tables and booths for picnic lunches. Rentals, instruction, refreshments, and accessory equipment sales are available. There is an area use charge of $2.50.

Driving directions: Coming from the north, take I-91 to the Bradley Field exit and go west on Route 20 to East Hartland. Turn left (south) onto Route 179 and continue for 2 miles to the Touring Center. From the south, take I-91 to I-84. Go west to the Farmington exit and take Route 10 north to Route 44. Turn left and drive west to Route 179, then north 12 miles to the Touring Center.

Suggestion courtesy of Bob Shaw, Pine Mountain Cross-Country Ski Touring Center, Route 179, East Hartland, Connecticut 06092 (203-653-4279).

Great World Ski Touring Center
West Simsbury, Connecticut
20 miles of trails
novice-intermediate-advanced
USGS: Avon

Great World maintains a wide network of trails through the West Simsbury Valley. In addition to these marked and groomed trails, there are others in nearby Stratton Brook State Park. Trail maps cost $.50.

The Touring Center includes a warming barn and offers rentals and EPSTI certified instruction. Sandwiches, snacks, and beverages are served. Trails are covered by a Nordic Ski Patrol. There is no trail fee, although donations for trail maintenance are encouraged.

Driving directions: From Routes 10 and 202 in Simsbury, turn west onto Farms Village Road (Route 309). Great World is located in the village of West Simsbury.

Suggestion courtesy of Chris Modisette, Great World Ski Touring Center, 250 Farms Village Road, West Simsbury, Connecticut 06092 (203-658-4461).

McLean Game Refuge
Granby, Connecticut
15 miles of trails/3400 acres
novice-intermediate
USGS: Tariffville/New Hartford

Skiing in the Refuge is on unplowed park roads and hiking trails, most of which are blazed. The terrain in the eastern section is fairly gentle. Four miles of unplowed roads wind through hemlock and pine woods, past two ponds, and along a brook. Some of the hiking trails are also skiable. The Summit Trail, to the top of Barndoor Hill, is negotiable by intermediates if snow cover is adequate. There are excellent views to the west and northwest from the top of the hill. West of the Firetown Road, the terrain is more rugged but offers good views. Snowmobiles are not permitted.

Trails are shown on a map in a pamphlet that is available at the Refuge. The *Connecticut Walk Book* also includes a description and a trail map.

Driving directions: From I-91, take Route 20 west to Granby, then go south approximately 1 mile on Route 10. There is a sign at the main entrance on the right (west). Enter and park in the plowed area.

Suggestion courtesy of McLean Game Refuge, Granby, Connecticut.

Cedar Brook Farms Ski Touring Center
West Suffield, Connecticut
2 miles of trails
novice
USGS: Windsor Locks/West Springfield

Cedar Brook is a family-operated Touring Center on a 200-acre working dairy farm. Trails wind across open fields, with some hills and wooded areas. They are well groomed, with set tracks. Trail signs with hand-painted pictures correspond with a trail map. Snowmobiles are not permitted in the area.

The Touring Center includes a warming hut with a small snack bar. Rentals, instruction, and moonlight tours are available. Trails are patrolled by the Nordic Ski Patrol. The trail fee is $3.00 on weekends and $2.00 on weekdays, with special group rates.

Driving directions: From Suffield, drive west on Route 168. About ¼ mile beyond the junction with Route 187 in West Suffield, turn right (north) onto Ratley Road. Continue for about 1½ miles to the Touring Center in a brown wooden building on the left.

Suggestion courtesy of Stanley and Barbara Falkowski, Cedar Brook Farms Ski Touring Center, 1481 Ratley Road, West Suffield, Connecticut 06093 (203-668-5026).

Northwest Park
Windsor, Connecticut
6.5 miles of trails
novice-intermediate
USGS: Windsor Locks

There are several nice trails in this 500-acre park, with excellent views of the Rainbow Reservoir. The forest is vigorous, mature timber; terrain is varied, with a few steep slopes. Trails are marked with color-coded signs, and there is a map posted at the park entrance. Maps are also available from the Windsor Recreation Department. Snowmobiling and hunting are not allowed in the park.

Driving directions: From I-91, take the Poquonock exit and go north on Route 75 to Prospect Hill Road (1½-2 miles). Turn left. Continue for just over a mile to Lang Road and turn right. Park at the end of the road.

Suggestion courtesy of Bob Levine, Windsor Recreation Department, Windsor, Connecticut.

West Hartford Reservoir Reservation
West Hartford, Connecticut
40 miles of trails/3000 acres
novice–intermediate–advanced
USGS: Avon

Situated within the metropolitan Hartford area, the West Hartford Reservoir Reservation is a vast, undeveloped tract including six reservoirs, several small ponds, and surrounding watershed lands. The forest is primarily hardwoods with some hemlock. Terrain varies from gentle and rolling to steep and rugged, with some interesting outcrops and unique geological features. There are good views from some of the higher elevations.

The Reservation is laced with about 40 miles of interconnecting trails, paths, and roads. Many of these are wide, well-cleared fire roads. Trails go around lakes and up wooded slopes to the west. One of the more rugged areas is along a section of the Metacomet Trail, part of the Connecticut Blue Trail System, which runs along a ridge. All intersections are marked with can lids: yellow letters on grey background. Snowmobiles are prohibited.

Litter barrels and rest rooms are available, but there are no shelters. Picnics without fires are permitted.

A good guide to the area is *Roads and Trails in the Reservoir,* which includes trail descriptions and maps, lists of birds, animals and wildflowers found in the area, historical information, and points of interest. Trail descriptions include comments on ski touring and other winter activities.

Driving directions, southern tract: From West Hartford Center, head west on Route 4 (Farmington Avenue) 2–3 miles to the entrance of the Reservoir. From I-84, get off at Exit 39 in Farmington and drive 2 miles east. Park by the administration building or by the fountain. This section of the Reservation has the greatest number of trails and the most varied terrain.

Driving directions, northern tract: From Bishop's Corners in West Hartford, follow Route 44 (Albany Avenue) west for 2 miles. Entrance is on the right.

Suggestion courtesy of David Kendall, West Hartford, Connecticut.

Winding Trails Recreation Area
Farmington, Connecticut
300 acres
novice–intermediate
USGS: New Britain

This area has a number of ski touring trails through wooded areas, along a former glacial deposit, and around a pond and a large lake. The beginner's loop follows a road from the cross-country hut north to a power line, turns right along the power line, then follows the first connecting trail through a pine wood back to the center. A number of excellent novice and intermediate trails go through deciduous and coniferous woods, many connecting to a north-south central path. All trails are marked and shown on a map available at the cross-country hut. A snowmobile is used to groom one trail; they are not otherwise permitted in the area.

The cross-country hut is heated by a potbellied stove and has picnic tables and rest rooms. There are picnic tables, grills, and campsites around the hut. Rentals, EPSTI certified instruction, and guided tours are available.

Driving directions: From the center of Farmington, drive west on Route 4 for about ½ mile. Entrance to the Recreation Area is on the right. Parking is available in the lot next to the cross-country hut, about 1 mile from the entrance.

Suggestion courtesy of Jim and Judy Shea, West Hartford, Connecticut.

Topsmead State Forest
Litchfield, Connecticut
513 acres
novice–intermediate
USGS: Litchfield/West Torrington

There are several trails and open meadows in the central part of Topsmead State Forest. The terrain is gently rolling, with occasional moderately steep hills. Trails are marked with numbered signs, and trail maps are available near the parking area. Snowmobiles are prohibited.

Driving directions: From Litchfield, take Route 118 east, turning right onto Old East Litchfield Road. After ½ mile, turn right onto Buell Road and continue ¼ mile to the State Forest entrance on the right.

Suggestion courtesy of Anthony Cantele, Connecticut Department of Environmental Protection, Pleasant Valley, Connecticut.

White Memorial Foundation
Litchfield, Connecticut
35 miles of trails/4000 acres
novice-intermediate-advanced
USGS: Litchfield

This large conservation preserve is primarily forested, with ponds (suitable for skating) and several streams. The terrain is gentle, varying from flat to moderately hilly. Some of the trails are logging and fire roads; others are hiking and riding trails. All are marked and color coded to a map, which is available for $.50 at the Foundation office. No snowmobiles are allowed.

The main area includes offices, the White Memorial Conservation Center, and a campground for primitive camping. The Center is open from Tuesday through Saturday during the winter. There are picnic tables and toilets. Dormitories with kitchen facilities are available for rent. Contact the Conservation Center for further information.

Driving directions: From Litchfield, take Route 202 west for 2½ miles to the White Memorial sign. Turn left and immediately right; continue for ½ mile to the central area. Park here or drive to other parking areas in the preserve.

Suggestion courtesy of Robert H. Shropshire, Superintendent, The White Memorial Foundation, Inc., Litchfield, Connecticut.

Woodbury Ski and Racquet
Woodbury, Connecticut
40 miles of trails/103 acres
novice-intermediate
USGS: Woodbury

This alpine area offers ski touring on 40 miles of trails plus a large open area at nearby Steep Rock Park. Facilities at the ski area include a ski shop, warming hut and snack bar, and courts for paddle and indoor tennis. Rental equipment, certified instruction, and guided tours are available.

Driving directions: Woodbury Ski and Racquet is north of Woodbury on Route 47.

Suggestion courtesy of Woodbury Ski and Racquet, Route 47, Woodbury, Connecticut 06798 (203-263-2203).

Seth Low Pierrepont State Park
Ridgefield, Connecticut
1.9 miles of trails
intermediate
USGS: Peach Lake/Bethel

Seth Low Pierrepont State Park is located by a lake, with skiing along the lake and over wooded upland areas providing good views. Trails are marked with rusty tin can lids nailed to trees and posts. Snowmobiles are prohibited. The southern location of this park makes snow conditions unpredictable.

Ski route: The main trail leaves Barlow Mountain Road just south of the lake. It starts in a level, newly overgrown field, passes the lake, and ascends through woods to rock outcrops. Here there are several possible downhill runs. Return to the road by the same route.

Driving directions: From I-84, take Route 7 south 4 miles to Route 35. Follow Route 35 to Route 116. Take 116 north for 1¾ miles, then turn right onto Barlow Mountain Road. Follow this road a short distance and take the left fork, which leads to Barlow Mountain School. Park alongside the road or at the school.

Suggestion courtesy of Edward Rizzotto, Connecticut Department of Environmental Protection, Middlebury, Connecticut.

Southford Falls State Park
Southbury, Connecticut
1.6 miles of trails/120 acres
novice–intermediate
USGS: Southbury

These are easy trails that go through mixed hardwood forest and over rolling, sometimes rocky terrain. The main trail loops around the park, and short side trails provide longer or shorter variations on this tour. All trails are marked with red tags or paint blazes. Maps are available at the park headquarters. Snowmobiles are not permitted.

The park has a heated shelter and sanitary facilities. There is a hill for sledding and a plowed pond for ice skating.

Ski route: From the old mill pond dam, the trail goes east along the shore of the pond and into a wooded area. It continues south along a route that bypasses the ledges and rounds the hill, affording views to the west. The trail continues down the side slope (now proceeding north), then runs parallel to the brook leading back to the dam. A short section of intermediate trail crosses from one side of the loop to the other, making a "figure 8." One side trail crosses a covered bridge and returns to the dam along the other side of the brook. Another side trail leads to a lookout tower with nice views.

Seth Low Pierrepont State Park

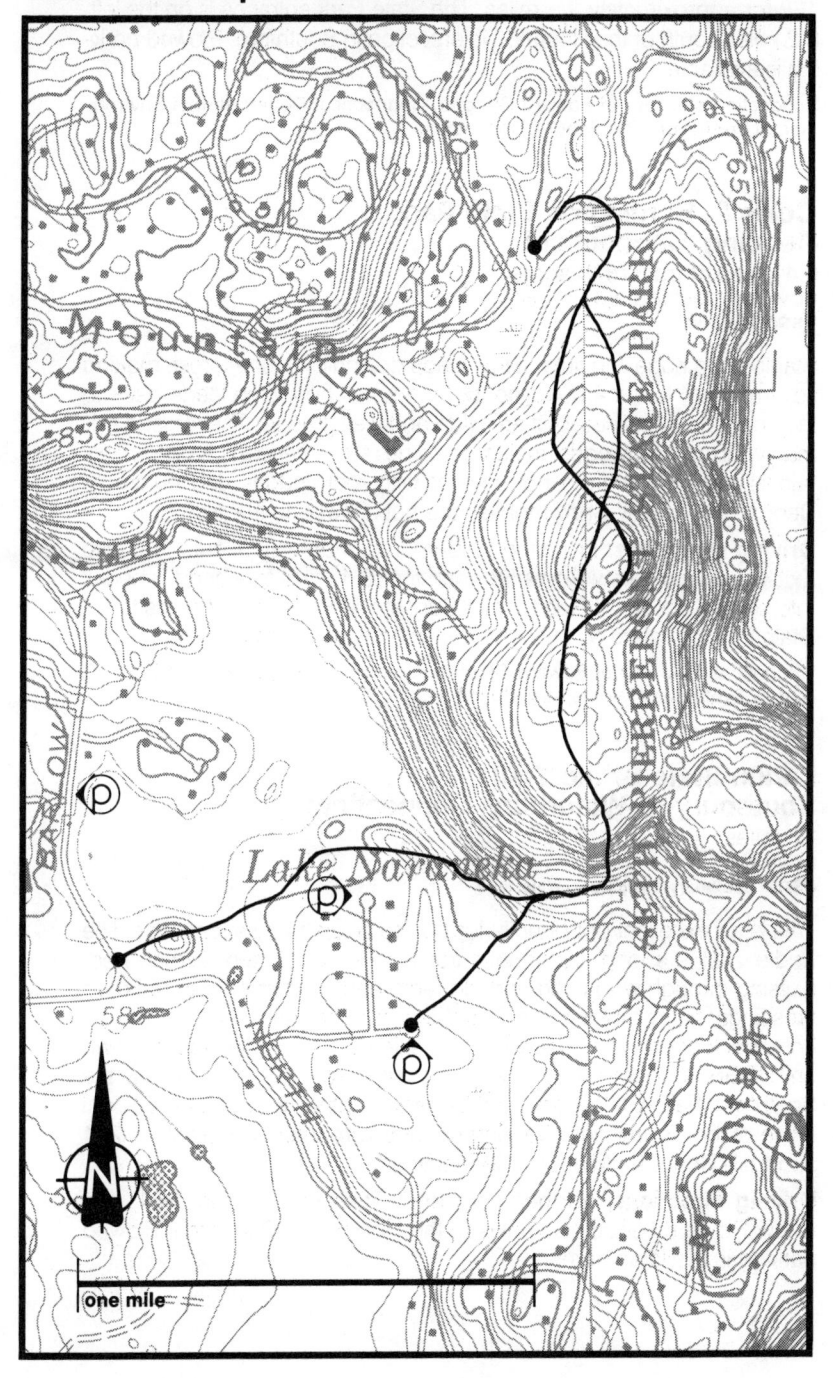

Connecticut

Driving directions: From I-84, take Exit 16 and head south on Route 188 for approximately 2½ miles. The State Park entrance is on the left, 0.2 miles south of the Route 67 intersection in Southford. Plowed parking is available.

Suggestion courtesy of Edward Rizzotto, Connecticut Department of Environmental Protection, Middlebury, Connecticut.

Collis P. Huntington State Park
Redding, Connecticut
6.4 miles of trails/878 acres
novice–intermediate
USGS: Botsford

Starting in a ridge-top field, a trail leads downhill into the forest, making several small loops around ponds and small hills, then leads back to the entrance. Most sections are wide and well graded. The forest is primarily mixed hardwoods, including some rare American chestnut. Terrain is irregular, though not severe, with rock ledges and outcrops. Deer are prevalent. Snowmobiles are not allowed in the park.

Driving directions: From the Wilbur Cross Parkway (Route 15), take Exit 44/45 and follow Route 58 north for 10.4 miles to a bend, where it intersects Sunset Hill Road. Take Sunset Hill Road for 0.7 miles to the State Park entrance on the right. Park alongside the road.

Suggestion courtesy of Edward Rizzotto, Connecticut Department of Environmental Protection, Middlebury, Connecticut.

Larkin State Bridle Trail
Southbury-to-Waterbury, Connecticut
11 miles
novice
USGS: Southbury/Naugatuck/Waterbury

This is an excellent opportunity for novice skiers to try a long tour. The Bridle Trail is a long, continuous trail on an abandoned railroad bed, passing through woodland and old farm lands. There are several road crossings. Snowmobiles are forbidden, but the trail may be used by horseback riders when snow cover is skimpy. The Bridle Trail is shown on USGS topographic maps. Handout maps are available at the Southford Falls State Park (see separate entry), and at the regional office of the Connecticut Department of Environmental Protection, 251 Judd Hill Road, Middlebury, Connecticut.

Driving directions, northeastern end: Take Exit 17 from I-84, and follow Route 63 south 1½ miles to the Hop Brook Dam area. Plowed parking is available here.

Collis P. Huntington State Park

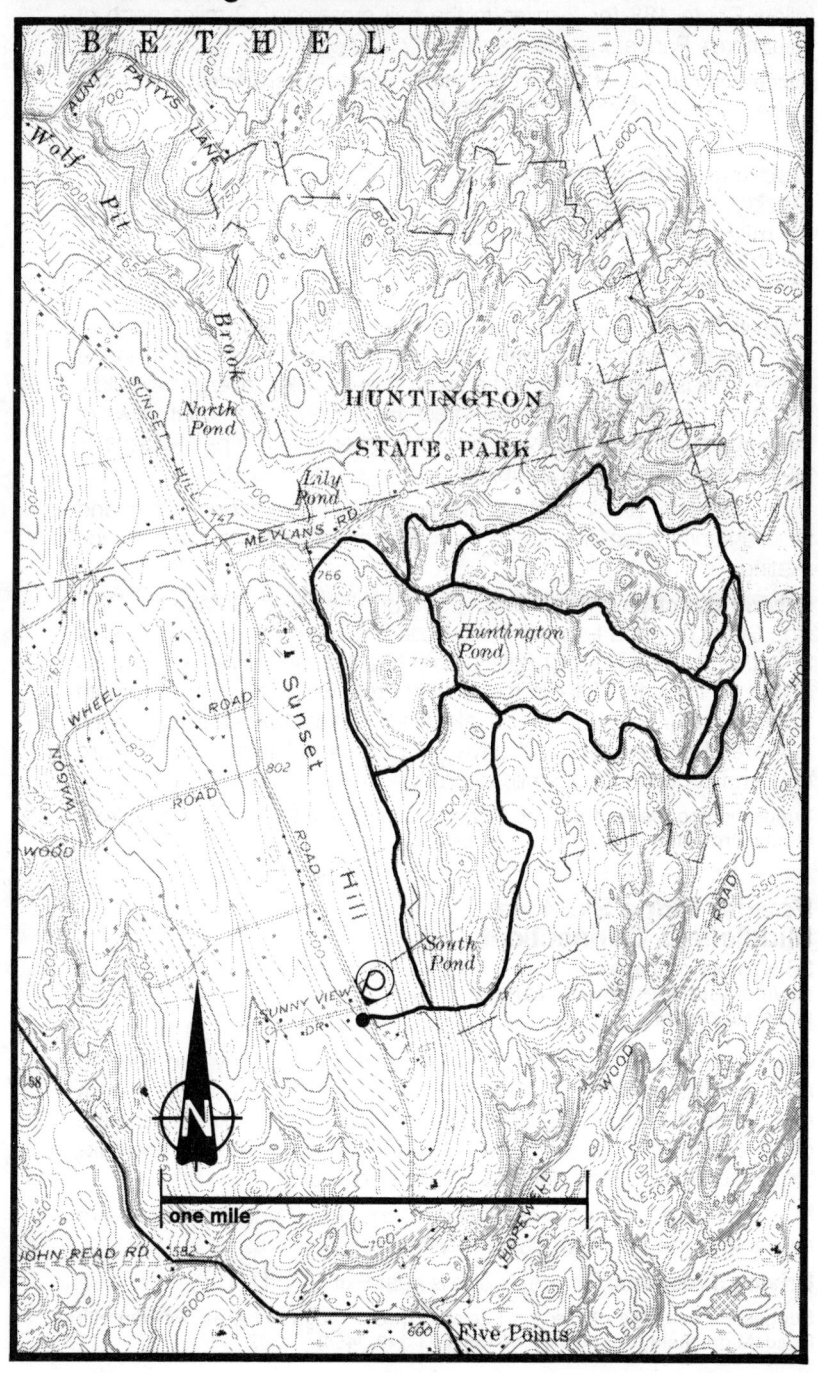

231   Connecticut

Driving directions, southwestern end: From I-84, take Exit 16 and follow Route 188 for 2 miles to the trail crossing (0.2 miles north of Southford). Park alongside the road.

Suggestion courtesy of Edward Rizzotto, Connecticut Department of Environmental Protection, Middlebury, Connecticut.

Osbornedale State Park
Derby, Connecticut
3.3 miles of trails/350 acres
intermediate
USGS: Ansonia

Trails in Osbornedale State Park are presently undergoing major revision. Primary trails have been completed; others will be added in the future. This is a former farming area, with open fields, overgrown fields, and mixed hard- and softwood forest. Higher elevations offer views of the Naugatuck River Valley. Trails are marked with red paint blazes or tags. Snowmobiles are prohibited.

There are picnic shelters with fireplaces, a food concession, and heated sanitary facilities at the Park. Pickett's Pond is cleared for ice skating.

Driving directions: From Derby, go north on Route 8; take the Division Street exit and turn left at the bottom of the ramp. Follow Division Street, which becomes Chadfield Street, to the park entrance 0.3 miles ahead on the right. Park in the plowed area. From the north, go south from Seymour on Route 8 and take the Wakelee Avenue exit. Turn left at the end of the ramp and drive 3½+ miles to Division Street. Turn right and continue for 0.3 miles to Park entrance on the right.

Suggestion courtesy of Edward Rizzotto, Connecticut Department of Environmental Protection, Middlebury, Connecticut.

Powder Ridge Ski Area
Middlefield, Connecticut
36+ miles of trails
novice-intermediate-advanced
USGS: Middletown

There are 6 miles of trails on the Powder Ridge property and over 30 miles of trails adjacent to the area. The Connecticut Blue Trail system runs along the ridge above the ski area; a trail use ticket entitles the cross-country skier to a ride on the lift for access. There is snowmaking on some trails, and one trail is lighted for night use.

Rental equipment, instruction, maps, food, and beverages are available at the Ski Area. There is a trail fee.

Driving directions: Powder Ridge is near Exit 16, off I-91.

Suggestion courtesy of George Fenich, Powder Ridge Ski Area, Powder Hill Road, Middlefield, Connecticut 06455 (203-349-3454).

Osbornedale State Park

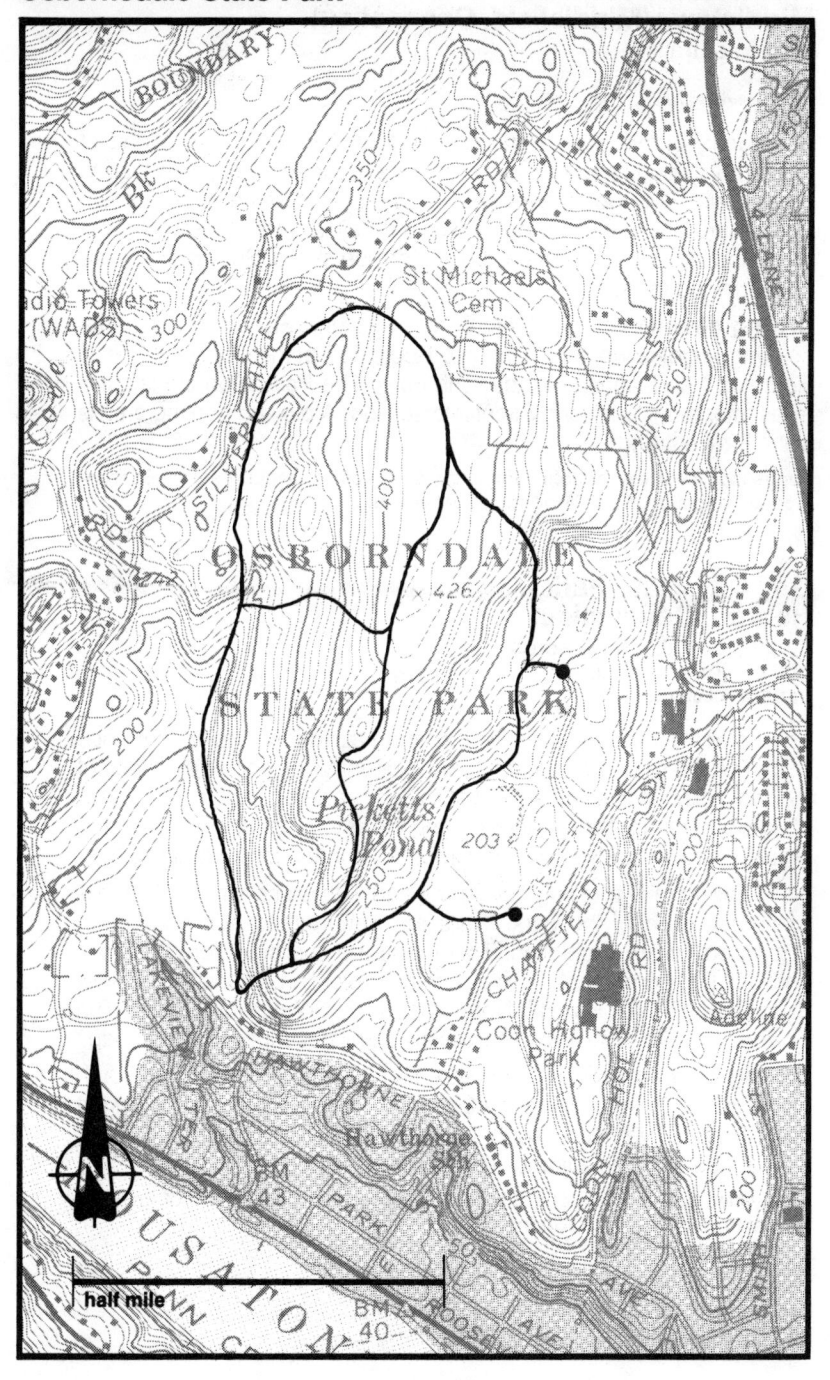

233 Connecticut

Wadsworth Falls State Park
Middletown/Middlefield, Connecticut
3 miles of trails
novice
USGS: Middletown

Ski touring in this State Park is through slightly rolling forestland of mixed hardwoods and hemlock. From the Park entrance, trails lead to Wadsworth Falls, going over several streams on stone bridge crossings. There are a few sections where the trail is steep; these are quite short and should pose no problem to novice skiers. Snowmobiles are not permitted in the Park.

Driving directions: Take Exit 18 from I-91 onto Route 66 east. After entering Middletown, turn right onto Route 157 at the stop light. Follow Route 157 and signs to Wadsworth Falls. The Park is on the left, 1½ miles after the Wadsworth Street intersection. A plowed parking area is at the Park entrance.

Suggestion courtesy of John Smutnick, Connecticut Department of Environmental Protection, North Windham, Connecticut.

Gay City State Park
Hebron, Connecticut
8 miles of trails/1569 acres
novice-intermediate
USGS: Marlborough

The name of the Park is derived from an abandoned town that once occupied the site. The peaceful, rolling countryside shows evidence of the zeal and business enterprise of its early settlers. Look for the crumbling stone foundations of the mill and the several cellar holes near the Blackledge River. Also note the tombstones in the town cemetery.

The terrain is mainly rolling lowland with some small hills in the western section of the park. Trails are well marked and numbered. Snowmobiles are prohibited. Trail maps are available from the Connecticut Department of Environmental Protection, Mansfield Hollow State Park, RR #2, Box 82, North Windham, Connecticut 06256. The *Connecticut Walk Book* also has detailed trail descriptions and a map.

Driving directions: From I-86, take Exit 97 onto Route 85. Go south on Route 85 for approximately 23 miles. The Park entrance is on the right. From Route 94, go north 1 mile on Route 85 to the Park. Most of the trails begin at the entrance road or near the pond.

Suggestion courtesy of John Smutnick, Connecticut Department of Environmental Protection, North Windham, Connecticut.

Wadsworth Falls State Park

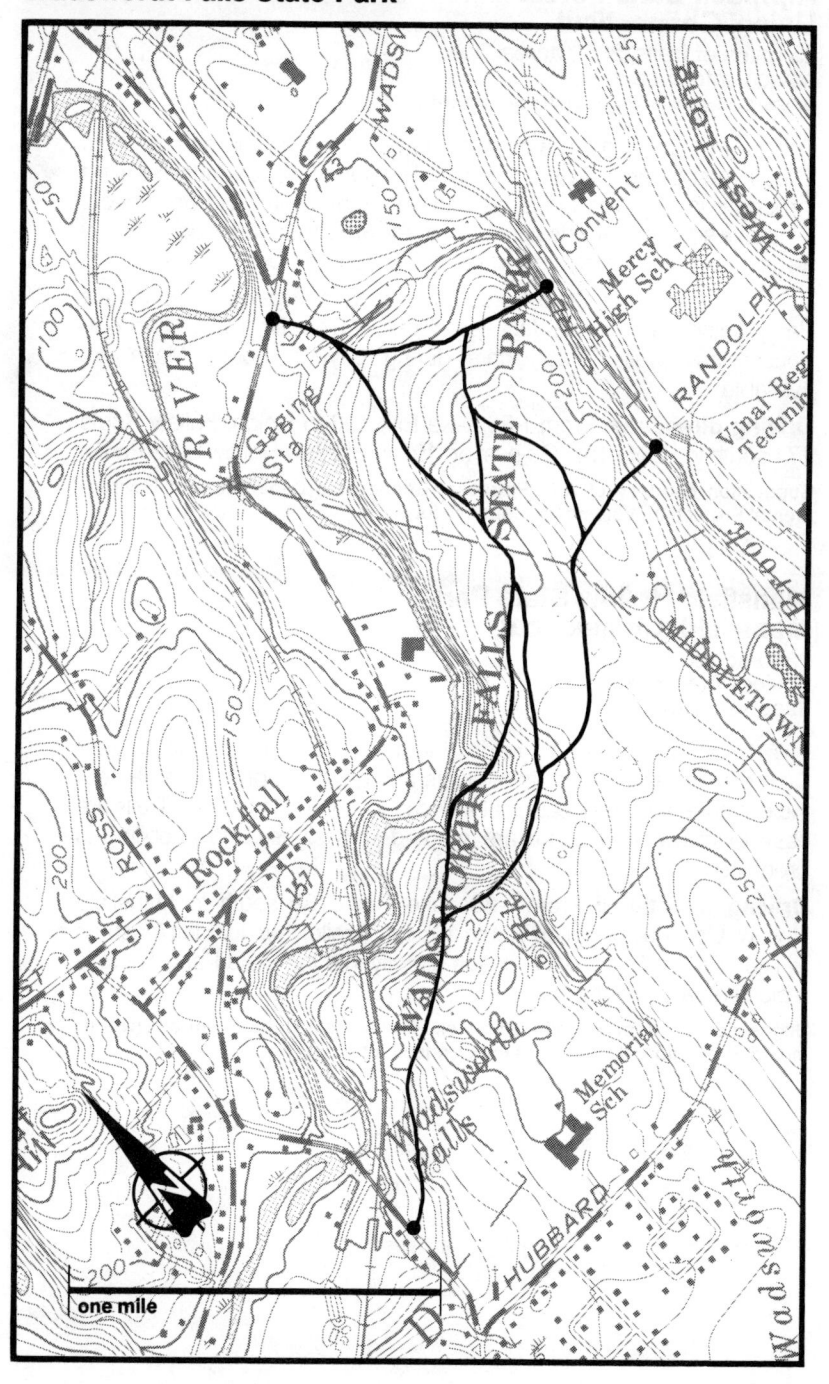

one mile

235 Connecticut

Nipmuck State Forest
Union, Connecticut
25 miles of trails/2000 acres
novice-intermediate
USGS: Southbridge/Wales/Eastford/Westford

This is a quasi-primitive area, with no development, on an estimated 2000 acres. Skiers may use the old, abandoned wood roads that wind through primarily wooded areas with stands of conifer and white birch. Nine miles of trails are designated for snowmobiles and receive heavy weekend use; other trails are reserved for foot use only.

Access to the State Forest trails is from Bigelow Hollow State Park, which has minimal facilities. Picnic tables, fireplaces, and outhouses are available to skiers during daylight hours. Maps are available.

Driving directions: From I-86, take Exit 106 in Union. Follow Route 171 south to Route 197. Go east on 197 to Bigelow Hollow State Park.

Suggestion courtesy of A.E. Petracco, Connecticut Department of Environmental Protection, Voluntown, Connecticut.

Mansfield Hollow State Park
Mansfield, Connecticut
2300 acres
novice-intermediate
USGS: Spring Hill

This is an area of open fields and forest surrounding an eastern Connecticut reservoir. It offers skiers a large, open practice area near the entrance and easy trails that stretch the length of the Park. Trails are easy to follow, and some are marked with signs. Snowmobiling is prohibited.

Driving directions: From I-86, take Route 89 south to Mansfield Hollow. Continue south on Route 195 for ¼ mile, then turn left (east) on Bassett Bridge Road, which leads directly into the State Park. There is a plowed parking area.

Suggestion courtesy of John Smutnick, Connecticut Department of Environmental Protection, North Windham, Connecticut

Mansfield Hollow State Park

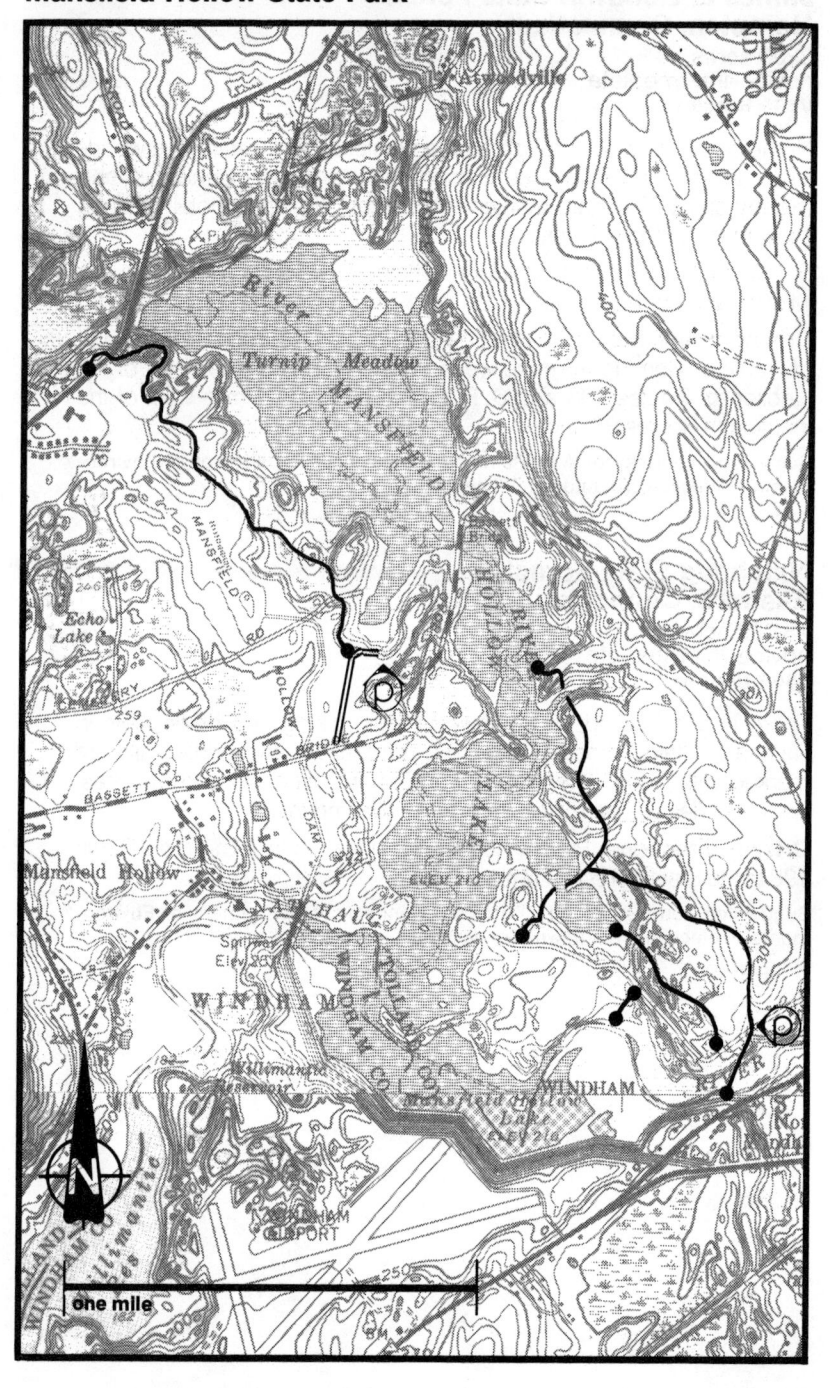

Connecticut

James L. Goodwin State Forest
Hampton, Connecticut
2200 acres
novice-intermediate
USGS: Hampton

Numerous trails wind through a pine plantation and deciduous woodlands around Pine Acre Lake. Terrain is moderate, with gentle hills and marshy areas. Trails are marked with blazes, and snowmobiling is not allowed in the State Forest.

The Goodwin Conservation Center offers education in forest, wildlife, and general conservation, and includes a small museum.

Driving directions: The State Forest is located on Potter Road, north of Route 6. Coming from the west, Potter Road is 3 miles east of the junction of Routes 198 and 6. From the east, it is 1 mile west of the junction of Routes 97 and 6.

Suggestion courtesy of A.E. Petracco, Connecticut Department of Environmental Protection, Voluntown, Connecticut.

Natchaug State Forest
Eastford, Connecticut
13,000 acres
novice-intermediate
USGS: Hampton

There is good skiing on unplowed roads, hiking and bridle trails in Natchaug State Forest. Hiking trails are blazed, and bridle trails are marked with signs. The area is wooded, with streams and marshes. Snowmobiles are permitted only on designated trails.

Driving directions: From Phoenixville, drive south 4 miles on Route 198 to the State Forest entrance.

Suggestion courtesy of A.E. Petracco, Connecticut Department of Environmental Protection, Voluntown, Connecticut.

Mashamoquet Brook State Park
Pomfret, Connecticut
950 acres
novice–intermediate–advanced
USGS: Danielson

Situated along Mashamoquet and Wolf Den Brooks, this State Park has a network of blazed hiking trails and several interesting features. In the southern part of the park are two rock formations: Table Rock and Indian Chair. From the Indian Chair there is a nice view of the valley with its many stone walls. Near the park entrance are the sites of a former cider mill, grist mill, and wagon shop. Snowmobiling is prohibited.

Driving directions: Mashamoquet Brook State Park is 5 miles southwest of Putnam on Route 44.

Suggestion courtesy of A.E. Petracco, Connecticut Department of Environmental Protection, Voluntown, Connecticut.

Pachaug State Forest
Voluntown, Connecticut
24,000 acres
novice–intermediate
USGS: Voluntown

There are numerous unplowed roads, hiking and bridle trails in this very large State Forest. Some are designated for snowmobile use; many others are available for ski touring. The landscape is rocky, but not too steep, with Atlantic white cedar swamps and a rare rhododendron sanctuary. Hiking trails are marked with blazes, snowmobile and bridle trails with signs. Maps for the Chapman and Green Falls area may be obtained at a self-help box at the Forest headquarters.

Driving directions: From Routes 138 and 165 in Voluntown, go north ¾ mile on Route 49 to the State Forest entrance.

Suggestion courtesy of A.E. Petracco, Connecticut Department of Environmental Protection, Voluntown, Connecticut.

Ski Touring Abandoned Railroad Grades

At the height of the "railroad era" in the late 19th century, main and branch railroad lines crisscrossed New England. As industry left the region and traffic dwindled, many routes were abandoned. The old grades that remain now provide scenic corridors for ski tourers that want to explore new territory. Some states, particularly Connecticut, have acquired miles of abandoned right-of-way for possible future development as transportation corridors. Currently, these state-owned routes serve as recreation trails, suitable for hiking and ski touring.

Abandoned railroad grades provide generally easy touring. Elevation changes are minimal, and former highway crossings provide frequent access points. Skiers should check out their touring location on a map, in advance. Recent editions of USGS maps often indicate abandoned grades specifically; on older maps, the shape of contour lines along a route offers the tourer a clue to track formerly in use.

Snowmobiles frequently use old grades, particularly where bridges are far apart. The tourer will find that missing bridges are likely to be the biggest obstacle en route. Generally, the older the abandonment, the more likely that the trackbed is overgrown, bridges are out, or civilization (housing developments, especially!) has encroached on the route. More recent abandonments are easy to follow, but the lack of small growth also makes these lines more attractive to the snowmobiler.

The legal status of abandoned rights-of-way is often uncertain. Skiers should respect private property that they may approach or cross while touring old grades.

Occasionally old grades will intersect active railroad trackage. Ski tourers should exercise extreme caution in these areas. DO NOT SKI ON ACTIVE TRACKS! Trains can approach with surprising silence on a snowy day, and a skier's equipment can make last-second evasive action impossible. (A ski tourer was fatally injured by a train in the Boston area, during the "Great Blizzard" of February, 1978.)

The text below, arranged by state, lists abandonments that may be suitable for ski touring. Few of these grades have been specifically field checked; they are presented as suggestions for exploration. Each entry shows the approximate end points and date of the abandonment, the railroad involved, the approximate mileage, and the USGS quadrangles on which the abandonment appears. Comments on the location are included where more information is available.

Abandoned Railroad Grades

Note: The numbers on this map correspond to the numbered trail descriptions that follow.

Abbreviations:

- B&M — Boston & Maine
- NH — New York, New Haven and Hartford (may also be identified on maps as New Haven, Penn Central or Conrail—see note).
- NYC — New York Central (also Penn Central or Conrail—see note).
- PC — Penn Central
- SV — Suncook Valley
- C&C — Claremont & Concord
- S&E — Sanford & Eastern
- M&WR — Montpelier & Wells River (also identified on maps as B&C—Barre & Chelsea)

Maps produced after 1969 generally show former NYC and NH lines with Penn Central identification; maps produced after 1976 are now giving Conrail (CR) identification. As maps are revised, CR identification will become more common.

Massachusetts

1. South Dennis-Provincetown (1960)   NH   38 miles
USGS: Dennis/Harwich/Orleans/Wellfleet/North Truro/Provincetown

Bridges out at Pilgrim Beach, Provincetown, and along beach on Cape Cod Bay side, North Truro.

2. West Wareham-Fairhaven (1955)   NH   13 miles
USGS: Snipatuit Pond/Marion/New Bedford North

3. Middleboro-Plymouth (c. 1935)   NH   15 miles
USGS: Bridgewater/Plympton/Plymouth

West end (from active tracks in Middleboro) to Middleboro town line apparently built over by U.S. Route 44. From the Waterville section of Middleboro, the route extends east to Carver (traceable by the line of USGS benchmarks along the route—this was quite common in earlier years). Route shows as abandoned grade on Plymouth USGS sheet, terminating at the Mass. 3 embankment in North Plymouth.

4. Hingham–Kingston (1960/1940)   NH   19 miles
USGS: Hingham/Cohasset/Scituate/Duxbury

From Hingham to Greenbush, sections of this grade appear in good condition. (Cohasset sheet shows parts as abandoned grade.) From Greenbush south, encroachments are more frequent. Bridges are out over the North and South Rivers, Marshfield. Paved or unpaved roads follow sections of the old grade in Duxbury.

5. Mansfield–Norton (1965)   NH   5 miles
USGS: Mansfield/Norton

6. Franklin–Blackstone (1968)   NH   8 miles
Blackstone–Putnam (Conn.) (1965)   25 miles
USGS: Franklin/Blackstone/Uxbridge/Oxford/Thompson, Conn./Putnam, Conn.

Former "Midland Division" (old New York & New England RR) direct route, with heavy curves and grades, between Boston and New Haven. (For extension see Putnam–Portland section under Connecticut railroad grades.)

7. Millis–Woonsocket (R.I.) (1968/1940)   NH   18 miles
USGS: Medfield/Holliston/Franklin/Blackstone

Section from West Medway (end of active track) to Millis abandoned fairly recently; the rest is overgrown. A housing development cuts across the grade in Bellingham, and roads interfere with skiing in Blackstone. Beware of active tracks at several railroad crossings in Milford and Woonsocket.

8. Easton–Taunton (1965)   NH   17 miles
USGS: Brockton/Taunton

Route starts at former Easton RR station.

9. Wrentham–Valley Falls (R.I.) (1970)   NH   12 miles
USGS: Wrentham/Attleboro/Pawtucket, R.I.

Grade begins at Plainville (may be further abandonments north of there) and continues into North Attleboro; it divides, with one branch running to Attleboro and another to Valley Falls. Although this abandonment is relatively recent, it is through a built-up area and may not be very scenic skiing.

10. West Hanover–Hanover (1940)   NH   approx. 2 miles
USGS: Hanover

11. Randolph-Stoughton Junction (c. 1940) NH approx. 5 miles
USGS: Blue Hills/Brockton

12. Barre Plains-Winchendon (1968) NYC 25 miles
USGS: Barre/Templeton/Winchendon

This recently abandoned line provides a long, scenic location for touring through relatively remote country, with few encroachments. At Baldwinville, the former high trestle has been removed and the route passes through the town and crosses active tracks of the Boston & Maine—probably unskiable. Route ends at Waterville, south of Winchendon, at active track operated by the B&M.

13. West Auburn-Webster (1940) NYC 10 miles
USGS: Worcester South/Leicester

Not shown as abandoned grade on the map, and may be hard to locate. Leaves Conrail (former NYC) main line south of Webster Jct. 6 miles west of Worcester.

14. Holliston-Milford (1970) NYC 6 miles
USGS: Holliston

15. South Middleton-Tewksbury (1940) B&M 18 miles
USGS: Reading/Wilmington/Billerica

Broken up at Wilmington Jct. (crossing of active tracks) by I-93 construction.

16. Topsfield-Newburyport (1960) B&M 15 miles
USGS: Georgetown/Newburyport West

Very clear, but not marked as old grade on USGS maps. Begins at end of active trackage (proposed for abandonment) in Topsfield and continues north and east, across I-95 to end near Route 1 rotary in Newburyport.

17. Swampscott-Marblehead (1970) B&M 4 miles
USGS: Lynn/Marblehead South/Marblehead North

Maps not very much help in locating grade through this built-up area.

18. Westford-Acton (1942) B&M 4 miles
USGS: Westford

19. Concord–Billerica (1965)   B&M   12 miles
USGS: Concord/Billerica

The Bedford–Billerica section of this line was the route of the first two-foot gauge railroad in America (abandoned 1878), later a branch of the B&M.

20. Marlboro–Maynard (1950/1972)   B&M   10 miles
USGS: Marlboro/Hudson

21. Ayer–Milford (N.H.) (1942)   B&M   20 miles
USGS: Ayer/Pepperell/South Merrimack, N.H./Milford, N.H.

Shows as abandoned grade on USGS maps. A very short section of track through Pepperell is still active.

22. Clinton–Hudson (1960/1975)   B&M   6 miles
USGS: Clinton/Hudson

Skiable section begins east of the abandoned Clinton tunnel. Track still exists, but is unserviceable, from Berlin to Hudson.

23. Sterling Jct.–Pratts Jct. (1940)   B&M/NH
USGS: Sterling/Clinton   approx. 5 miles

24. Gardner–Winchendon (1955)   B&M   9 miles
USGS: Gardner/Templeton/Winchendon

Route 140 reconstruction about 1975 has cut across parts of this line.

25. West Townsend–Greenville (N.H.) (1979)   B&M   11 miles
USGS: Townsend/Milford, N.H.

Out of service (but not dismantled) since 1971 and legally abandoned in 1979, this branch provides new opportunities for skiers to explore. Growth appears substantial in sections. Stay off the high trestle at Greenville.

26. Oakdale-Barre (1939)   B&M   20 miles
USGS: Sterling/Worcester North/Paxton/North Brookfield/Barre
Continuation: Ware/Warren/Palmer/Ludlow/Belchertown

The middle section of the B&M Central Massachusetts Branch from Oakdale to Wheelwright was abandoned in 1939, and in 1974 to a junction with the Boston & Albany (now Conrail) in Barre.

    Beyond Barre, the Central Massachusetts continued on an old grade (abandoned 1932) roughly paralleling the active Ware River branch of Conrail (formerly the Penn Central and New York Central). The Central Mass. grade extends south to Forest Lake. There is active track west to Canal Junction, on the Central Vermont Railway. From there to Norwottock, the Central Mass. grade parallels the active line of the Central Vermont. These two sections of parallel lines total 25 miles.

27. Bondsville-Ludlow (1914)   B&M   15 miles
USGS: Ludlow/Palmer

The Hampden Railroad, one of the most ambitious construction projects of the early 20th century, ran from Athol Junction on the New York Central to a connection with the Central Mass. (B&M) at Bondsville. Constructed to the highest standards, it cost nearly $250,000 a mile to build, but was never used and was eventually dismantled. The Mass. Turnpike disrupts the old grade east of Ludlow.

Rhode Island

28. Pascoag-Providence (c. 1960)   NH   approx. 15 miles
USGS: Chepachet/Georgiaville/North Scituate/Providence

Continues northwest from Pascoag to obscure junction in Uxbridge with former Midland Division route (see Blackstone-Putnam, Conn. section under Mass. abandoned grades).

29. West Warwick-Moosup (Conn.) (c. 1970)   NH   20 miles
USGS: Crompton/Coventry Center/Oneco, Conn./Plainfield, Conn.

A state recreation trail, this route shows on Rhode Island highway maps as suited for snowmobiling. End of active tracks is at West Warwick town line.

30. Wood River Junction-Hope Valley (c. 1950)   WRB/NH
                                                                            approx. 5 miles
USGS: Carolina/Hope Valley

Formerly the Wood River Branch Railroad. Grade is obscure on USGS maps.

Connecticut

31. Putnam–Portland (1965) NH approx. 50 miles
USGS: Putnam/Danielson/Hampton/Spring Hill/Willimantic/Columbia/Colchester/Moodus/Middle Haddam

Active tracks through Willimantic.

32. Middletown–Chester (1970) NH approx. 15 miles
USGS: Middletown/Middle Haddam/Haddam/Deep River

Portions operated by Valley Railroad tourist line, operating from Essex to Deep River. Stay away from active tracks!

33. Melrose–Rockville (1940) NH approx. 5 miles
USGS: Broad Brook/Ellington/Rockville

34. Vernon–Willimantic (1976) NH approx. 19 miles
USGS: Rockville/Marlborough/Columbia

Includes a tunnel (presumably unskiable).

35. Hawleyville–Litchfield (c. 1960) NH approx. 35 miles
USGS: Newtown/Roxbury/New Preston/Litchfield

Southern sections partially flooded out by Shepaug Reservoirs.

36. Botsford–Trumbull (1970) NH 5 miles
USGS: Botsford/Long Hill/Bridgeport

Not clear on maps on southern part.

New Hampshire

37. Hudson–Rochester (1943) B&M 45 miles
USGS: Nashua North/Windham/Haverhill 15'/Mt. Pawtuckaway/Dover West/Berwick

This route includes a short section of active track between Epping and Fremont.

38. Hooksett–Center Barnstead (1955) SV 25 miles
USGS: Suncook 7½'/Gossville/Gilmanton

Reconstruction of N.H. 28 through the Suncook Valley has cut up the old grade that shows on the USGS maps. Investigation before touring is recommended.

39. Goffstown–Henniker (1940)   B&M   17 miles
USGS: Goffstown/Weare/Hillsboro (also Concord 15′)

The former North Weare Branch shows as "abandoned" on the 15′ Concord USGS map (dated 1942). The old grade shows on the Hillsboro sheet from Henniker Junction to the east edge of the map. Flood control reservoirs in the Henniker area have obliterated sections.

    Portions of the former New Boston Branch (abandoned 1935) that left this line at Parkers, west of Goffstown, and followed the Piscataquog River south to New Boston, may also be skiable.

40. Contoocook–Bennington (1965/1940/1979) C&C/B&M   23 miles
USGS: Hopkinton/Hillsboro/Peterborough

Parts of the northern section of this line have been flooded out by new reservoirs. The northern section, abandoned in 1965, may currently be the best for skiing; however, the 7-mile Hillsboro–Bennington section is now legally abandoned as far south as the paper mill at Bennington, and provides new territory for skiers to explore.

41. Concord–Claremont (1960/1965/1978)   B&M/C&C   54 miles
USGS: Concord 7½′/Penacook/Hopkinton/Hillsboro/
Mt. Kearsarge/Sunapee/Claremont

This B&M branch existed for a few years as an independent short line before piecemeal abandonment. The section from Concord to Contoocook was torn up in 1960, after a key bridge washed out. The Contoocook to Newport section was eliminated in 1965. Dismantling is presently underway (1979) on the section from Newport to Claremont, including two wooden covered bridges. Construction of I-89 has disrupted sections of the old grade between Contoocook and Warner. Any old wooden bridges remaining on this line should be crossed with *extreme care*.

42. Winchendon (Mass.)–North Walpole (1972) B&M   45 miles
USGS: Winchendon, Mass./Royalston, Mass./Monadnock/Keene/Bellows Falls

This line, the B&M Cheshire Branch, has been legally abandoned, but the track and bridges have not yet been dismantled. The track is becoming overgrown, and substantial snow cover is necessary for skiing over the rails and ties. Through Keene, the line is presumably unskiable, and intersects active trackage.

43. West Ossipee–Conway (1972)   B&M   10 miles
USGS: Ossipee Lake

This segment of the Conway Branch has been legally abandoned although parts of the track still remain. Trackage at both ends is active, from West Ossipee station south, and the Conway town line north. Snowmobiles frequently use this long straight corridor.

44. Plymouth–Haverhill (1954)   B&M   30 miles
USGS: Plymouth/Rumney 7½'/Wentworth/Warren/ East Haverhill/Newbury

While parts of this line have been built over by N.H. Route 25, sections away from the highway still remain. New USGS maps clearly indicate the abandoned grade.

Vermont

45. Wells River–Montpelier (1955)   M&WR/B&C   32 miles
USGS: Barre/East Barre/Plainfield/Groton/Woodsville 7½'

This line was abandoned in the mid-1950s. This route, formerly the Montpelier and Wells River, and Barre and Chelsea Railway, follows Vt. 12 out of Montpelier, and is recognizable from maps. The Plainfield and Woodsville 15' USGS sheets, both older, show this line as it was operated until abandoned. Woodsville sheet is out-of-print.

46. Burlington–Alburg (1964)   Rutland   40 miles
USGS: Colchester Point/South Hero/North Hero/Rouses Point

This line of the abandoned Rutland Railway was removed after 1964 when the state of Vermont purchased the line south of Burlington. The route crosses several sections of Lake Champlain on riprapped causeways. Bridges on these sections were removed. From these causeways the line runs generally north, "island-hopping" to Alburg.

Maine

47. Kittery–Portland (1943)   B&M   38 miles
USGS: Dover 15'/North Berwick 7½'/Kennebunk/ Old Orchard Beach/Prouts Neck

The former Eastern Railroad route from Portsmouth to Portland, known as the "Old Eastern," appears on the USGS quads as an old grade. The Dover sheet does not identify it as such. From the Piscataqua River bridge to Jewett it has been used as a highway route and is unskiable. From Jewett to North Berwick the route appears clear for about 7 miles. On the northeastern side of North Berwick, active trackage exists for some distance towards Highpine, where the Old Eastern grade starts again at Bald Hill Crossing. The line extends through Kennebunk and Arundel to the outskirts of Biddeford; it is interrupted by the Maine Turnpike in Kennebunk. On the outskirts of Saco, the Old Eastern grade reappears. Although used in part for power lines, it is likely skiable until the crossing of the deep, tidal Scarboro River. Beyond the river crossing, after a few miles, the line rejoins active trackage in South Portland.

48. Rochester (N.H.)–Cumberland Mills (1956/1970)   B&M/S&E   40 miles
USGS: Berwick/Kennebunk/Buxton/Portland 15'

By 1956 the Rochester, N.H.–Alfred, Me. section had been abandoned; the rest followed by 1970. The route is clear on all quads: the Berwick, Kennebunk, and Portland sheets refer to the S&E; the Buxton to the B&M. From South Lebanon to East Lebanon (Berwick sheet) the grade has been used for U.S. 202.

Contributing to Future Editions

The *Ski Touring Guide to New England* has been written and updated with help from many skiers who have taken the time to make suggestions or write about areas with which they are familiar. Because information in any guidebook is subject to change and because there are many other ski trails in New England, there is a constant need for new input. We welcome suggestions for new places to ski and appreciate comments on areas already described in this edition.

Please send any correspondence to:
    Editor, *Ski Touring Guide to New England*
    Eastern Mountain Sports
    Vose Farm Road
    Peterborough, New Hampshire 03458

Entries in this edition

There is a special need for trail information where a detailed description of the ski route is given. Even if a route is described well, a comment to that effect is helpful. If reporting a problem or suggesting a change, please state with area you are writing about and be specific about the changes that need to be made. Be sure to send your name and address in case we have any questions.

New areas

When suggesting a new area, please send your name and address and include an address to which we can write for further information (a touring center, state park headquarters, managing agency, or other source), if at all possible. Even if you cannot supply detailed trail information, once we know of a possible area, we can try to get information from other sources. If describing a new area yourself, please answer the questions listed below. Be sure to state whether or not there are any maps that show the trails.

    Your name and address.
    Name of area.
        address.
        telephone number.
Name and address of landowner or public agency managing the area.
Trail information:
Total miles of trails and/or acreage of area.
Grading, according to difficulty (novice, intermediate, advanced).
How are trails marked?

Are trails maintained or groomed?
What USGS topographic map covers the area?
What other maps of the area are available?
General description (terrain, vegetation, scenery, outstanding features).
Ski route (if applicable, give a detailed account of the trail including difficult spots or places where one might lose the trail).
Are snowmobiles permitted on the trails?
What is the extent of snowmobile use?

Facilities:
Describe any buildings or physical facilities at the area that may be used by ski tourers.
Is the area affiliated with an inn or alpine ski area?
Is there a ski shop? waxing room? rental equipment? instruction? guided tours?
Are there any other programs or services at the area?
Is there a fee for parking? trail use? maps?
Driving directions (from nearest town or numbered route).
Parking directions.

Bibliography

General Ski Touring

Caldwell, John. *Caldwell on Competitive Cross-Country Skiing.* Brattleboro, Vermont: The Stephen Greene Press, 1979.

Caldwell, John. *Cross-Country Skiing Today.* Brattleboro, Vermont: The Stephen Greene Press, 1977.

Freeman, Cortlandt. *Steve Reischl's Ski-Touring for the Fun of It.* Boston: Little, Brown and Company, 1974.

Lederer, William and Wilson, Joe Pete. *Complete Cross-Country Skiing and Ski Touring.* New York: W.W. Norton and Company, Inc., 1972.

Tapley, Lance. *Ski Touring in New England and New York.* Lexington, Massachusetts: Stone Wall Press, 1976.

Ski Touring Guides

Ford, Sally and Daniel. *25 Ski Tours in the Green Mountains.* Somersworth, New Hampshire: New Hampshire Publishing Company, 1978.

Ford, Sally and Daniel. *25 Ski Tours in the White Mountains.* Somersworth, New Hampshire: New Hampshire Publishing Company, 1977.

Frado, John; Lawson, Richard; and Coy, Robert. *25 Ski Tours in Western Massachusetts.* Somersworth, New Hampshire: New Hampshire Publishing Company, 1978.

Griswold, Whit. *Berkshire Trails for Walking and Ski Touring.* Charlotte, North Carolina: East Woods Press, 1979.

SKI Magazine. *Guide to Cross-Country Skiing.* New York: Times Mirror Magazines, Inc. (published annually).

Ski Touring Guide. Troy, Vermont: Ski Touring Council (published annually).

Tapley, Lance. *Ski Touring in New England and New York.* See above.

Wass, Stan with Alvord, David W. *25 Ski Tours in Connecticut.* Somersworth, New Hampshire, 1978.

Mountaineering and Winter Camping

Danielson, John. *Winter Hiking and Camping.* Glens Falls, New York: Adirondack Mountain Club, 1977.

Ferber, Peggy. *Mountaineering: The Freedom of the Hills.* Seattle, Washington: The Mountaineers, 1974.

Steck, Allen and Tejada-Flores, Lito. *Wilderness Skiing.* New York: Sierra Club, 1972.

First Aid and Emergency Care

American National Red Cross. *Advanced First Aid and Emergency Care.* New York: Doubleday and Company, Inc., 1973.

American National Red Cross. *Standard First Aid and Personal Safety.* New York: Doubleday and Company, Inc., 1973.

American Academy of Orthopaedic Surgeons. *Emergency Care and Transportation of the Sick and Injured.* Chicago: American Academy of Orthopaedic Surgeons, 1977.

Wilkerson, James A., M.D., ed. *Medicine for Mountaineering.* Seattle, Washington: The Mountaineers, 1975.

Hiking Guides

AMC Guide to Mount Washington and the Presidential Range. Boston: Appalachian Mountain Club, 1979.

AMC Maine Mountain Guide. Boston: Appalachian Mountain Club, 1976.

AMC Massachusetts and Rhode Island Trail Guide. Boston: Appalachian Mountain Club, 1978.

AMC Trail Guide to Mount Desert Island. Boston: Appalachian Mountain Club, 1978.

AMC White Mountain Guide. Boston: Appalachian Mountain Club, 1979.

Appalachian Trail Guide: Maine. Augusta, Maine: Maine Appalachian Trail Club, Inc., 1978.

Appalachian Trail Guide: Massachusetts and Connecticut. Harpers Ferry, West Virginia: Appalachian Trail Conference, Inc., 1978.

Appalachian Trail Guide: New Hampshire and Vermont. Harpers Ferry, West Virginia: Appalachian Trail Conference, Inc., 1979.

Baldwin, Henry I., ed. *Monadnock Guide.* Concord, New Hampshire: Society for the Protection of New Hampshire Forests, 1970.

Blaisdell, Paul H. *25 Walks in the Lakes Region of New Hampshire.* Somersworth, New Hampshire: New Hampshire Publishing Company, 1977.

Butcher, Russell D. *Field Guide to Acadia National Park.* Pleasantville, New York: Reader's Digest Press, 1977.

Clark, Stephen. *Guide to Baxter State Park and Katahdin.* Fort Halifax Publishing Company, 1979.

Connecticut Walk Book. East Hartford, Connecticut: Connecticut Forest and Park Association, Inc., 1975.

Costecke, Diane M., ed. *Franconia Notch: An In-Depth Guide.* Concord, New Hampshire: Society for the Protection on New Hampshire Forests, 1975.

Day Hiker's Guide to Vermont. Montpelier, Vermont: Green Mountain Club, 1978.

Doan, Daniel. *Fifty Hikes: Walks, Day Hikes, and Backpacking Trips in New Hampshire's White Mountains.* Somersworth, New Hampshire: New Hampshire Publishing Company, 1977.

Doan, Daniel. *Fifty More Hikes in New Hampshire.* Somersworth, New Hampshire: New Hampshire Publishing Company, 1978.

Fisher, Alan. *Country Walks Near Boston.* Boston: Appalachian Mountain Club, 1976.

Gibson, John. *Fifty Hikes in Maine.* Somersworth, New Hampshire: New Hampshire Publishing Company, 1976.

Gibson, John. *Walking the Maine Coast.* Camden, Maine: Down East Magazine, 1977.

Griswold, Whit. *Berkshire Trails for Walking and Ski Touring.* Charlotte, North Carolina: East Woods Press, 1973.

Guide Book of the Long Trail. Montpelier, Vermont: Green Mountain Club, 1977.

Guide to the Metacomet–Monadnock Trail. Berkshire Chapter, Appalachian Mountain Club, 1976 (available through Walter Banfield, Pratt Corner Road, Amherst, Massachusetts 01002).

Hardy, Gerry and Sue. *Fifty Hikes in Connecticut.* Somersworth, New Hampshire: New Hampshire Publishing Company, 1978.

Henley, Thomas A. and Sweet, Neesa. *Hiking Trails in the Northeast.* Matteson, Illinois: Greatlakes Living Press, 1976.

Kendall, David. *Roads and Trails in the Reservoir.* West Hartford, Connecticut: Committee to Save the Reservoir, 1975.

Keyarts, Eugene. *Short Walks in Connecticut, Volume 1.* Chester, Connecticut: The Globe Pequot Press, 1968.

Keyarts, Eugene. *Short Walks in Connecticut, Volume 2.* Chester, Connecticut: The Globe Pequot Press, 1972.

Keyarts, Eugene. *Short Walks in Connecticut, Volume 3.* Chester, Connecticut: The Globe Pequot Press, 1973.

Kibling, Mary L. *25 Walks in the Dartmouth–Lake Sunapee Region.* Somersworth, New Hampshire, New Hampshire Publishing Company, 1979.

Mitchell, J.H. and Griswold, Whit. *Hiking Cape Cod.* Charlotte, North Carolina: East Woods Press, 1978.

Sadlier, Paul and Ruth. *Fifty Hikes in Massachusetts.* Somersworth, New Hampshire: New Hampshire Publishing Company, 1975.

Sadlier, Paul and Ruth. *Fifty Hikes in Vermont.* Somersworth, New Hampshire: New Hampshire Publishing Company, 1974.

Sadlier, Paul and Ruth. *Short Walks on Cape Cod and the Vineyard.* Chester, Connecticut: The Globe Pequot Press, 1976.

Sadlier, Paul and Ruth. *Short Walks Along the Maine Coast.* Chester, Connecticut: The Globe Pequot Press, 1977.

SLA Trails Guide. Plymouth, New Hampshire: Squam Lakes Association, 1973.

Thomas, Bill. *Eastern Trips and Trails.* Harrisburg, Pennsylvania: Stackpole Books, 1975.

A Trail Guide to Mount Moosilauke. Hanover, New Hampshire: Dartmouth Outing Club, 1978.

Weber, Ken. *25 Walks in Rhode Island.* Somersworth, New Hampshire: New Hampshire Publishing Company, 1978.

Index to Trails

Acadia National Park, *Bar Harbor, ME* 27
Akers Ski, Pineland Ski Club, *Andover, ME* 20
Allis State Park, *Brookfield, VT* 116
Amity Pond Natural Area, *Pomfret, VT* 125
Anderson, Larz, Park, *Brookline, MA* 177
Andover Village Improvement Society, *Andover, MA* 158
Appalachian Trail on Saddle Ball Mountain, *Adams, MA* 194
Auburn Ski Touring Center, *Auburn, ME* 23
Bald Hill-Wood Hill Reservation, *Andover, MA* 159
Barrows House Ski Touring Center, *Dorset, VT* 131
Battel Trail, *Lincoln, VT* 112
Baxter State Park, *Millinocket, ME* 16
Beach Pond Parks, *Exeter/West Greenwich, RI* 182
Bear Brook State Park, *Allenstown, NH* 77
Bearsden Conservation Area, *Athol, MA* 208
Bellows Pipe Trail, *North Adams, MA* 190
Birches Ski Touring Center, The, *Rockwood, ME* 17
Birch Hill Wildlife Management Area, *Winchendon/Royalston/Templeton, MA* 209
Blackberry River Ski Touring Center, *Norfolk, CT* 220
Blue Hills Reservation, *Milton/Quincy/Canton/Randolph, MA* 179
Blueberry Hill Ski Touring Center, *Goshen, VT* 117
Bolles Trail, Mount Chocorua Area, *Albany, NH* 64
Bolton Valley Ski Resort, *Bolton, VT* 106
Borderland State Park, *Easton/Sharon, MA* 180
Boxford State Forest, *Boxford/North Andover, MA* 160
Boxford Wildlife Sanctuary, *Boxford, MA* 160
Bradbury Mountain State Park, *Pownal, ME* 23
Bradley Palmer State Park, *Topsfield/Hamilton, MA* 167
Brattleboro Country Club Ski Touring Center, *Brattleboro, VT* 143
Breadloaf Touring Center, *Ripton, VT* 118

Breakheart Reservation, *Saugus/Wakefield, MA* 173
Bretton Woods Touring Center, *Bretton Woods, NH* 49
Broad Brook Trail, *Pownal, VT* 138
Brookline Reservoir, *Brookline, MA* 176
Bucksteep Manor Ski Touring Center, *Washington, MA* 200
Burke Mountain Recreation, Inc., Touring Center, *East Burke, VT* 109
Burklyn Ski Touring Center, *East Burke, VT* 108
Butternut Ski Touring, *Great Barrington, MA* 204
Callahan, R.J., State Park, *Framingham, MA* 172
Camden Hills State Park, *Lincolnville, ME* 26
Camden Snow Bowl, *Camden, ME* 26
Camp Allen, New England Center for Outdoor Education at, *Bedford, NH* 87
Cannon Mountain/Franconia Notch State Park, *Franconia, NH* 46
Caratunk Wildlife Refuge, *Seekonk, MA* 182
Carrabassett Valley Touring Center, *Carrabassett, ME* 18
Carrigain Notch, Wilderness Trail-Sawyer River Road, *Lincoln, NH* 51
Carter Notch, Nineteen Mile Brook Trail to, *Pinkham Notch, NH* 41
Cedar Brook Farms Ski Touring Center, *West Suffield, CT* 224
Cedar Brook, Hancock Notch-Wilderness Loop, *Lincoln, NH* 53
Center at Foxhollow, The, *Lenox, MA* 202
Charles River, *Boston/Cambridge, MA* 175
Charles W. Ward Reservation, *Andover, MA* 159
Charmingfare Ski Touring Center, *Candia, NH* 77
Church Pond Loop, *Albany, NH* 54
Churchill House Ski Touring Center, *Brandon, VT* 116
Collis P. Huntington State Park, *Redding, CT* 230
Conway State Forest, *Conway, MA* 200
Cortina Inn Ski Touring Center, *Killington, VT* 120
Country Club Cross-Country Touring Center, *West Dover, VT* 138

Crackerbarrel Ski Shop, *Rawsonville, VT* 136
Craftsbury Nordic Ski Center, *Craftsbury Common, VT* 107
Cram Hill, *Brookfield, VT* 115
Crane Pond Wildlife Management Area, *Newbury/Georgetown/Groveland, MA* 163
Cross-Country Ski Shop and Trail System at Grafton, *Grafton, VT* 136
Cummington Farm Ski Touring Center, *Cummington, MA* 196
D.A.R. State Forest, *Goshen, MA* 197
Deer Farm Ski Touring Center, *Kingfield, ME* 19
Dexter's Inn and Nordic Ski Center, *Sunapee, NH* 75
Dome Trail, *Pownal, VT* 137
East Branch Saco River and Wild River Valleys, *Chatham, NH* 57
East Hill Farm, The Inn at, *Troy, NH* 87
Eastman Ski Touring Center, *Grantham, NH* 73
Edson Hill Ski Touring Center, *Stowe, VT* 105
Ethan Pond Trail, Zealand Road-Zealand Trail-, *Carroll, NH* 49
Evergreen Valley Ski Touring Center, *East Stoneham, ME* 21
Farm Resort, The, *Morrisville, VT* 104
Fernald Hill Farm, *Cornish, NH* 72
Flat Mountain Pond, Guinea Pond Trail to, *Sandwich, NH* 63
Foss Mountain Ski Touring, *Snowville, NH* 65
Foxfollow, The Center at, *Lenox, MA* 202
Fox Run Resort, *Ludlow, VT* 130
Fox State Forest, *Hillsboro, NH* 75
Franconia Inn Cross-Country Ski Center, *Franconia, NH* 45
Franconia Notch State Park, Cannon Mountain, *Franconia, NH* 46
Freetown-Fall River State Forest, *Assonet, MA* 183
Gap Mountain, *Troy, NH* 87
Gay City State Park, *Hebron, CT* 234
Glover Brook Trail, *Woodstock, NH* 58
Goodwin, James L., State Forest, *Hampton, CT* 238
Gray Ledges Farm, *Grantham, NH* 72
Great Island, *Wellfleet, MA* 185
Great Meadows National Wildlife Refuge, *Concord, MA* 170
Great World Ski Touring Center, *West Simsbury, CT* 223
Greeley Ponds Trail, *Lincoln/Waterville Valley, NH* 62

Green Mountain Touring Center, *Randolph, VT* 118
Green Trails Ski Touring Center, *Brookfield, VT* 115
Guinea Pond Trail to Flat Mountain Pond, *Sandwich, NH* 63
Gunstock Touring Center, *Gilford, NH* 70
Hale Reservation, *Westwood, MA* 178
Hancock Notch-Cedar Brook-Wilderness Loop, *Lincoln, NH* 53
Hancock Notch Trail-Sawyer River Trail, *Lincoln, NH* 52
Harold Parker State Forest, *Andover/North Andover, MA* 158
Hartwell Hill, *Littleton, MA* 154
Haystack Ski Touring Center, *Wilmington, VT* 140
Hazen's Notch Ski Touring Center, *Montgomery Center, VT* 101
Hermitage Ski Touring Center, *Wilmington, VT* 140
Hermon Meadow Ski Center, *Bangor, ME* 24
Hickory Hill Touring Center, *Worthington, MA* 202
Highland Lodge Ski Touring Center, *Greensboro, VT* 108
Holbrook Island Sanctuary, *Brooksville, ME* 28
Holiday Inn, *Intervale, NH* 55
Hollis Hof Ski Touring Center, *Hollis, NH* 94
Hopper Trail, *South Williamstown, MA* 191
Horsford Ski Touring, *Charlotte, VT* 102
Hubbard Brook Experimental Forest Area, *West Thornton, NH* 60
Hubbardston Wildlife Management Area, *Hubbardston, MA* 213
Human Environment Institute/Sargent Camp, *Peterborough, NH* 86
Huntington, Collis P., State Park, *Redding, CT* 230
Hyland Hill, *Westmoreland, NH* 80
Inn at East Hill Farm, The, *Troy, NH* 87
Jackson Ski Touring Foundation, *Jackson, NH* 56
James L. Goodwin State Forest, *Hampton, CT* 238
Jay Peak Touring Center, *Jay, VT* 101
John Minetto State Park, *Torrington, CT* 221
Kents Island, *Newbury, MA* 163
Kilkenny Area, *Kilkenny/Berlin/Randolph, NH* 39
Larkin State Bridle Trail, *Southbury-to-Waterbury, CT* 230
Larz Anderson Park, *Brookline, MA* 177
Lincoln Conservation Commission and Lincoln Land Trust, *Lincoln, MA* 171

Lincoln Guide Service, *Lincoln, MA* 171
Little Lyford Pond Camps,
  Brownville, ME 16
Living Memorial Park Cross-Country Trail,
  Brattleboro, VT 142
Long Trail to Stratton Pond,
  Stratton, VT 134
Longwood Ski Touring Center, Center
  Harbor, NH 71
Loon Mountain Ski Touring Center,
  Lincoln, NH 61
Lowell-Dracut State Forest,
  Lowell, MA 156
Lye Brook Wilderness,
  Manchester, VT, 135
Lynn Woods, *Lynn, MA* 174
Lynn Woods Ski Touring Center,
  Lynn, MA 174
Main Stream Touring Center, *Pleasant Valley, CT* 221
Manning State Forest, *Billerica, MA* 154
Mansfield Hollow State Park,
  Mansfield, CT 236
Mashamoquet Brook State Park,
  Pomfret, CT 239
McLean Game Refuge, *Granby, CT* 223
Metacomet-Monadnock Trail, *Southwick, MA to Jaffrey, NH* 209
Middlesex Fells Reservation, *Stoneham/ Medford/Winchester/Melrose/ Malden, MA* 173
Minetto, John, State Park,
  Torrington, CT 221
Missisquoi National Wildlife Refuge,
  Swanton, VT 100
Monadnock State Park, *Jaffrey, NH* 90
Moose Mountain Lodge, *Etna, NH* 68
Moosehorn National Wildlife Refuge,
  Calais and Dennysville, ME 28
Mount Abram Ski Slopes,
  Locke Mills, ME 22
Mount Ascutney Ski Area,
  Brownsville, VT 131
Mount Blue State Park, *Weld, ME* 20
Mount Cardigan, *Alexandria, NH* 68
Mount Chocorua Area, Bolles Trail,
  Albany, NH 64
Mount Greylock State Reservation, *South Williamstown/North Adams/ Adams, MA* 190-194
Mount Mansfield Ski Touring Center,
  Stowe, VT 106
Mount Moosilauke,
  Warren/Benton, NH 58
Mount Orient and Poverty Mountain,
  Pelham, MA 210
Mount Pawtuckaway Area,
  Deerfield, NH 78

Mount Sunapee State Park,
  Sunapee, NH 74
Mount Watatic Ski Touring Center,
  Ashby, MA 150
Mount Willard, *Crawford Notch, NH* 50
Mountain Meadows Ski Touring Center,
  Killington, VT 121
Mountain Top Ski Touring Center,
  Chittenden, VT 120
Myles Standish State Forest,
  Plymouth/Carver, MA 183
Nansen Ski Touring Trails, *Berlin, NH* 40
Narrow Gauge Cross-Country Trail,
  Bigelow, ME 19
Natchaug State Forest, *Eastford, CT* 238
New England Center for Outdoor Education at Camp Allen, *Bedford, NH* 87
Newton Recreation Areas,
  Newton, MA 176
Nickerson State Park, *Brewster, MA* 184
Nineteen Mile Brook Trail to Carter Notch, *Pinkham Notch, NH* 41
Nipmuck State Forest, *Union, CT* 236
Nobscot Scout Reservation, *Framingham/ Sudbury, MA* 172
Nordic Inn Ski Touring Center,
  Londonderry, VT 133
Nordic Skier, The, *Wolfeboro, NH* 71
Norsk Ski Touring Center,
  New London, NH 73
North Country Ski Touring Center,
  Carlisle, MA 156
Northfield Mountain Ski Touring Center,
  Northfield, MA 206
Northland Ski Touring Center,
  North Hero, VT 100
Northwest Park, *Windsor, CT* 224
Notch Road, *North Adams, MA* 190
Notchvill Reservation, *Windsor, MA* 196
Oak Hill, *Littleton, MA* 152
Oak n' Spruce Resort, *South Lee, MA* 203
Okemo Mountain, Inc., *Ludlow, VT* 130
Old Town Hill Reservation,
  Newbury, NH 162
Ole's Cross-Country, *Warren, VT* 113
Osbornedale State Park, *Derby, CT* 232
Otis Ridge Ski Center, *Otis, MA* 205
Owl's Head Area, *Lincoln, NH* 48
Pachaug State Forest, *Voluntown, CT* 240
Paine Mountain Trails, *Northfield, VT* 114
Palmer, Bradley, State Park,
  Topsfield/Hamilton, MA 167
Parker, Harold State Forest, *Andover/ North Andover, MA* 158
Parker River National Wildlife Refuge,
  Newburyport, MA 166
Peaceful Acres Touring Center,
  Hubbardston, MA 212

Pemi Trail, *Franconia/Lincoln, NH* 46
Pemigewasset Valley Ski Touring Center, *Franklin, NH* 74
Peru Outdoor Recreation Commission, *Peru/Landgrove, VT* 132
Pierrepont, Seth Low, State Park, *Ridgefield, CT* 228
Pine Mountain, *Martin's Location, NH* 41
Pine Mountain Cross-Country Ski Touring Center, *East Hartland, CT* 222
Pineland Ski Club/Akers Ski, *Andover, ME* 20
Pinkham Notch Area, *Gorham, NH* 42
Plymouth Village Ski Touring Center, The *Plymouth Union, VT* 126
Pole and Pedal Ship, *Henniker, NH* 76
Ponkapoag Outdoor Center, *Canton, MA* 180
Ponkapoag Pond, *Canton/Randolph, MA* 179
Poverty Mountain, Mount Orient and, *Pelham, MA* 210
Powder Ridge Ski Area, *Middlefield, CT* 232
Puddledock Ski Touring Trails, *Granville, VT* 114
Pulaski State Park, *Burrillville, RI* 181
Purgatory Falls, *Mont Vernon, NH* 88
Putterham Meadows Golf Course, *Brookline, MA* 177
Quaboag Wildlife Management Area, *Brookfield/West Brookfield, MA* 214
R.J. Callahan State Park, *Framingham, MA* 172
R.R.R. Brooks Trail, *Williamstown, MA* 188
Rabbit Hill Inn Ski Touring Center, *Lower Waterford, VT* 109
Red Fox Ski Touring Center, *New Marlborough, MA* 205
Red Ridge on Middle Moat Mountain, *North Conway, NH* 55
Riverbend Cross-Country Ski Shop, *South Newbury, VT* 119
Riverrunning and Ski Touring, *Falls Village, CT* 220
Riverrun North, *Sheffield, MA* 204
Riverwood Ski Touring Center, *Winchendon, MA* 150
Road's End Farm, *Chesterfield, NH* 80
Rocky Woods Reservation, *Medfield, MA* 178
Rose Mountains, Winn and *Lyndeborough/Greenfield, NH* 84
Rossignol, Sugarbush Inn/, Ski Touring Center, *Warren, VT* 113
Russell Pond, Tripoli Road-, *Woodstock, NH* 61

Saddle Ball Mountain, Appalachian Trail on, *Adams, MA* 194
Saddleback Mountain Ski Area, *Rangeley, ME* 18
Sagamore-Hampton Ski Touring Center, *North Hampton, NH* 78
Sandy Neck, *Barnstable, MA* 184
Sargent Camp, Human Environment Institute/, *Peterborough, NH* 86
Sawyer River Road, Wilderness Trail-Carrigain Notch-, *Lincoln, NH* 51
Sawyer River Road Area, *Hart's Location, NH* 53
Sawyer River Trail, Hancock Notch Trail-, *Lincoln, NH* 52
Sebago Lake State Park, *Naples, ME* 23
Seth Low Pierrepont State Park, *Ridgefield, CT* 228
Sitzmark Ski Touring Center, *Wilmington, VT* 142
Skatukee and Thumb Mountains, *Hancock, NH* 82
Ski Hostel Lodge, *Waterbury Center, VT* 107
Sky Line Trail, *Barnard/Pomfret, VT* 121
Smugglers' Notch, Village of, *Jefferson, VT* 103
Southford Falls State Park, *Southbury, CT* 228
Spruce Hill, *Florida/Savoy, MA* 194
Squaw Mountain Ski Area, *Greenville, ME* 17
Standish, Myles, State Forest, *Plymouth/Carver, MA* 183
Stark Farm Ski Touring Center, *Westford, VT* 102
Stow Town Forest, *Stow, MA* 170
Stratton Mountain Tour, *Northfield/Warwick, MA* 206
Stratton Pond, Long Trail to, *Stratton, VT* 134
Stratton Ski Touring Center, *Stratton, VT* 135
Stump Sprouts Ski Touring, *Charlemont, MA* 195
Sugarbush Inn/Rossignol Ski Touring Center, *Warren, VT* 113
Summer's Ski Touring Center, *Dublin, NH* 82
Sunday River Ski Touring Center, *Bethel, ME* 21
Sunset Hill Touring Center, *Sugar Hill, NH* 45
Taconic Crest Trail, *Petersburg, NY* 188
Teddybear Touring Trails, *North Turner, ME* 22
Temple Mountain Ski Area, *Peterborough, NH* 91

Tenney Mountain Ski Area, Plymouth, NH 69
Thayer Woods Reservation, Whitney and, Cohasset/Hingham, MA 181
Thumb Mountains, Skatutakee and, Hancock, NH 82
Timberlane Touring Trails, Woodford, VT 137
Topnotch Ski Touring Area, Stowe, VT 105
Topsmead State Forest, Litchfield, CT 226
Tory Pines Ski Touring Center, Francestown, NH 86
Townsend State Forest, Townsend, MA 151
Trapp Family Lodge, Stowe, VT 104
Tripoli Road-Russell Pond, Woodstock, NH 61
Tucker Hill Ski Touring Center, Waitsfield, VT 112
Tulip Tree Inn, Chittenden, VT 119
Tunxis State Forest, Hartland, CT 221
Turnpike Road, Thetford 126
Tyringham Cobble Reservation, Tyringham, MA 203
University Forest, Stillwater, ME 24
Viking Ski Touring Center, Londonderry, VT 133
Village of Smugglers' Notch, Jeffersonville, VT 103
Wachusett Mountain Ski Area, Princeton, MA 152
Wadsworth Falls State Park, Middletown/Middlefield, CT 234
Walden Pond State Reservation, Concord, MA 170
Walnut Lane Cross-Country Skiing, Middleton, MA 162
Wapack Trail, Ashburnham, MA to Greenfield, NH 91
Ward, Charles W., Reservation, Andover, MA 159
Ware River Watershed, Hubbardston/Barre/Rutland/Oakham, MA 212
Waterville Valley Ski Touring Center, Waterville Valley, NH 62
Weir Hill Reservation, North Andover, MA 154
West Hartford Reservoir Reservation, West Hartford, CT 225
West Hill Ski Touring Center, Putney, VT 143
West Mountain Inn, Arlington, VT 134
Weston Ski Track, Weston, MA 175
White House Touring Center, Wilmington, VT 141
White Memorial Foundation, Litchfield, CT 227
White Mountain Country Club, Ashland, NH 70
White Mountain School, Littleton, NH 44
Whitney and Thayer Woods Reservation, Cohasset/Hingham, MA 181
Wilder Ski Track, Springfield, MA 213
Wilderness Loop, Hancock Notch-Cedar Brook-, Lincoln, NH 53
Wilderness Ski Area, Dixville Notch, NH 38
Wilderness Trail-Carrigain Notch-Sawyer River Road, Lincoln, NH 51
Wild River Valleys, East Branch Saco River and, Chatham, NH 57
Wild Wings Ski Touring Center, Peru, VT 132
Willard Brook State Forest, West Townsend Ashby, MA 151
Willowdale State Forest, Ipswich, MA 166
Windblown, New Ipswich, NH 93
Winding Trails Recreation Area, Farmington, CT 226
Winn and Rose Mountains, Lyndeborough/Greenfield, NH 84
Woodbound Ski Touring Center, Jaffrey, NH 90
Woodbury Ski and Racquet, Woodbury, CT 227
Wood Hill, Bald Hill-, Reservation, Andover, MA 159
Woodstock Ski Touring Center, Woodstock, VT 127
World's End, Hingham, MA 180
York Pond Trail, Lancaster/Berlin, NH 38
Zealand Road-Zealand Trail-Ethan Pond Trail, Carroll, NH 49